THE CASTLE

ADAPTED FROM THE ORIGINAL NOVEL BY
FRANZ KAFKA
ADAPTED BY
DAVID ZANE MAIROWITZ
ILLUSTRATED BY
JAROMÍR 99

First published 2013
by SelfMadeHero
5 Upper Wimpole Street
London W1G 6BP
www.selfmadehero.com

© 2013 SelfMadeHero

Adaptor: David Zane Mairowitz
Artist: Jaromír 99

Editorial & Production Manager: Lizzie Kaye
Sales & Marketing Manager: Sam Humphrey
Publishing Director: Emma Hayley
With thanks to: Johana Zikova, Lukas Horky,
Nick de Somogyi and Dan Lockwood

A CIP record for this book is available from the British Library

ISBN: 978-1-906838-67-6

10 9 8 7 6 5 4 3 2 1

Printed and bound in Slovenia

Introduction

The Castle is another of Kafka's many great "unfinished" works. There are always two theoretical options: either the story follows the unending Kafkaian labyrinth, with each plot-line spawning a host of other ones, each question then raising response, counter-response and then another question, or... it just stops. Not "ends", but rather collapses from sheer exhaustion, as *The Castle* does in mid-sentence.

The Castle is often interpreted as depicting a blind, totalitarian bureaucracy casting an iron grip on the snow-bound village at the story's centre. But as with much of Kafka criticism, this is mostly beside the point. What counts is the Castle's inaccessibility, and the hunger which its mystery creates for servility. There can be no greater role in life than to serve the Castle as does (or thinks he does) the messenger Barnabas; no more powerful emotion than that resulting from delivering an incoherent, pointless letter from the Castle authority to the novel's central figure K., the "land surveyor" (who is not really a land surveyor, nor does the village even need one). Or for the family of Amalia, Barnabas's sister, vulgarly insulted by a minor Castle "official", which – its life now in ruins – grovels before the Castle authority to "beg pardon" for its daughter rejecting the obscene proposition.

At the centre stands the lonely K., who has arrived from more or less nowhere with only a walking stick. K. is as much "Kafka" as the earlier Joseph K. of *The Trial*. Unlike Joseph K., just-"K." does not strike out against an unfathomable Authority, but rather does his utmost to integrate in the village, to serve, in the vain hope of one day being admitted to the Castle. On this pointless quest, he encounters the enigmatic Frieda, inspired by the Czech Milena Jesenská, one of the key female figures in Kafka's life. But he will never meet Klamm, the Castle official (who may not be a Castle official at all and whose physical identity is even in doubt), to whom all subordinates defer and to whom all village women spring if summoned.

Nearly every aspect of *The Castle* has its counterface. Nothing is really as it seems, or even as anyone says it is. And nothing is ever really within K.'s grasp. He is plagued to wander in the snowy village, moving through a series of erotic temptations which, though chiefly unachieved, leave him empty and discharged, infinitely older than when the book began, although, in fact, not even one week has actually transpired.

Note on the text: Finding a definitive version of a Kafka text is like looking for the Castle: the roads are seemingly endless and labyrinthine. I have used several versions to make my own English translation. The ending used here is the one found in Kafka's manuscript draft, not in the original printed version.

David Zane Mairowitz

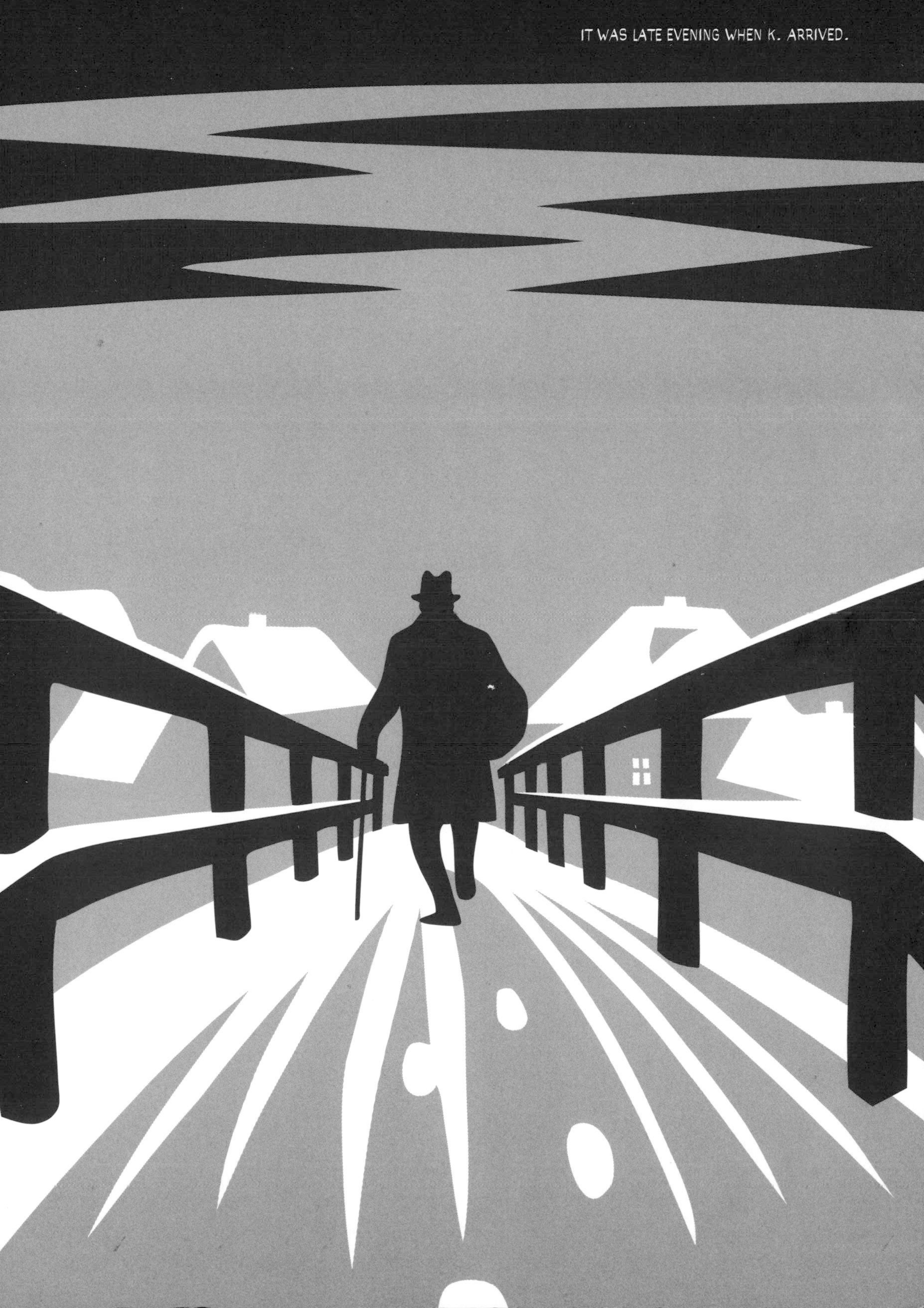
IT WAS LATE EVENING WHEN K. ARRIVED.

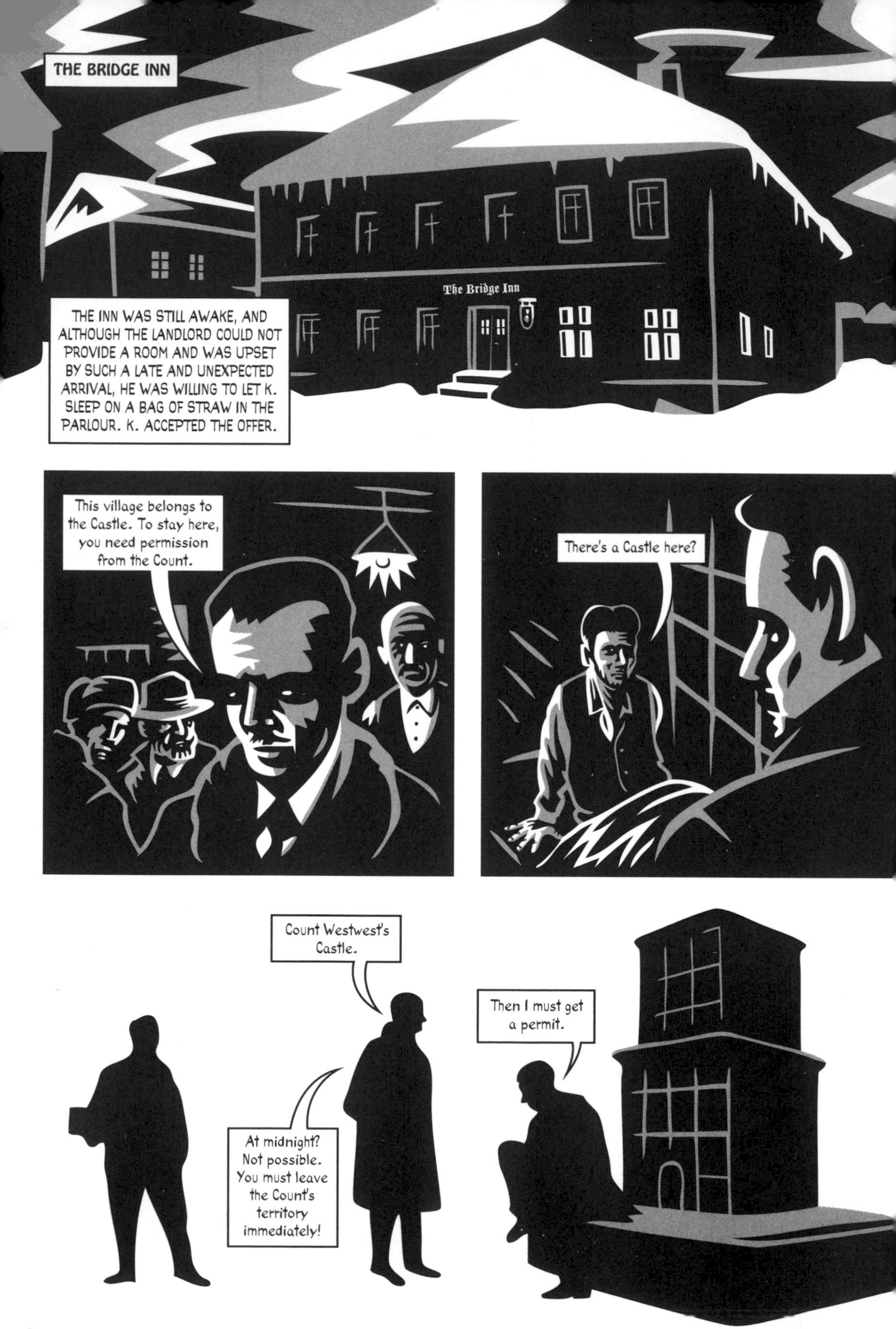
THE BRIDGE INN
The Bridge Inn
THE INN WAS STILL AWAKE, AND ALTHOUGH THE LANDLORD COULD NOT PROVIDE A ROOM AND WAS UPSET BY SUCH A LATE AND UNEXPECTED ARRIVAL, HE WAS WILLING TO LET K. SLEEP ON A BAG OF STRAW IN THE PARLOUR. K. ACCEPTED THE OFFER.
This village belongs to the Castle. To stay here, you need permission from the Count.
There's a Castle here?
Count Westwest's Castle.
Then I must get a permit.
At midnight? Not possible. You must leave the Count's territory immediately!

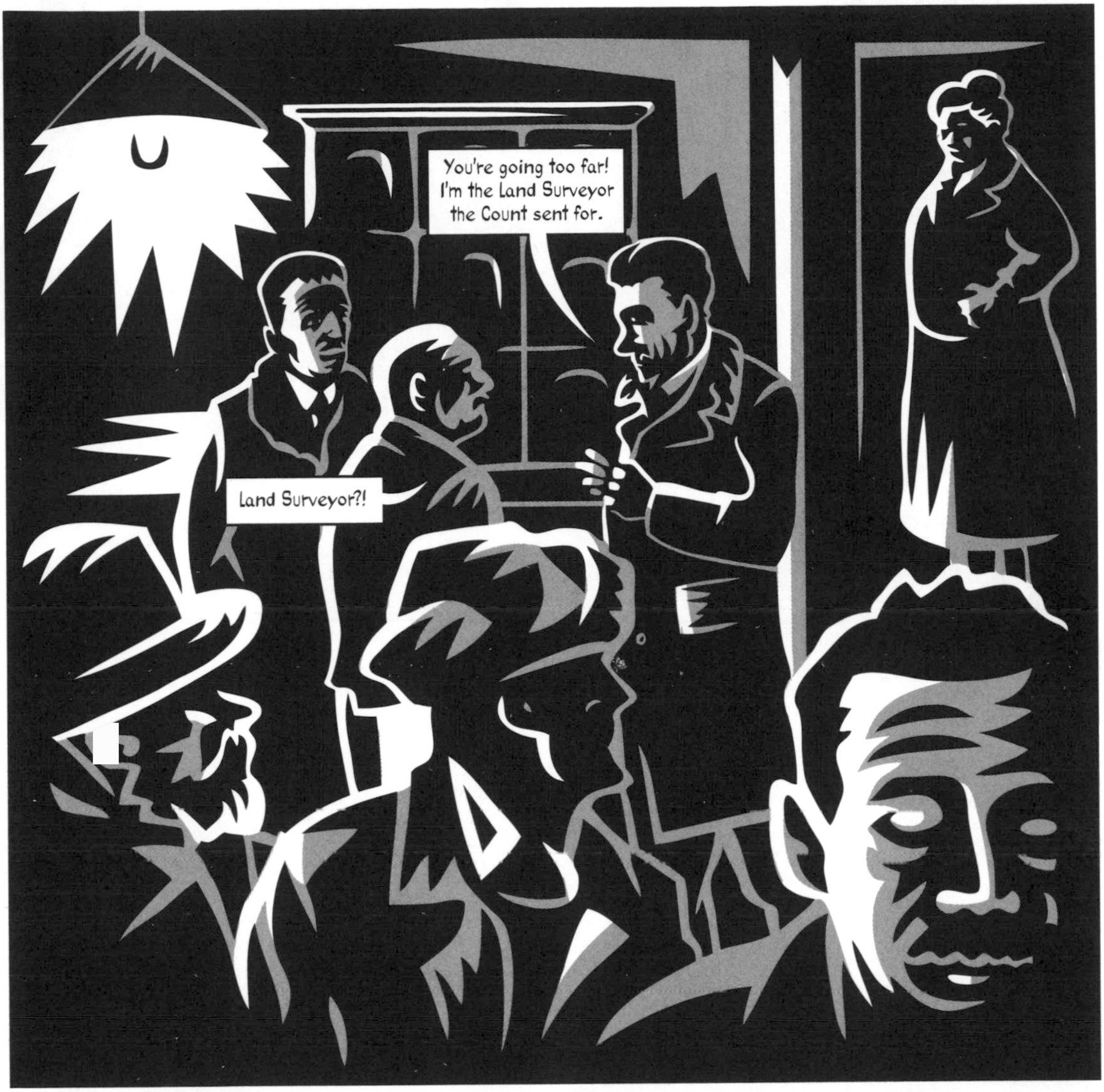
You're going too far! I'm the Land Surveyor the Count sent for.
Land Surveyor?!

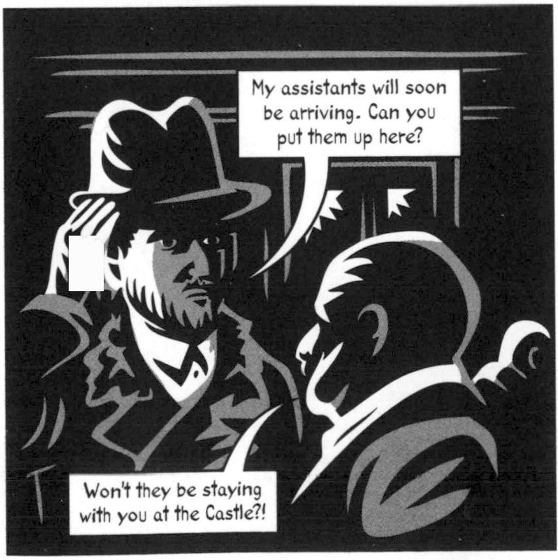
My assistants will soon be arriving. Can you put them up here?
Won't they be staying with you at the Castle?!

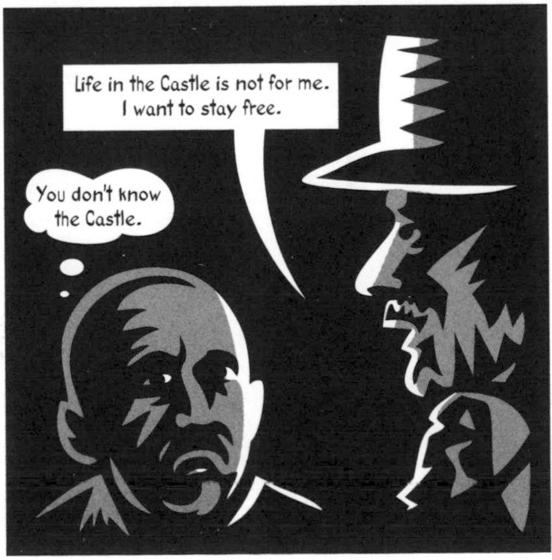
Life in the Castle is not for me. I want to stay free.
You don't know the Castle.

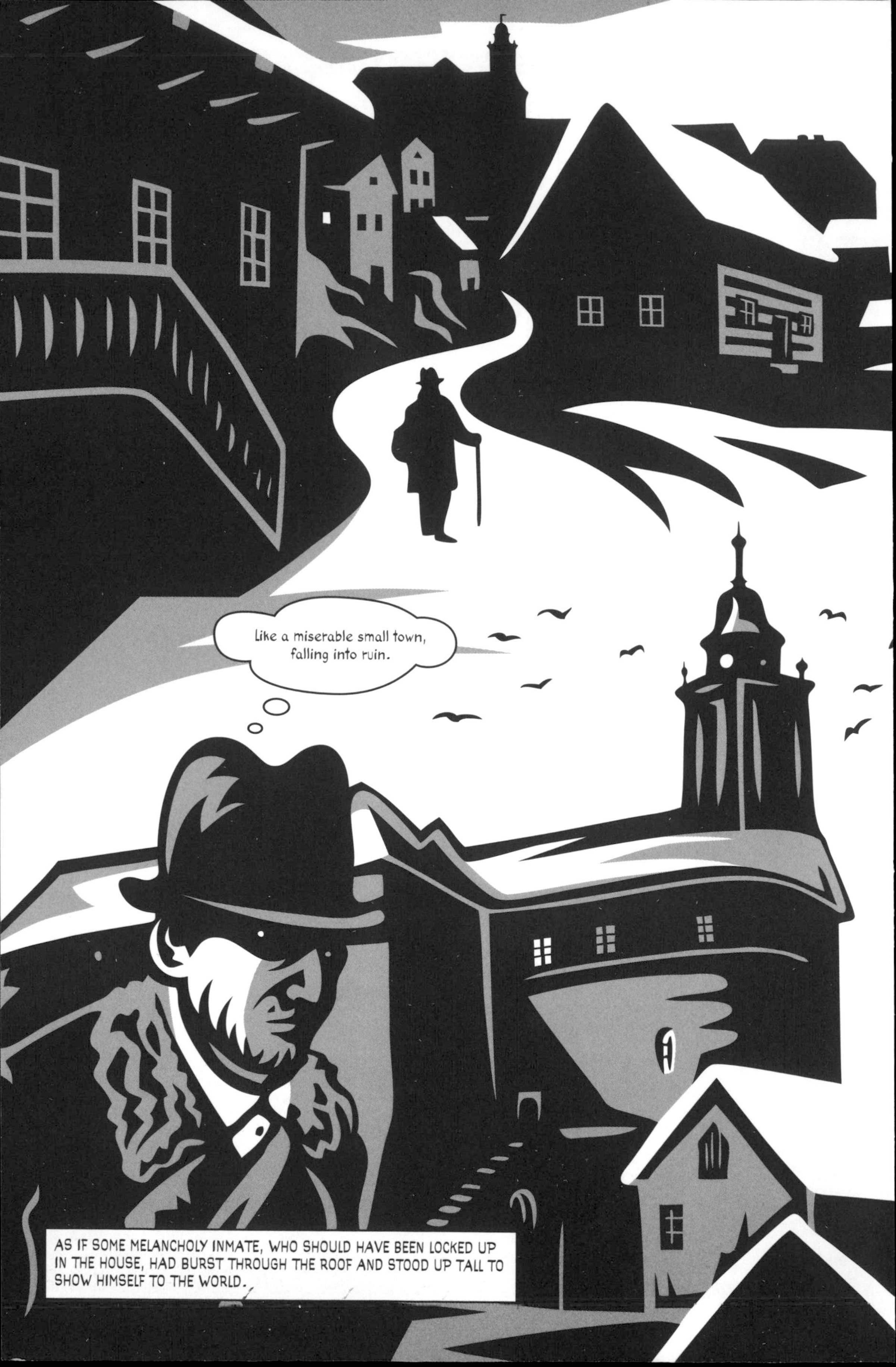
Like a miserable small town,
falling into ruin.
AS IF SOME MELANCHOLY INMATE, WHO SHOULD HAVE BEEN LOCKED UP
IN THE HOUSE, HAD BURST THROUGH THE ROOF AND STOOD UP TALL TO
SHOW HIMSELF TO THE WORLD.

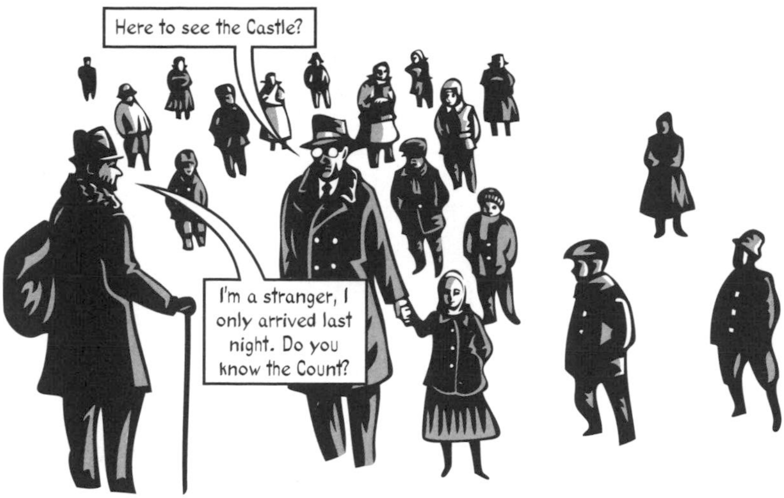
Here to see the Castle?
I'm a stranger, I only arrived last night. Do you know the Count?

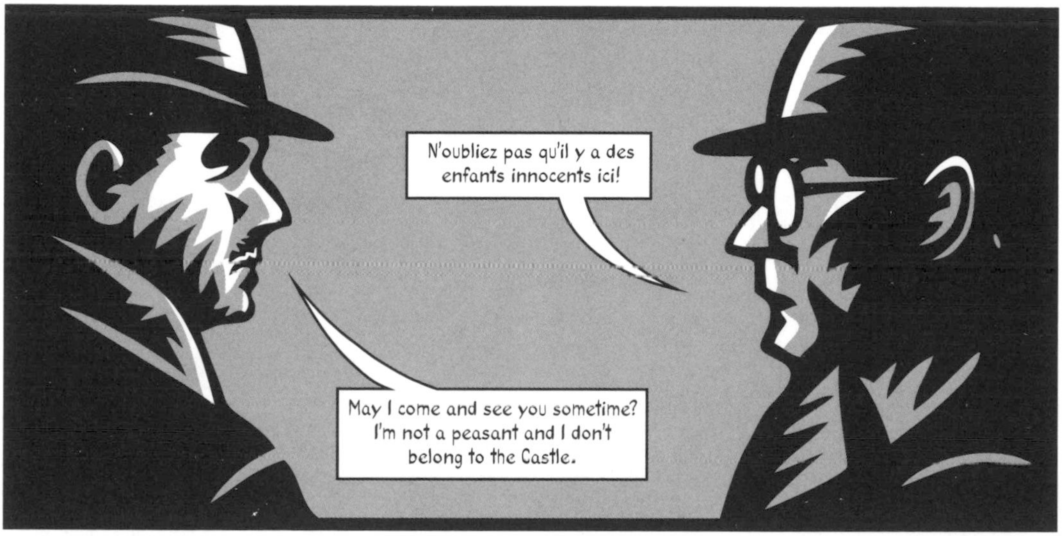
N'oubliez pas qu'il y a des enfants innocents ici!
May I come and see you sometime? I'm not a peasant and I don't belong to the Castle.

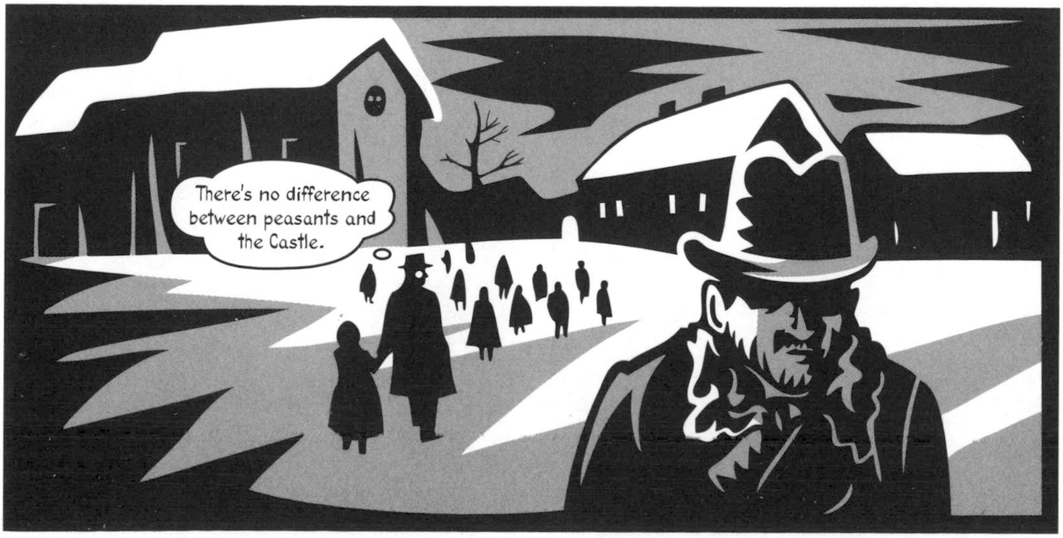
There's no difference between peasants and the Castle.

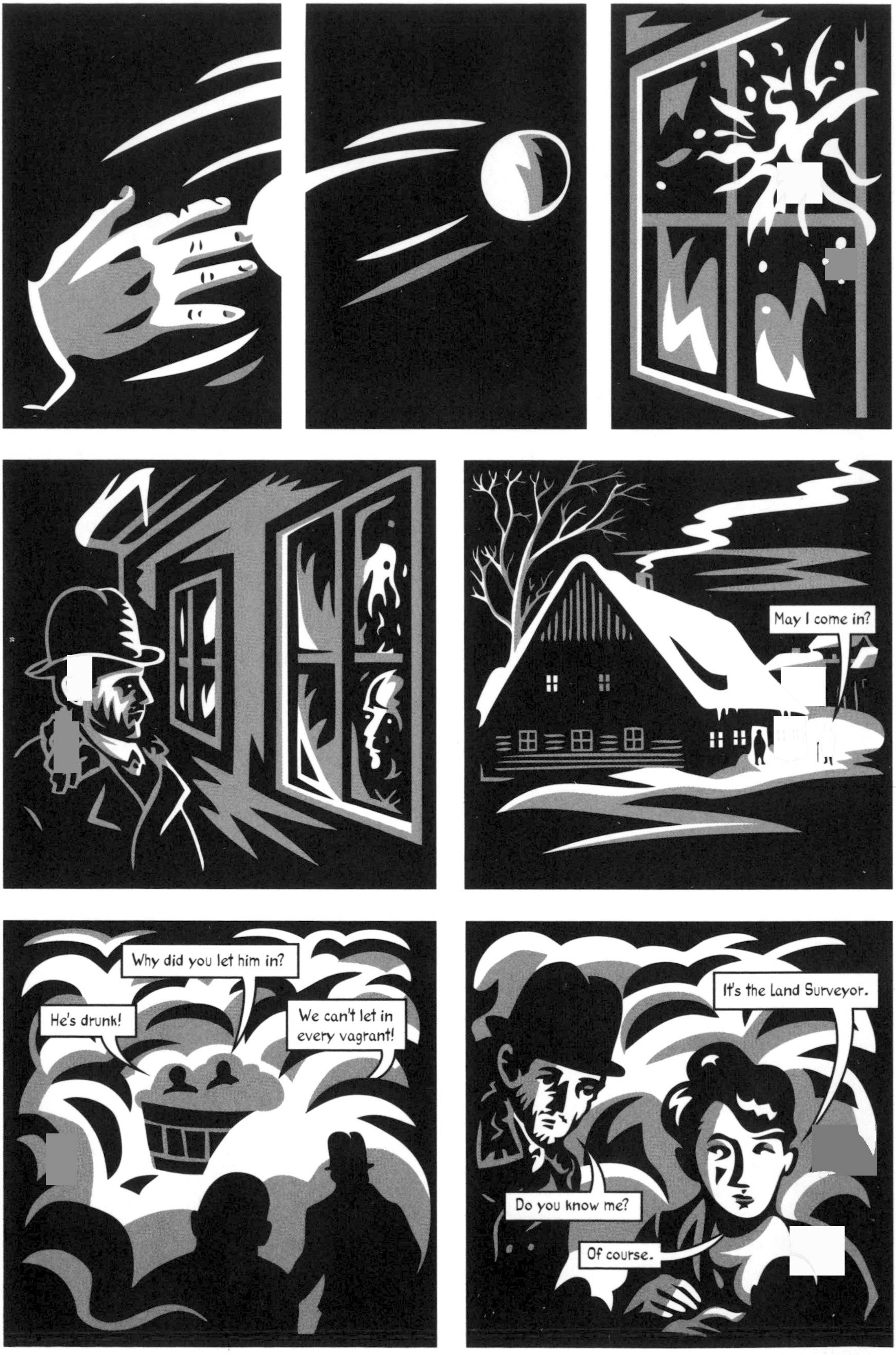
May I come in?
Why did you let him in?
He's drunk!
We can't let in every vagrant!
It's the Land Surveyor.
Do you know me?
Of course.

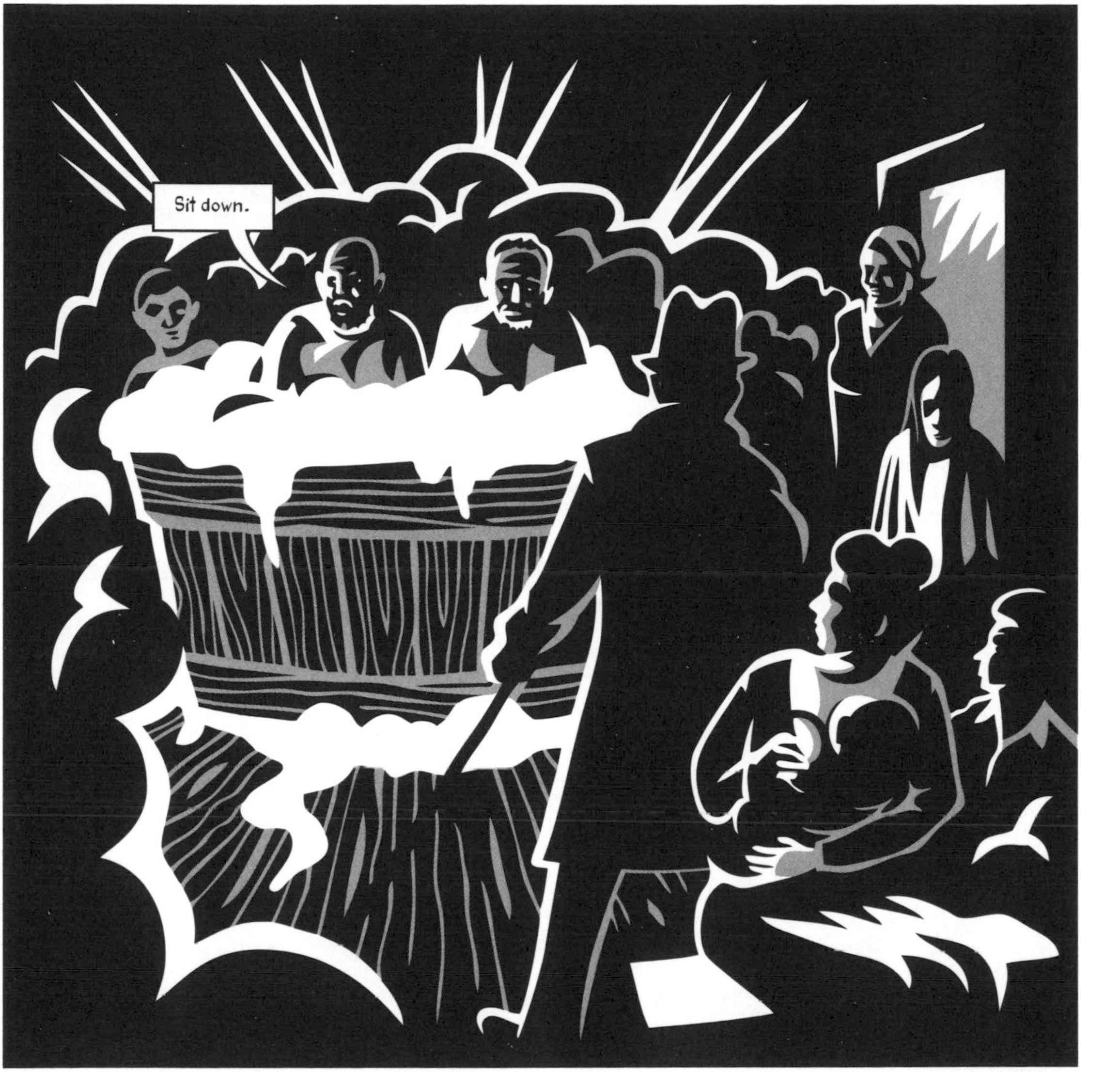
Sit down.

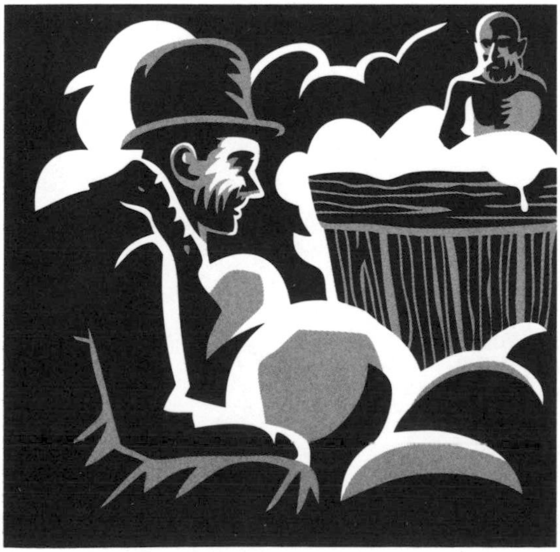

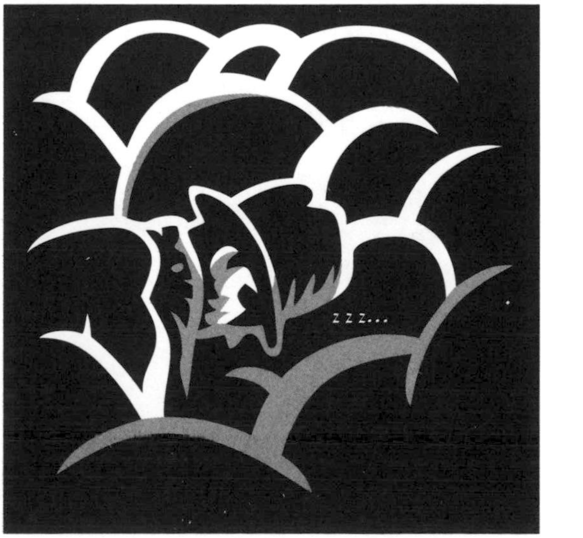
Z Z Z...

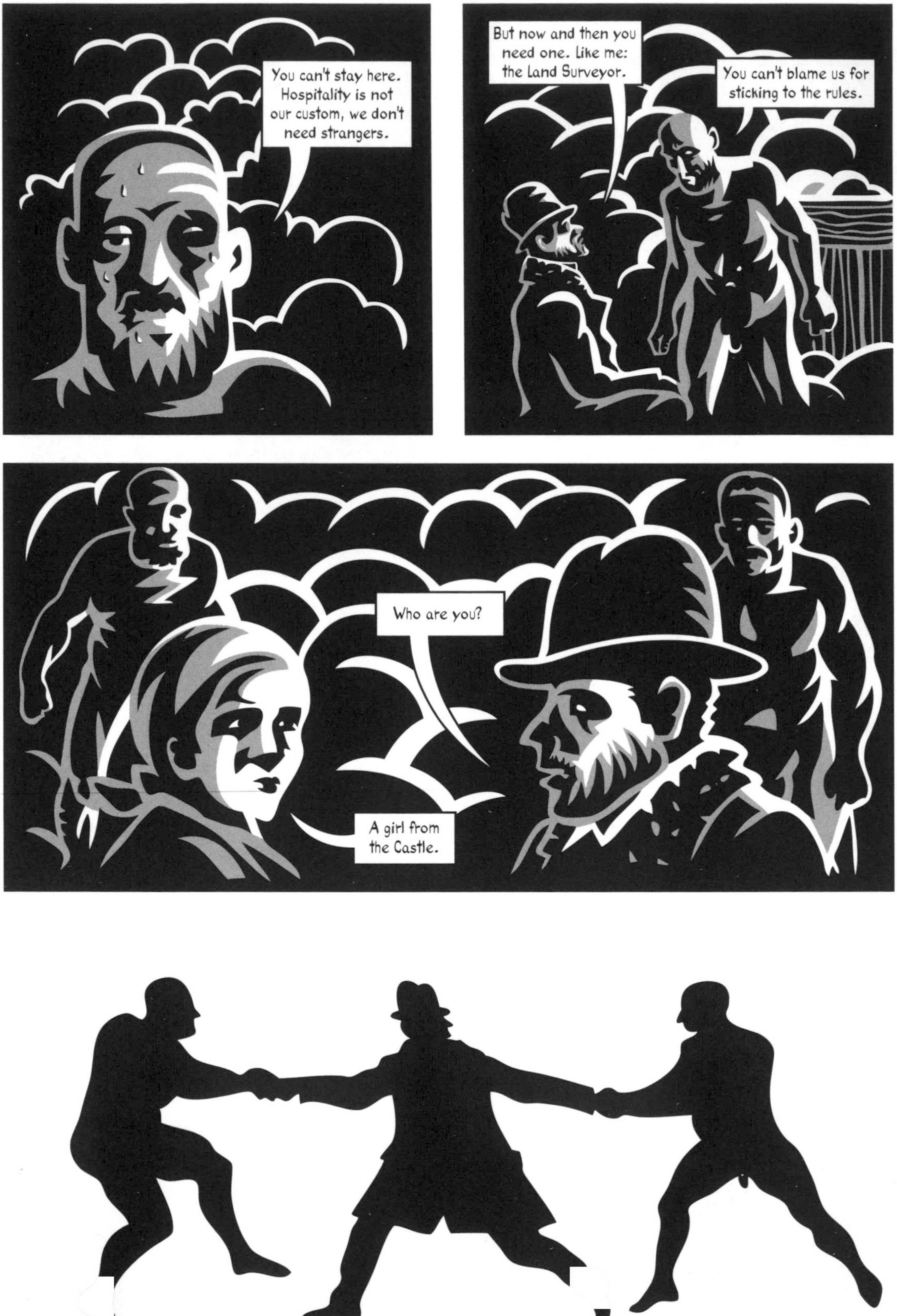
You can't stay here. Hospitality is not our custom, we don't need strangers.
But now and then you need one. Like me: the Land Surveyor.
You can't blame us for sticking to the rules.
Who are you?
A girl from the Castle.

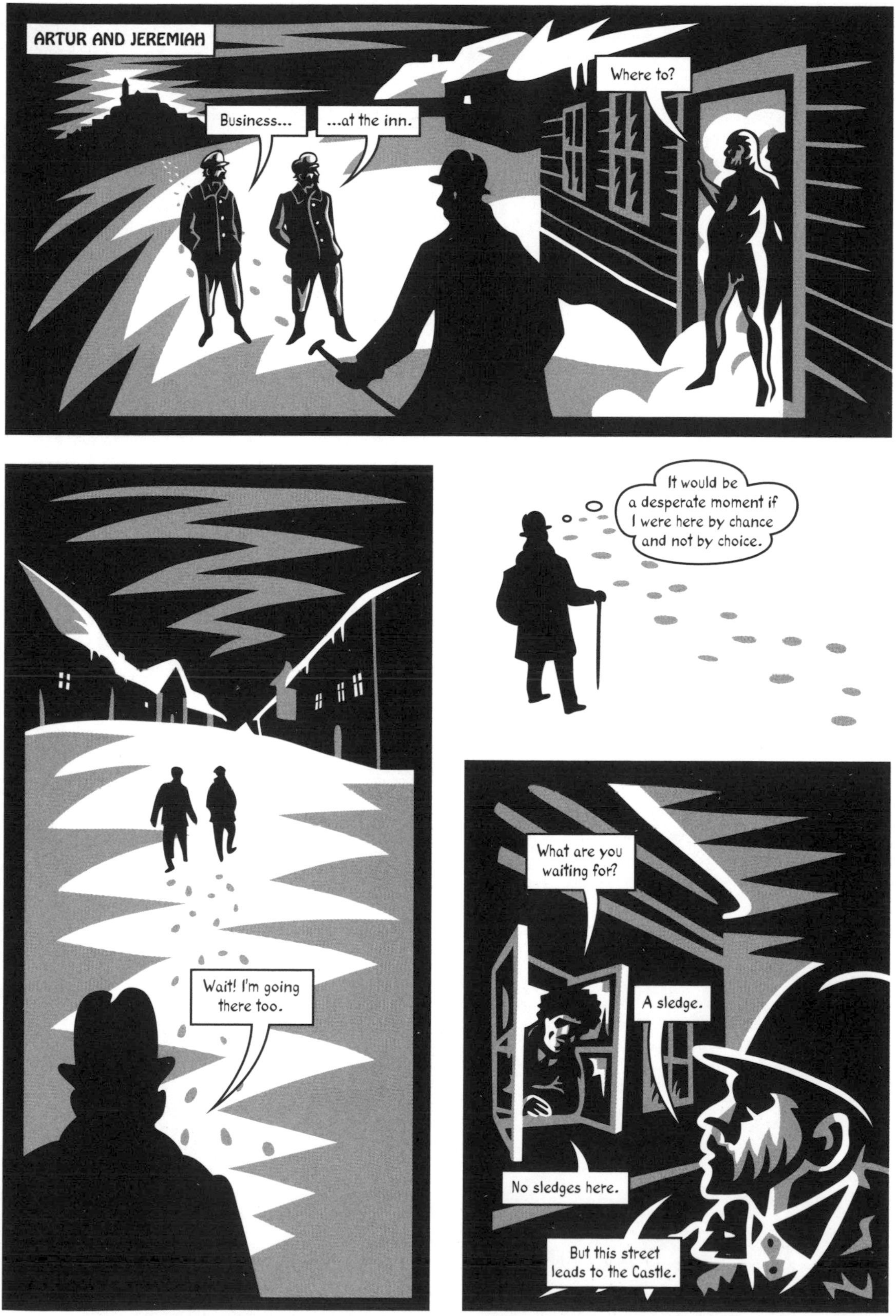
ARTUR AND JEREMIAH
Business...
...at the inn.
Where to?
Wait! I'm going there too.
It would be a desperate moment if I were here by chance and not by choice.
What are you waiting for?
A sledge.
No sledges here.
But this street leads to the Castle.

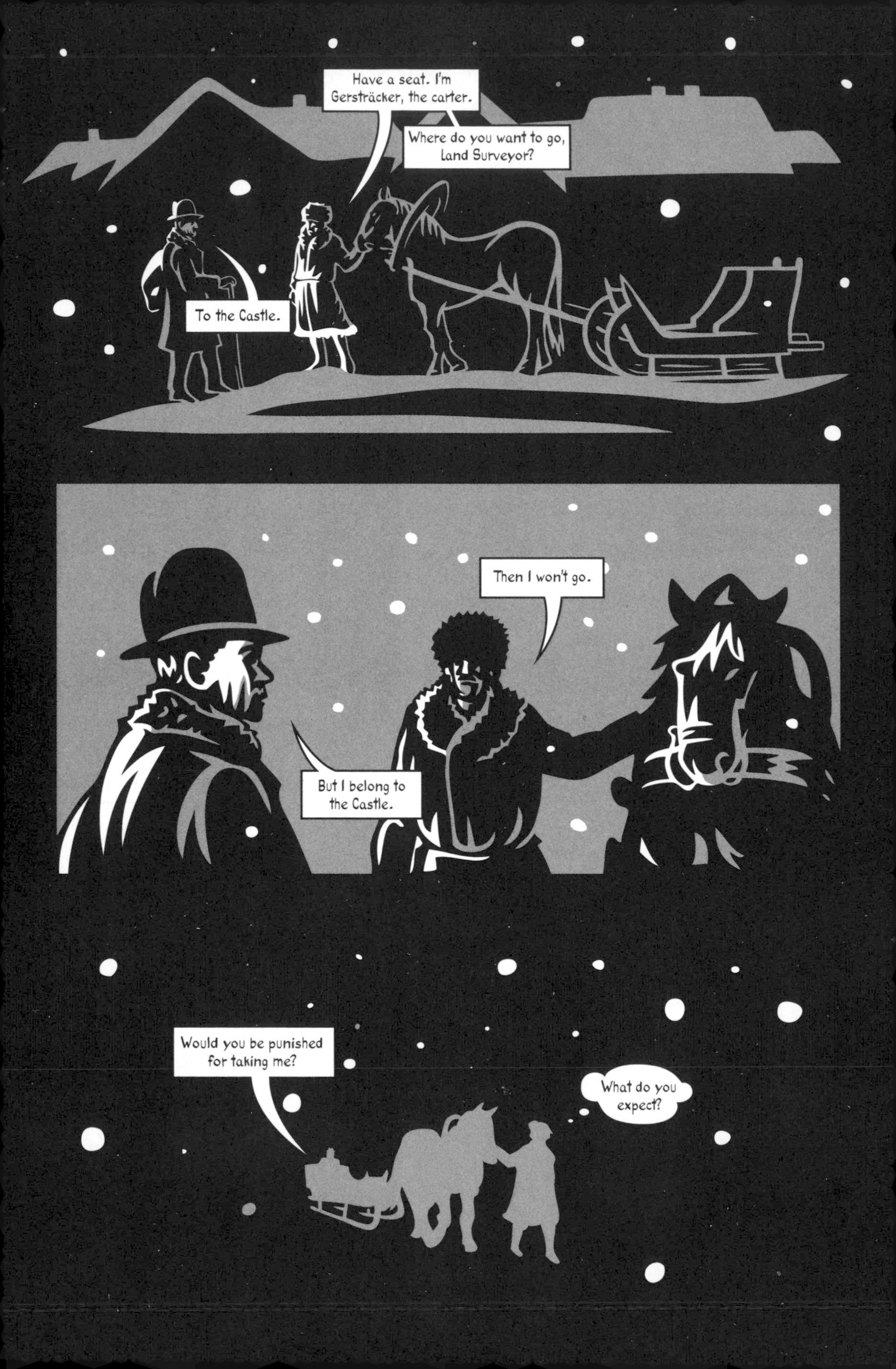
Have a seat. I'm Gersträcker, the carter.
Where do you want to go, Land Surveyor?
To the Castle.
Then I won't go.
But I belong to the Castle.
Would you be punished for taking me?
What do you expect?

Who are you?
Your...
...assistants.
What? My old assistants Artur and Jeremiah? Whom I've been expecting?

You're late. You've been negligent!
It was...
...a long way!
But I just met you coming from the Castle!

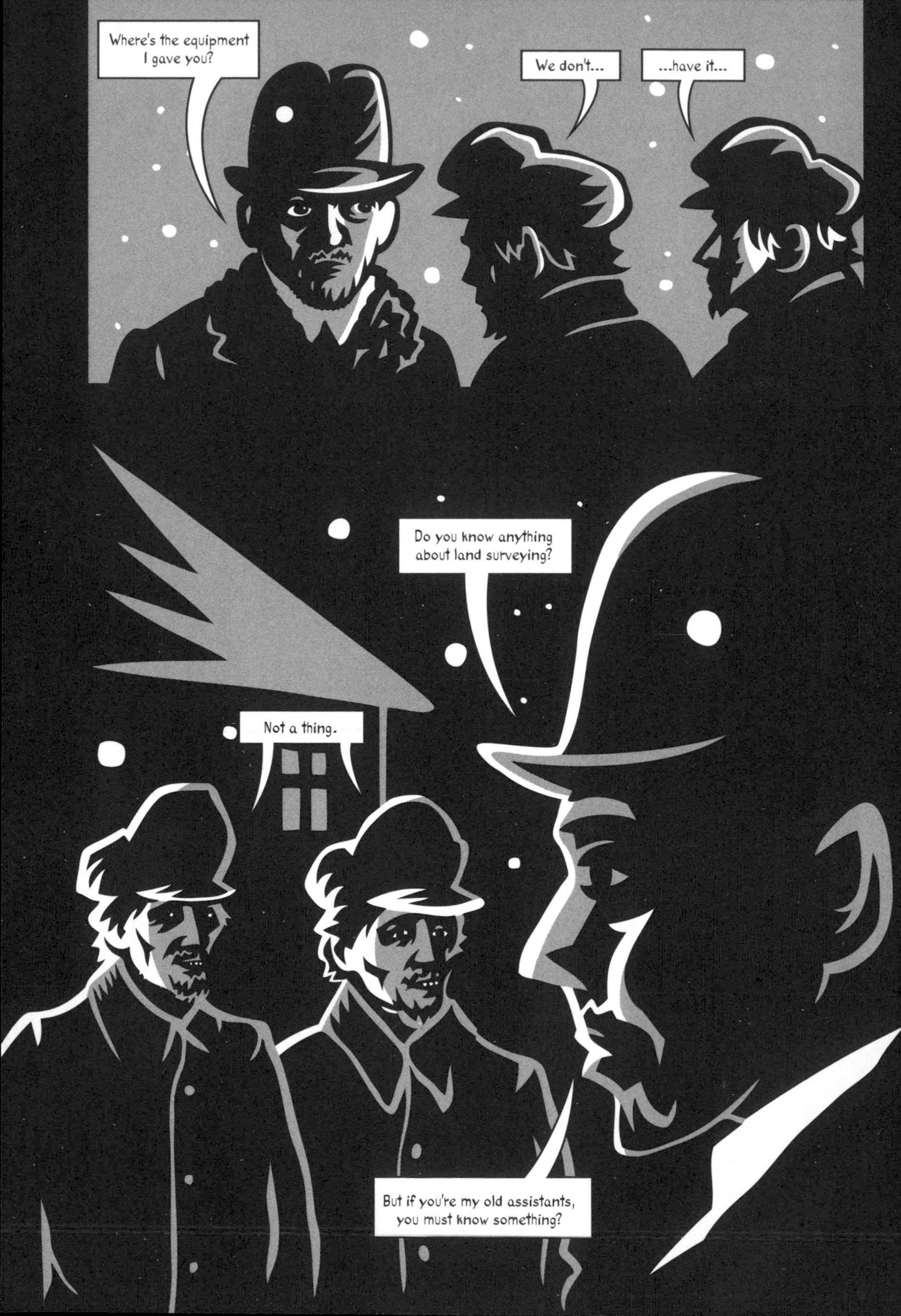
Where's the equipment I gave you?
We don't...
...have it...
Do you know anything about land surveying?
Not a thing.
But if you're my old assistants, you must know something?

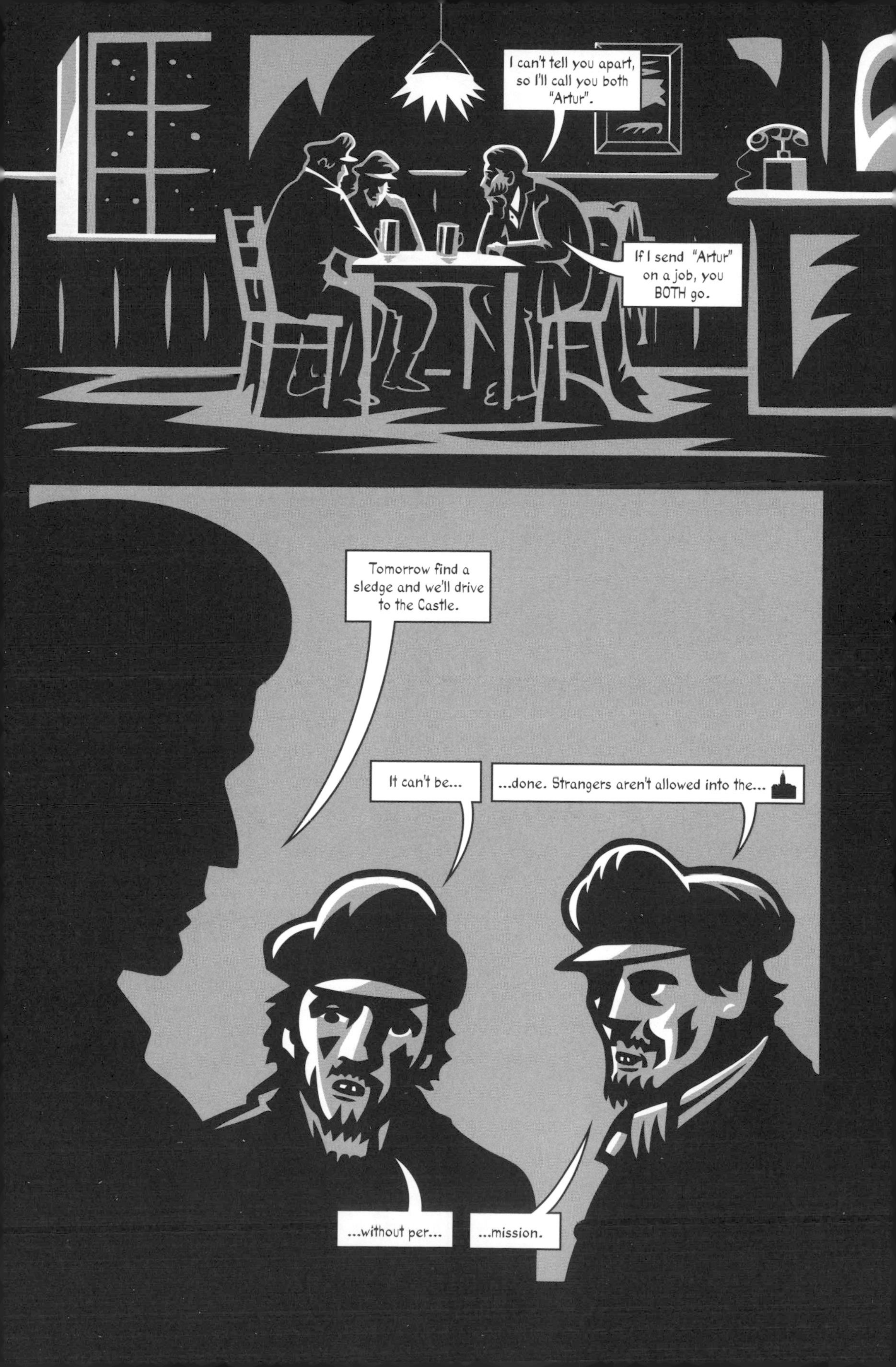
I can't tell you apart, so I'll call you both "Artur".
If I send "Artur" on a job, you BOTH go.
Tomorrow find a sledge and we'll drive to the Castle.
It can't be...
...done. Strangers aren't allowed into the...
...without per...
...mission.

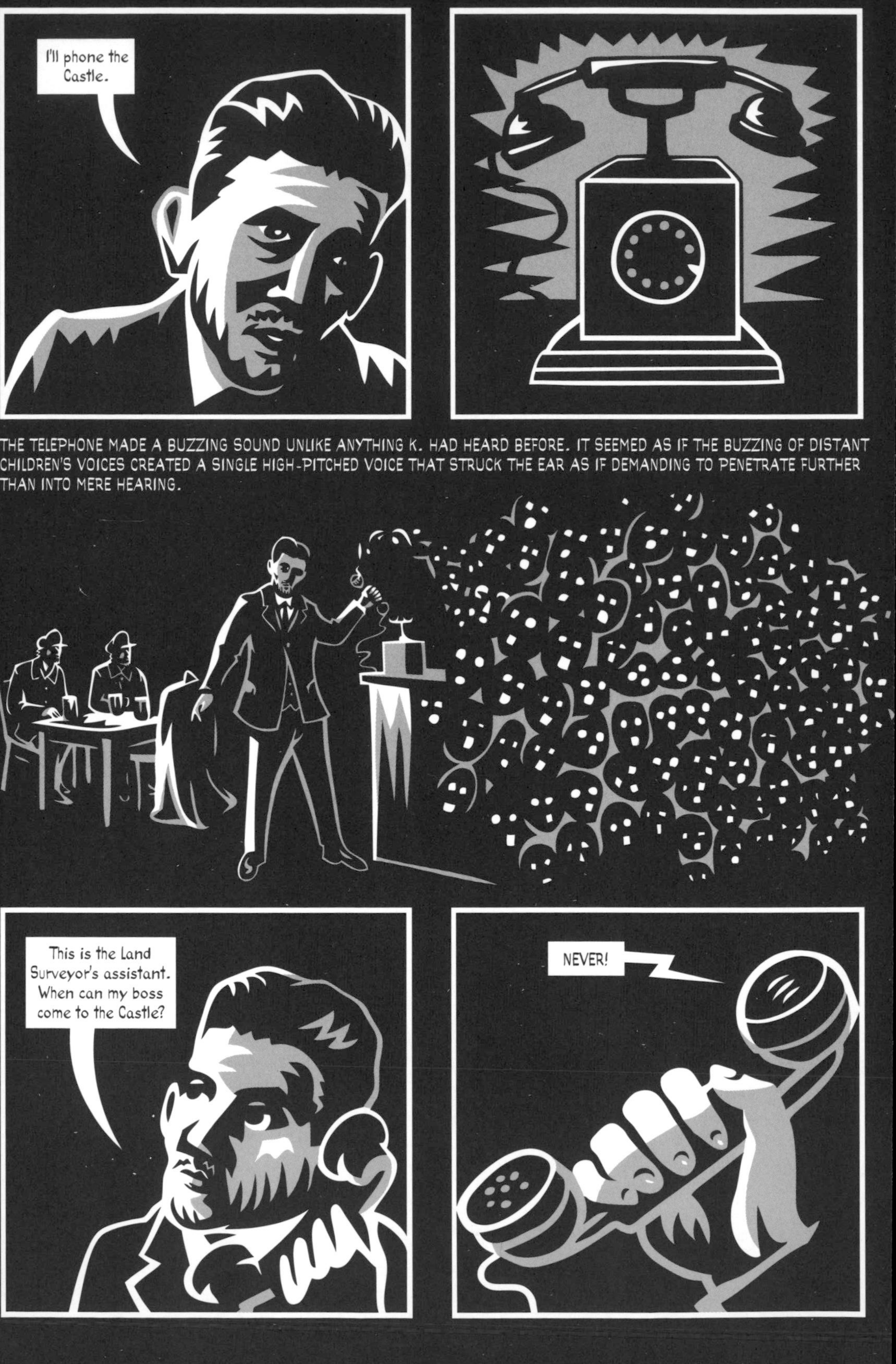
I'll phone the Castle.
THE TELEPHONE MADE A BUZZING SOUND UNLIKE ANYTHING K. HAD HEARD BEFORE. IT SEEMED AS IF THE BUZZING OF DISTANT CHILDREN'S VOICES CREATED A SINGLE HIGH-PITCHED VOICE THAT STRUCK THE EAR AS IF DEMANDING TO PENETRATE FURTHER THAN INTO MERE HEARING.
This is the Land Surveyor's assistant. When can my boss come to the Castle?
NEVER!

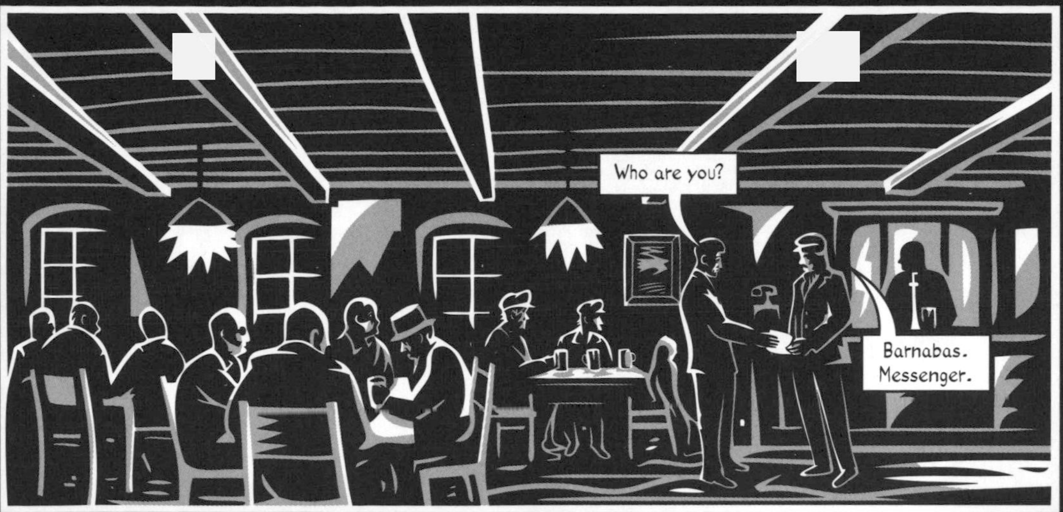
Who are you?
Barnabas. Messenger.

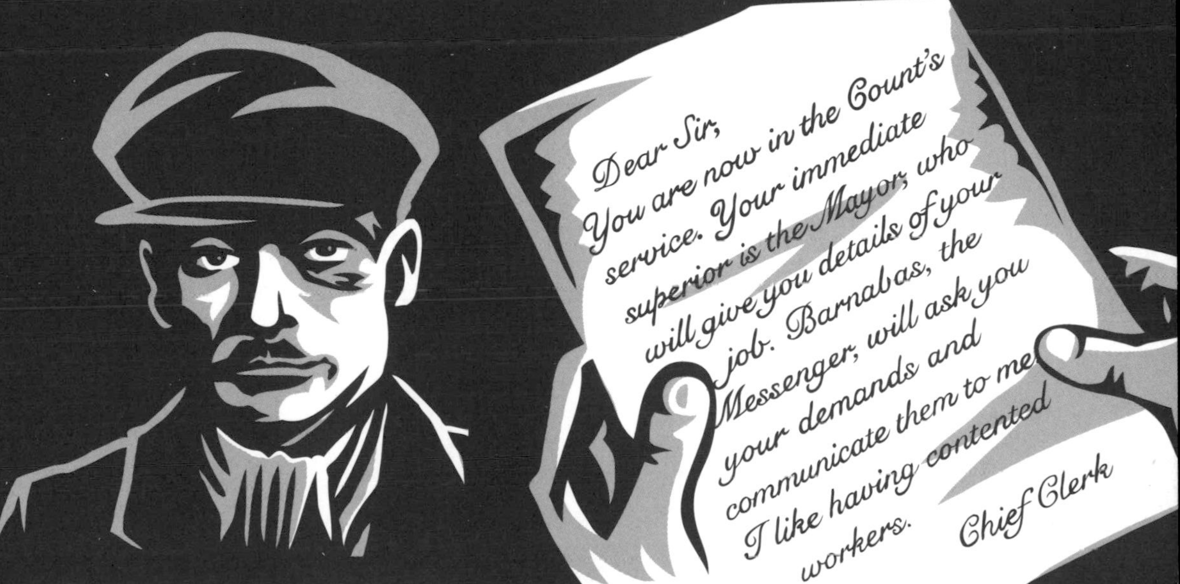
Dear Sir,
You are now in the Count's service. Your immediate superior is the Mayor, who will give you details of your job. Barnabas, the Messenger, will ask you your demands and communicate them to me. I like having contented workers.
Chief Clerk

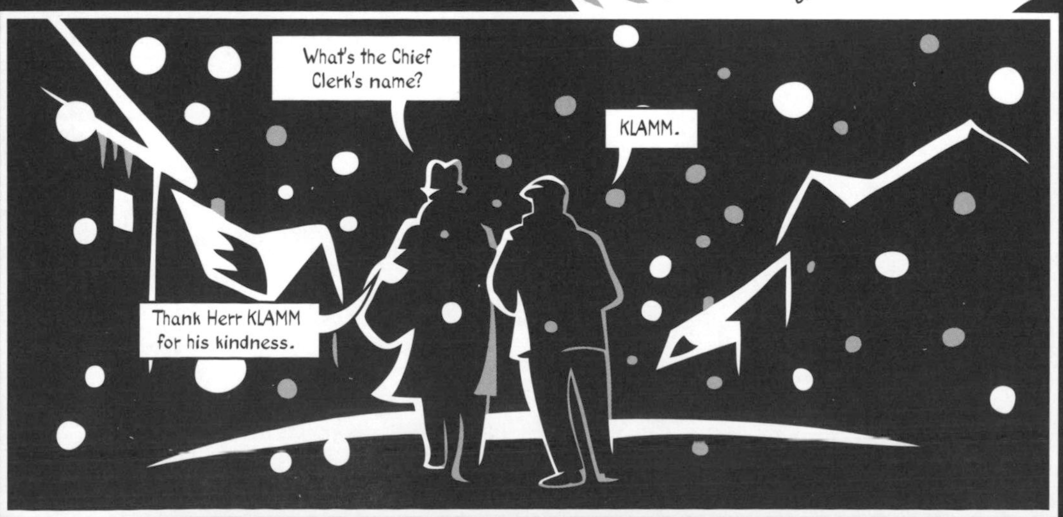
What's the Chief Clerk's name?
KLAMM.
Thank Herr KLAMM for his kindness.

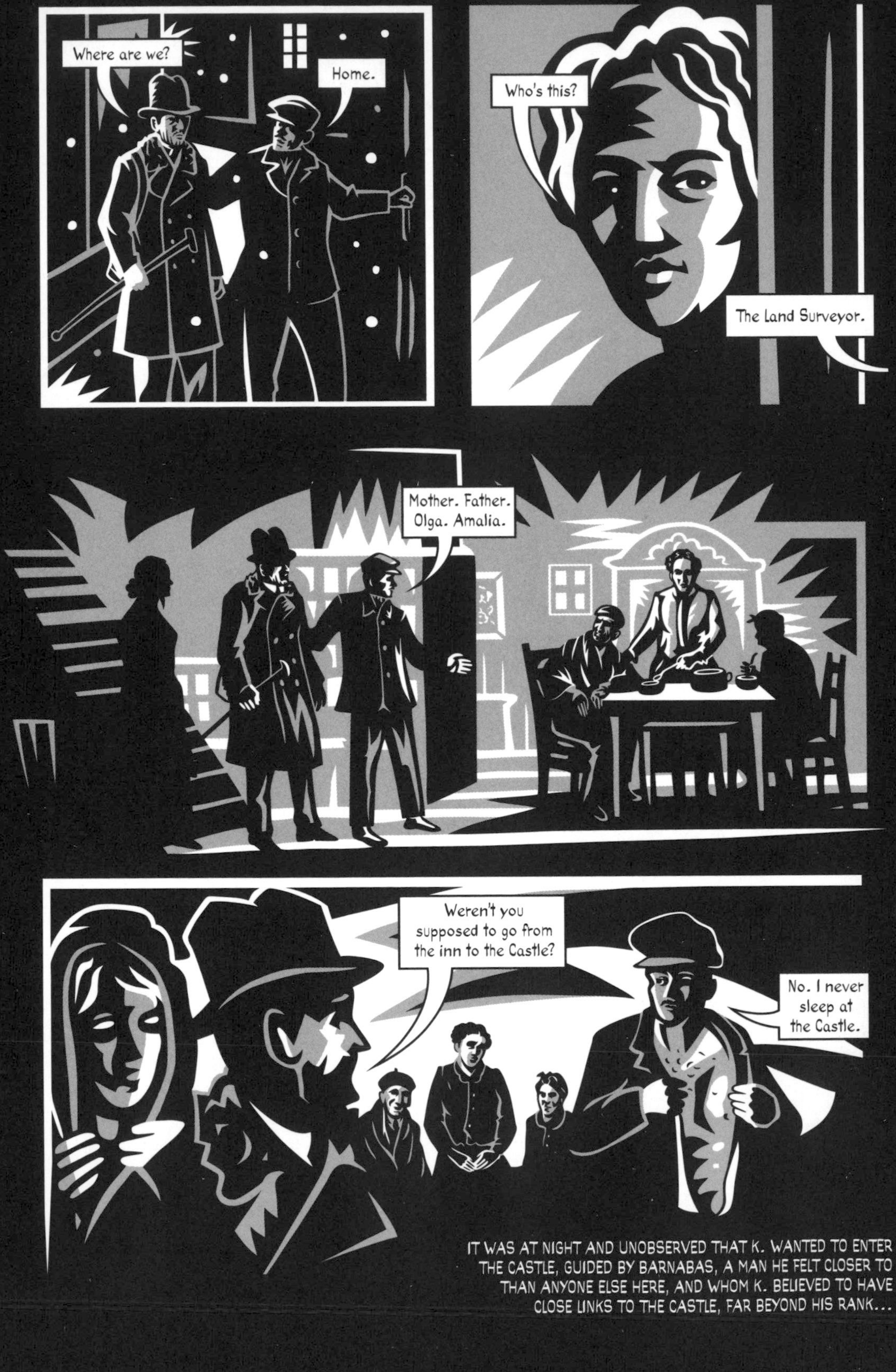

Where are we?
Home.
Who's this?
The Land Surveyor.
Mother. Father. Olga. Amalia.
Weren't you supposed to go from the inn to the Castle?
No. I never sleep at the Castle.
IT WAS AT NIGHT AND UNOBSERVED THAT K. WANTED TO ENTER THE CASTLE, GUIDED BY BARNABAS, A MAN HE FELT CLOSER TO THAN ANYONE ELSE HERE, AND WHOM K. BELIEVED TO HAVE CLOSE LINKS TO THE CASTLE, FAR BEYOND HIS RANK...

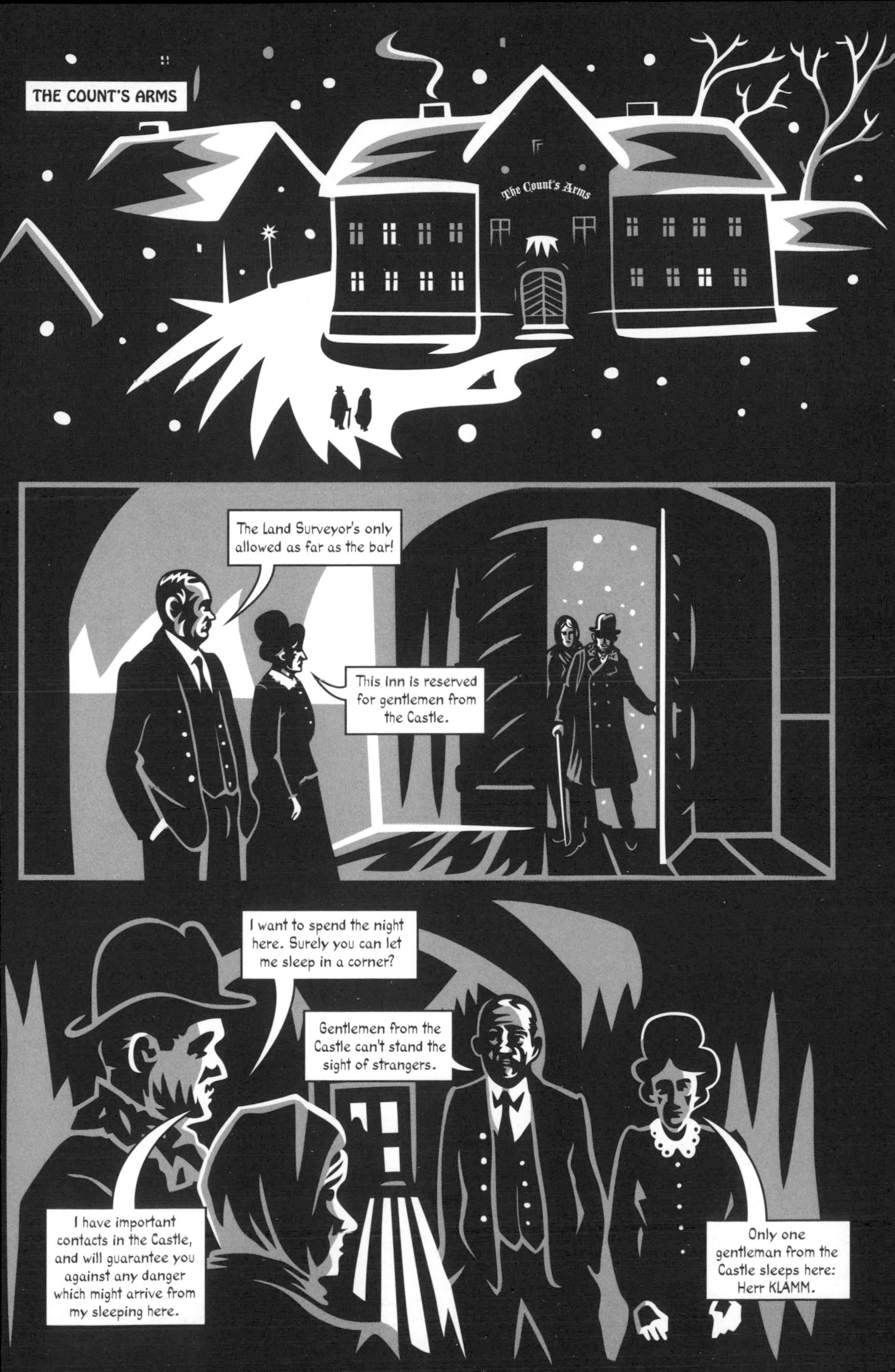
THE COUNT'S ARMS
The Count's Arms
The Land Surveyor's only allowed as far as the bar!
This Inn is reserved for gentlemen from the Castle.
I want to spend the night here. Surely you can let me sleep in a corner?
Gentlemen from the Castle can't stand the sight of strangers.
I have important contacts in the Castle, and will guarantee you against any danger which might arrive from my sleeping here.
Only one gentleman from the Castle sleeps here: Herr KLAMM.

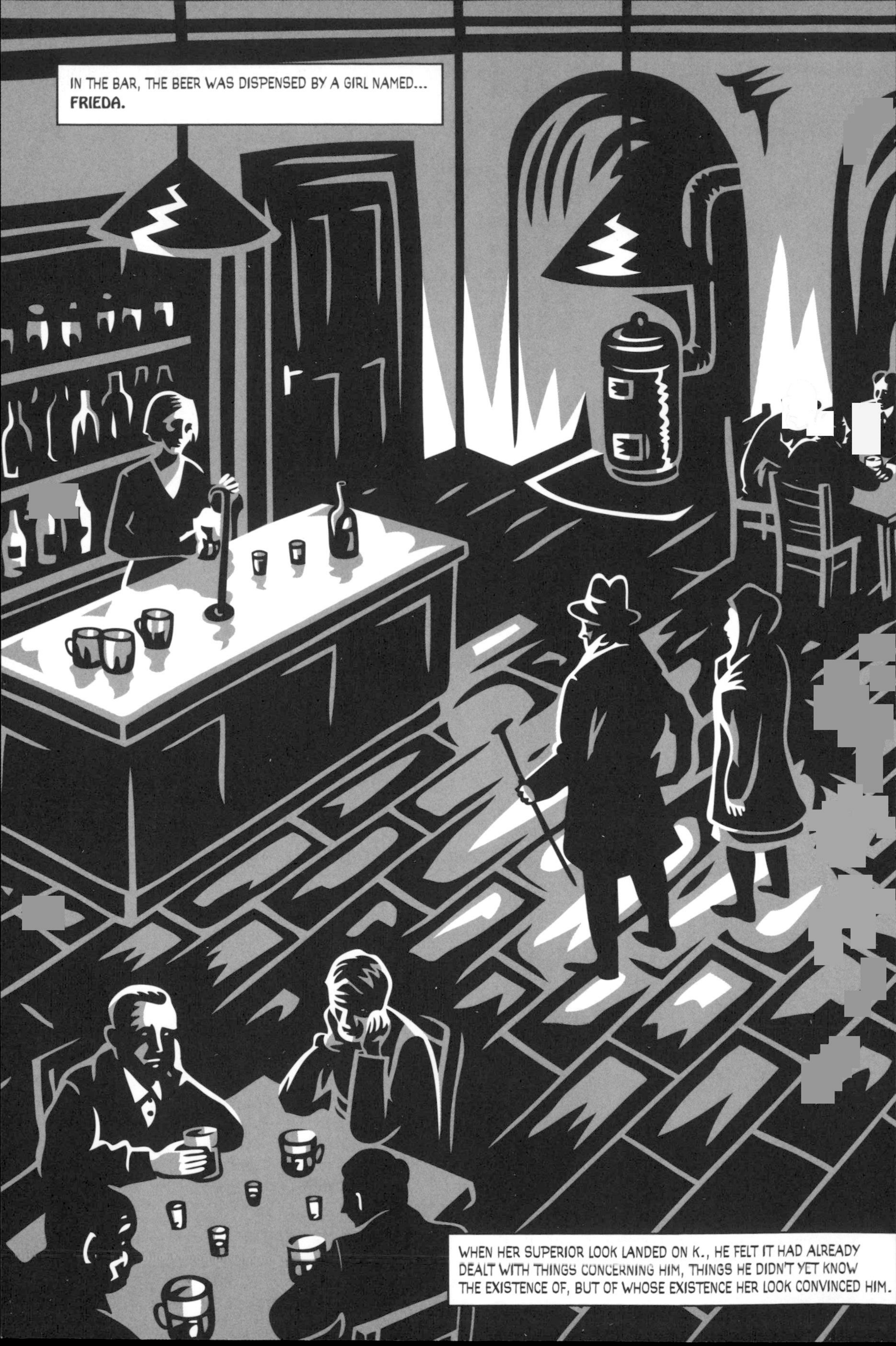
IN THE BAR, THE BEER WAS DISPENSED BY A GIRL NAMED... FRIEDA.
WHEN HER SUPERIOR LOOK LANDED ON K., HE FELT IT HAD ALREADY DEALT WITH THINGS CONCERNING HIM, THINGS HE DIDN'T YET KNOW THE EXISTENCE OF, BUT OF WHOSE EXISTENCE HER LOOK CONVINCED HIM.

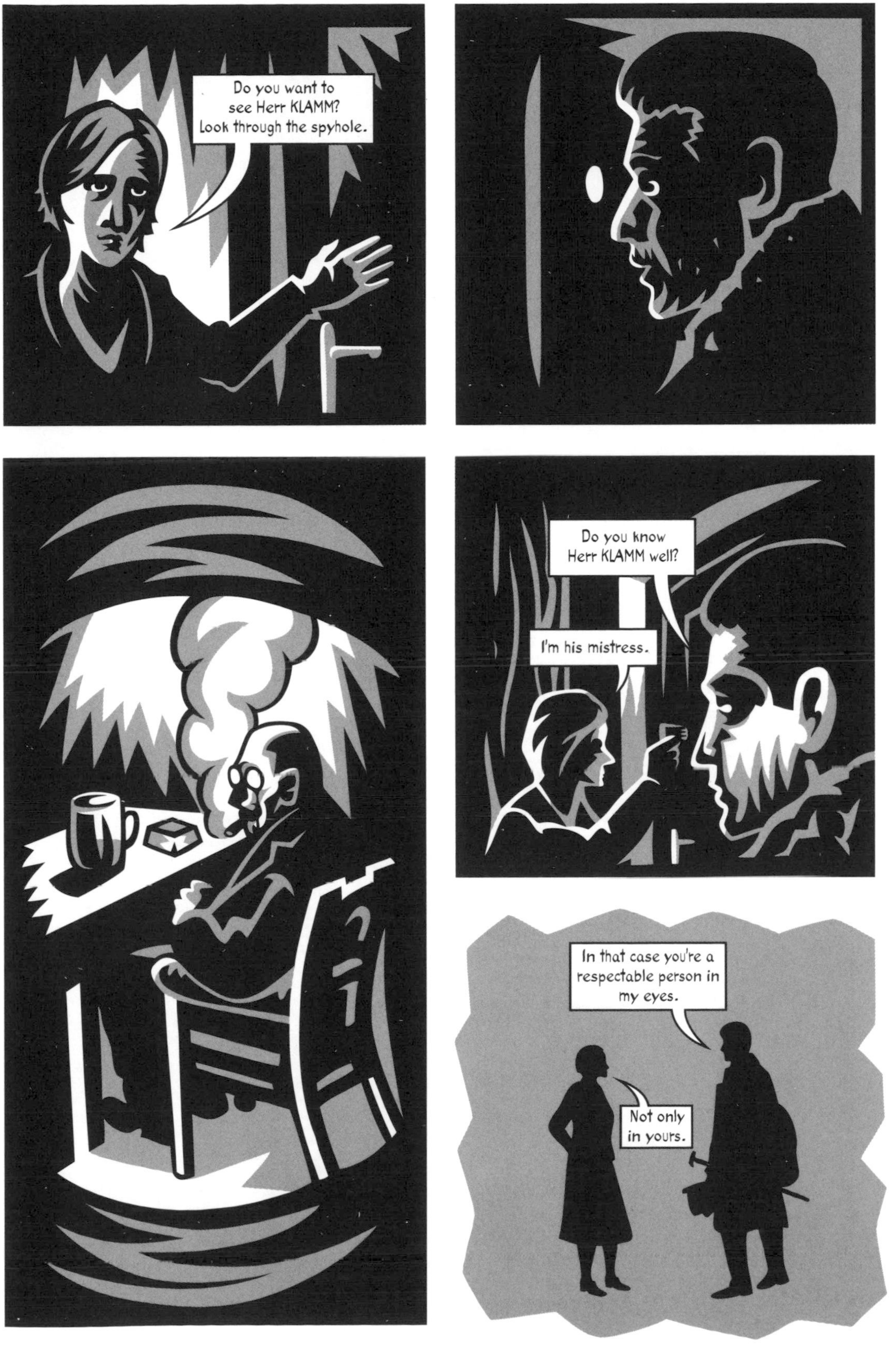
Do you want to see Herr KLAMM? Look through the spyhole.
Do you know Herr KLAMM well?
I'm his mistress.
In that case you're a respectable person in my eyes.
Not only in yours.

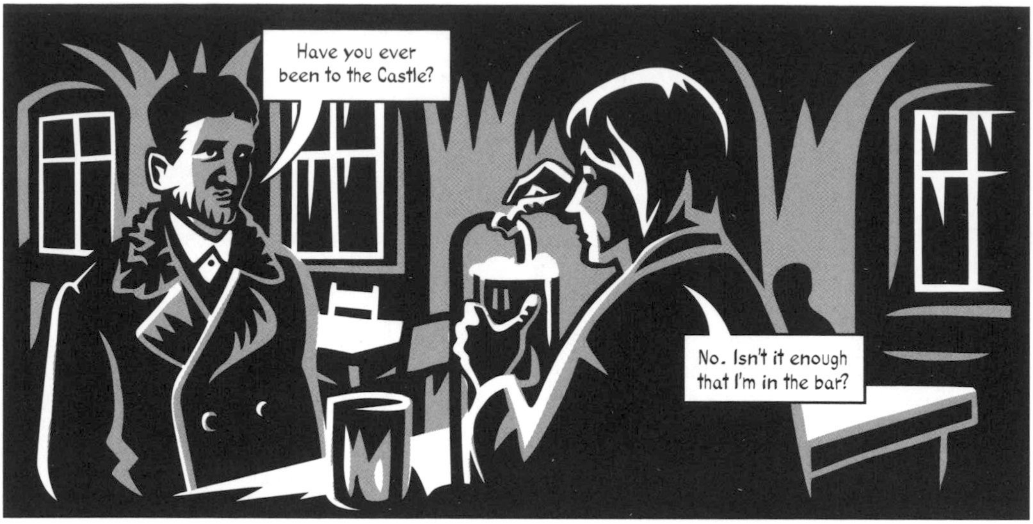
Have you ever been to the Castle?
No. Isn't it enough that I'm in the bar?

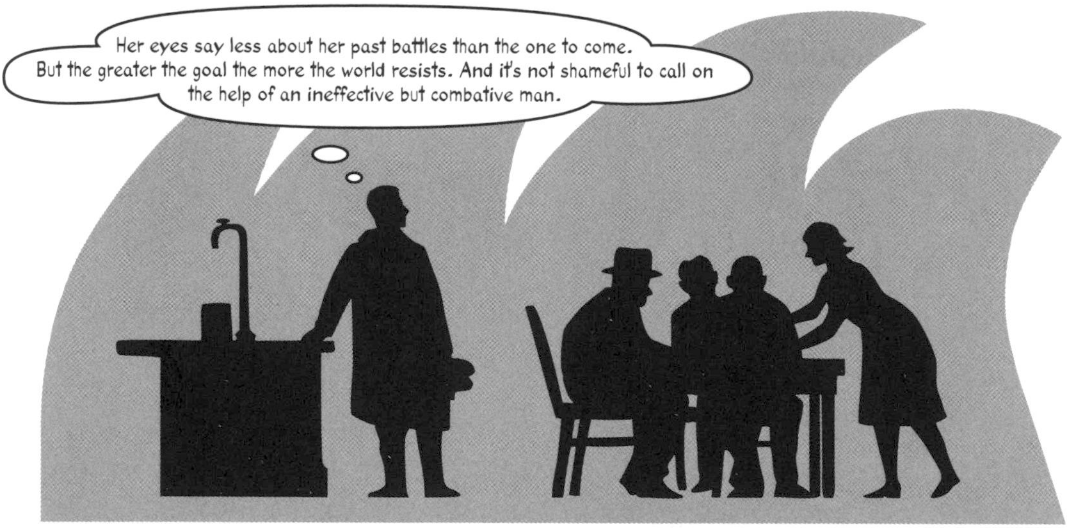
Her eyes say less about her past battles than the one to come. But the greater the goal the more the world resists. And it's not shameful to call on the help of an ineffective but combative man.

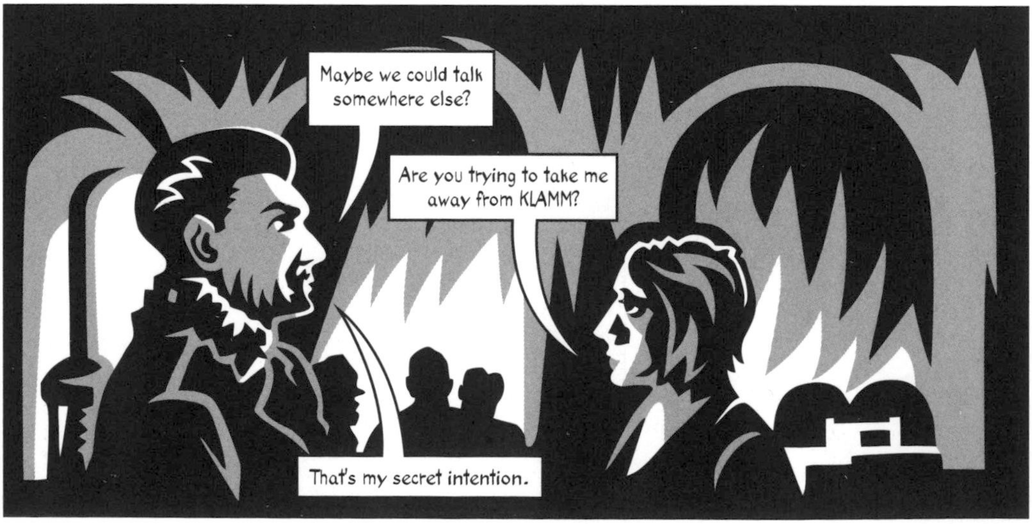
Maybe we could talk somewhere else?
Are you trying to take me away from KLAMM?
That's my secret intention.

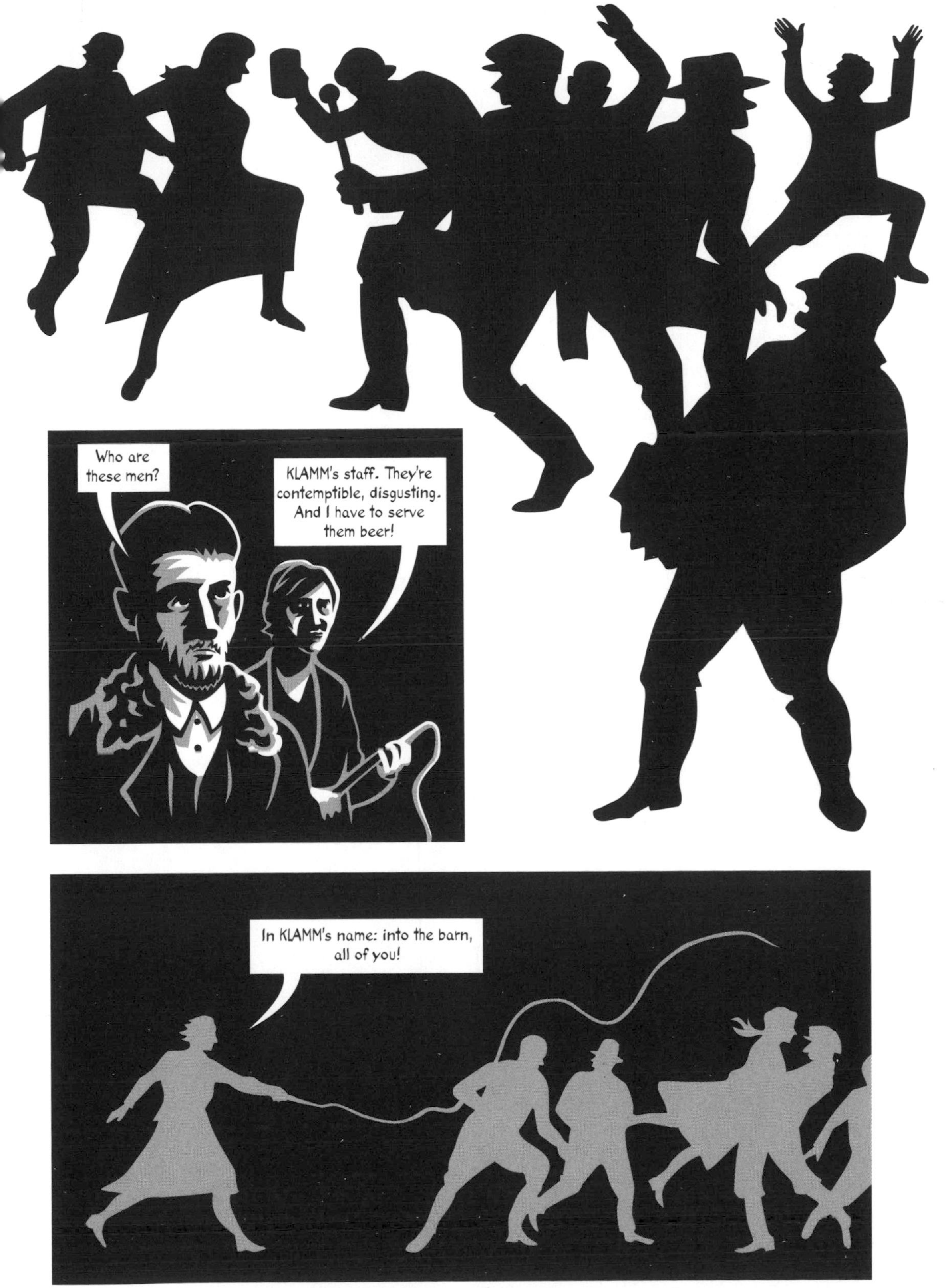
Who are these men?
KLAMM's staff. They're contemptible, disgusting. And I have to serve them beer!
In KLAMM's name: into the barn, all of you!

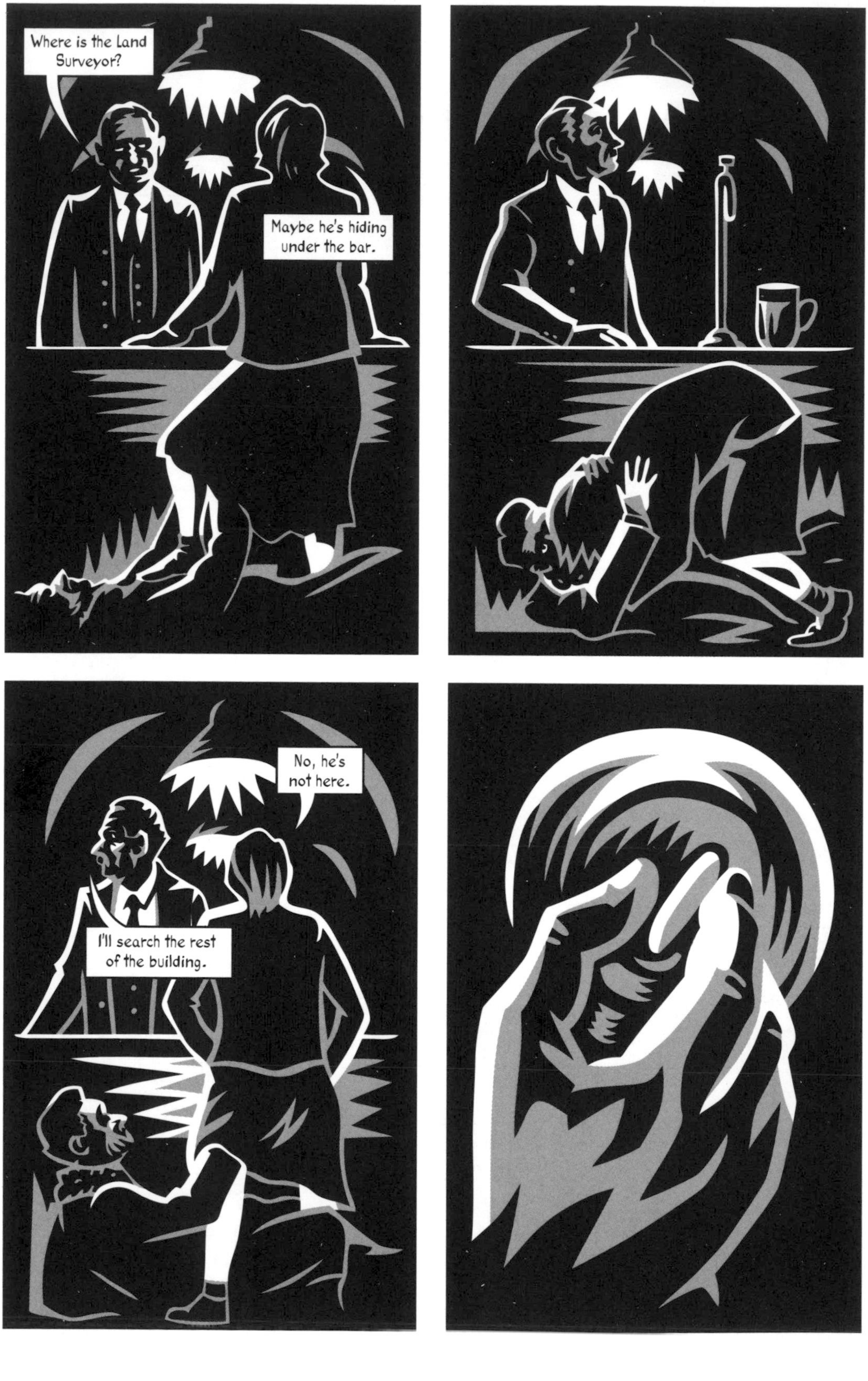
Where is the Land Surveyor?
Maybe he's hiding under the bar.
No, he's not here.
I'll search the rest of the building.

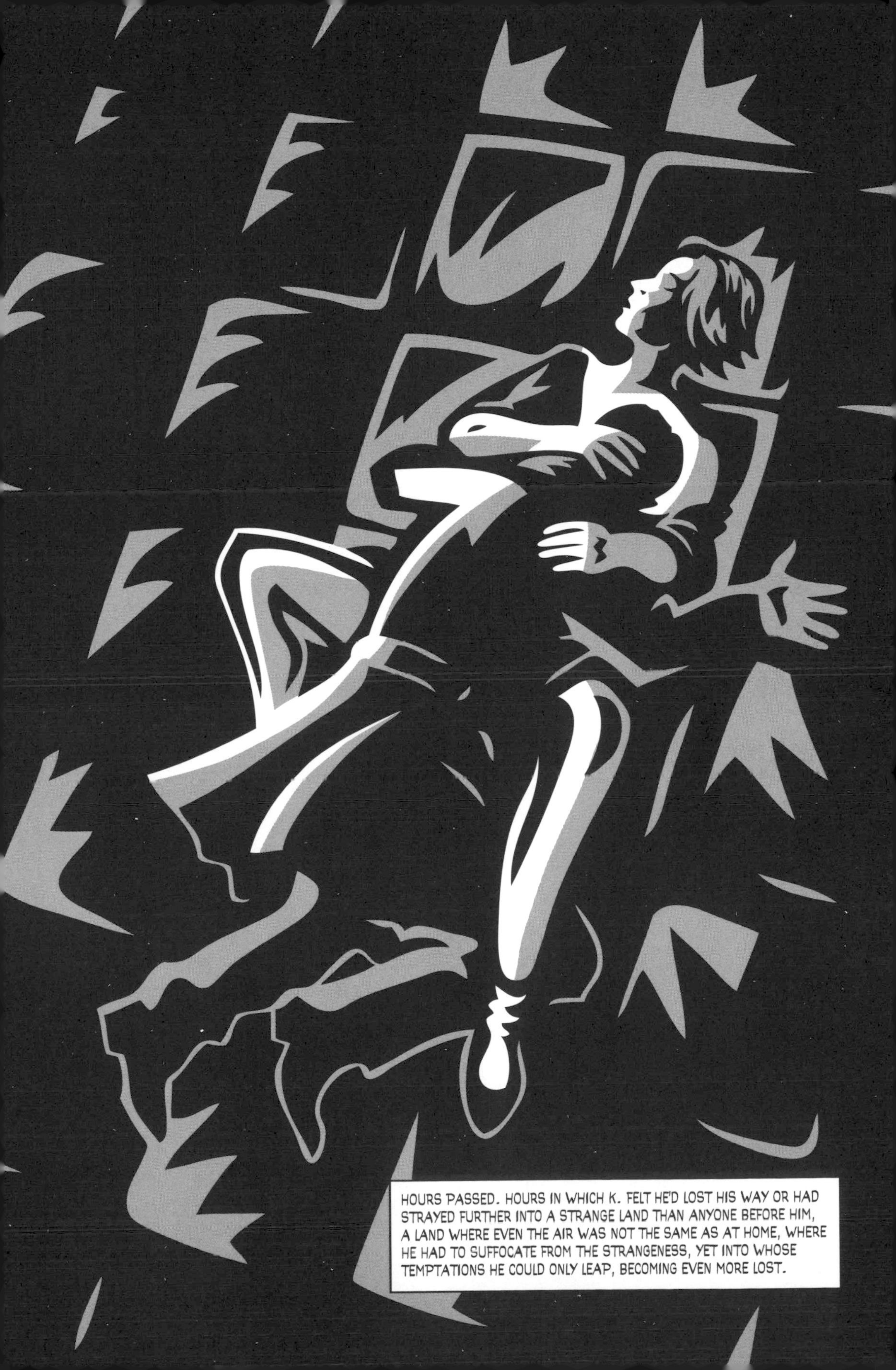
HOURS PASSED. HOURS IN WHICH K. FELT HE'D LOST HIS WAY OR HAD STRAYED FURTHER INTO A STRANGE LAND THAN ANYONE BEFORE HIM, A LAND WHERE EVEN THE AIR WAS NOT THE SAME AS AT HOME, WHERE HE HAD TO SUFFOCATE FROM THE STRANGENESS, YET INTO WHOSE TEMPTATIONS HE COULD ONLY LEAP, BECOMING EVEN MORE LOST.

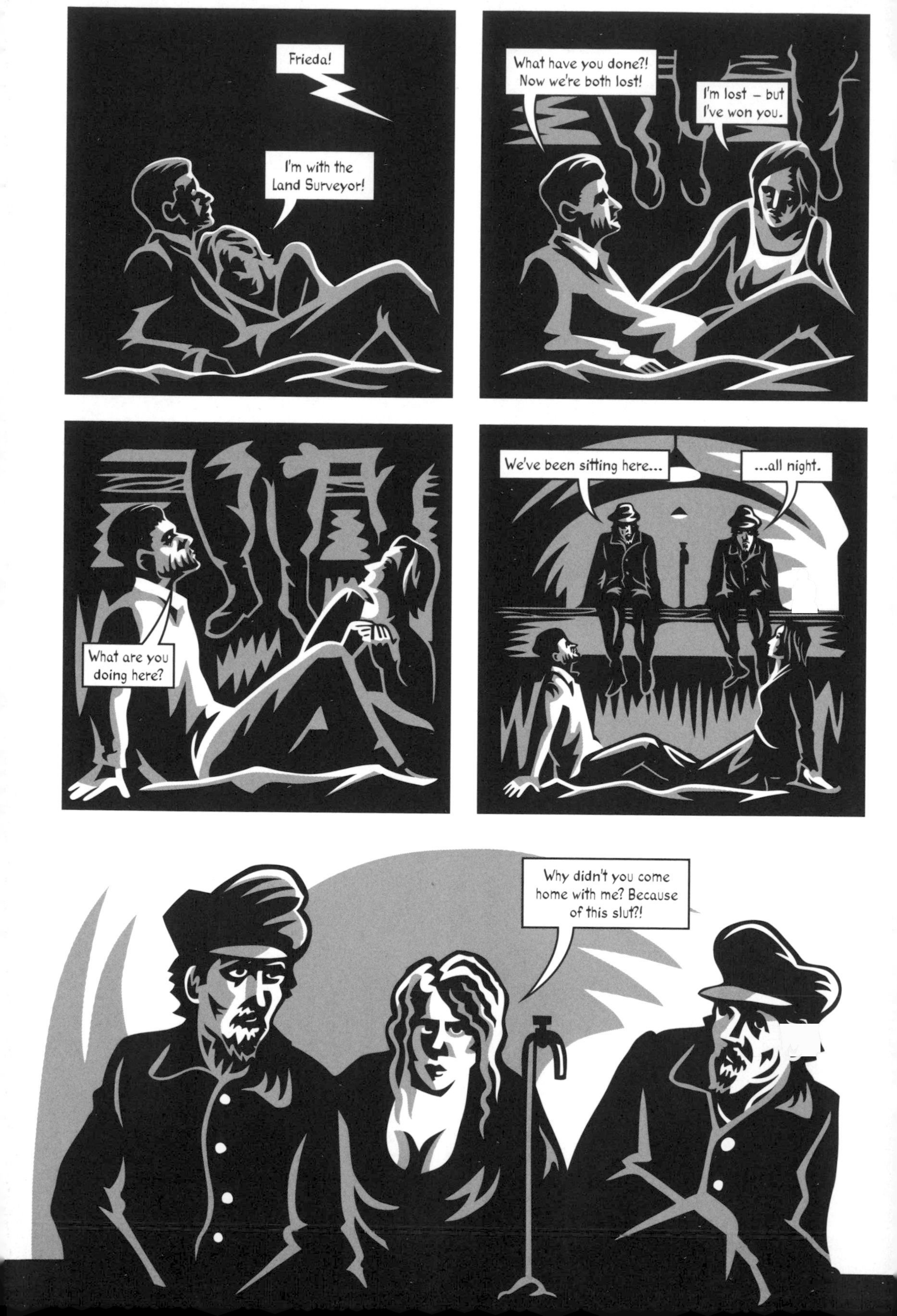
Frieda!
I'm with the Land Surveyor!
What have you done?! Now we're both lost!
I'm lost – but I've won you.
What are you doing here?
We've been sitting here...
...all night.
Why didn't you come home with me? Because of this slut?!

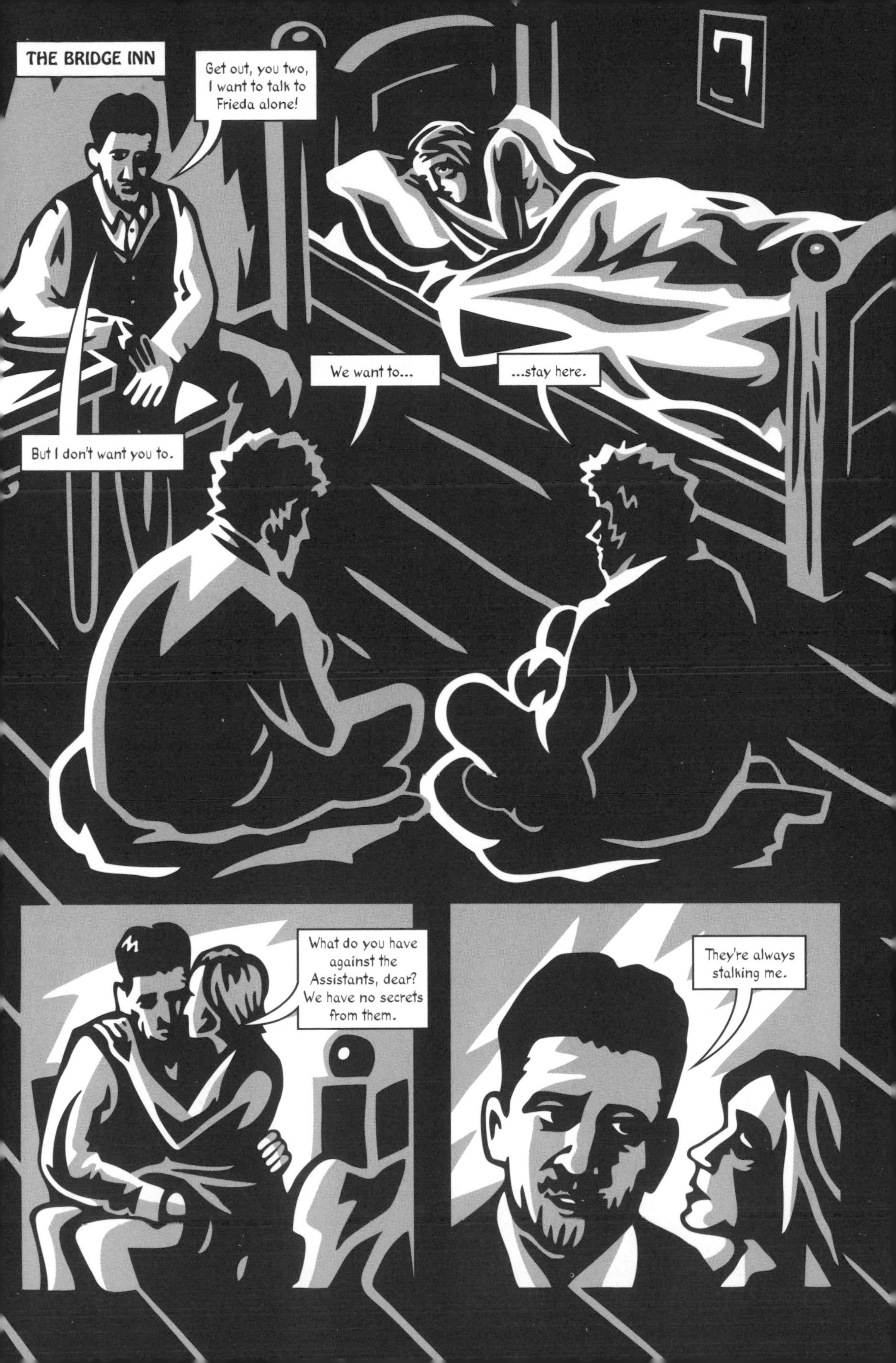
THE BRIDGE INN
Get out, you two, I want to talk to Frieda alone!
We want to...
...stay here.
But I don't want you to.
What do you have against the Assistants, dear? We have no secrets from them.
They're always stalking me.

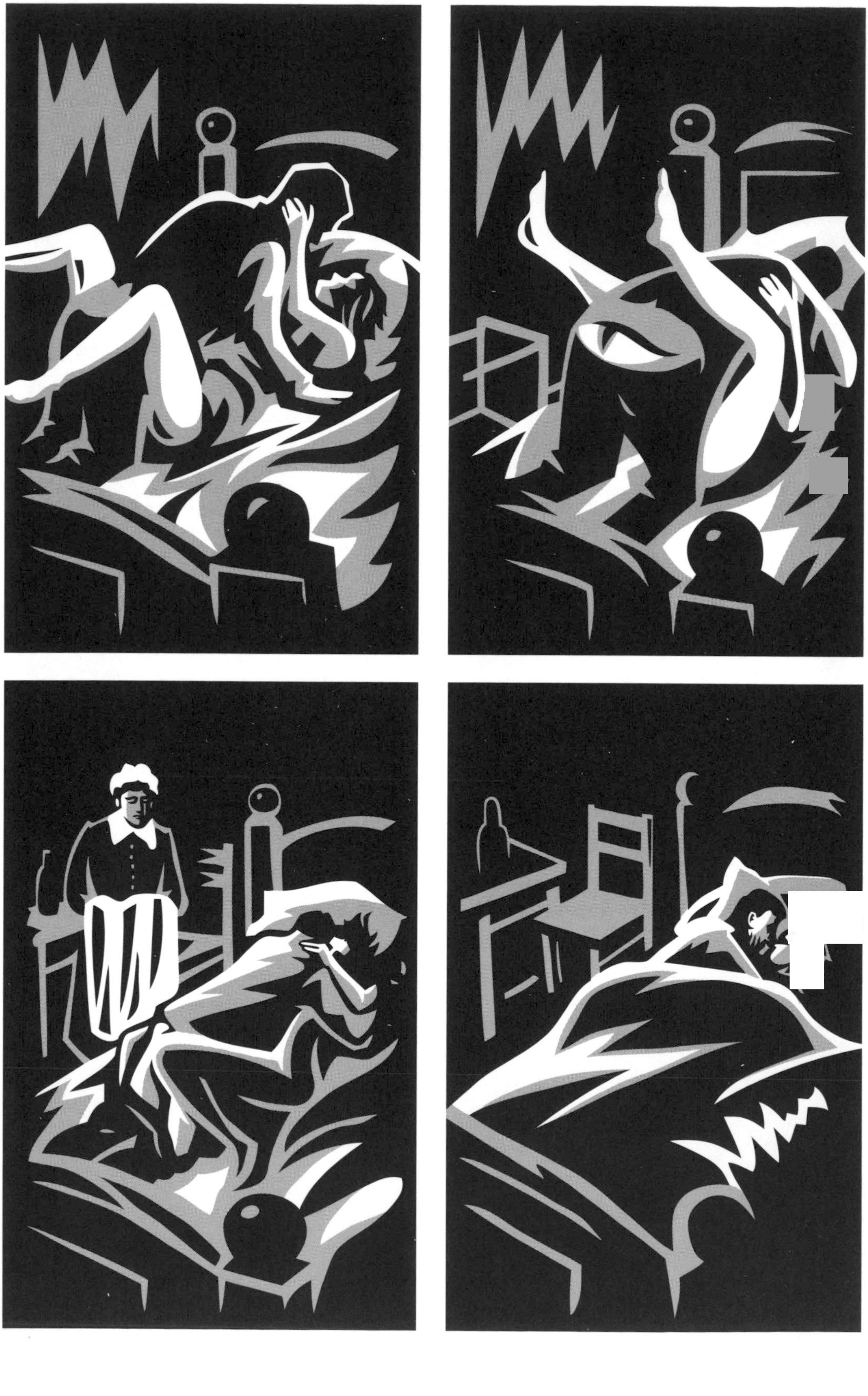

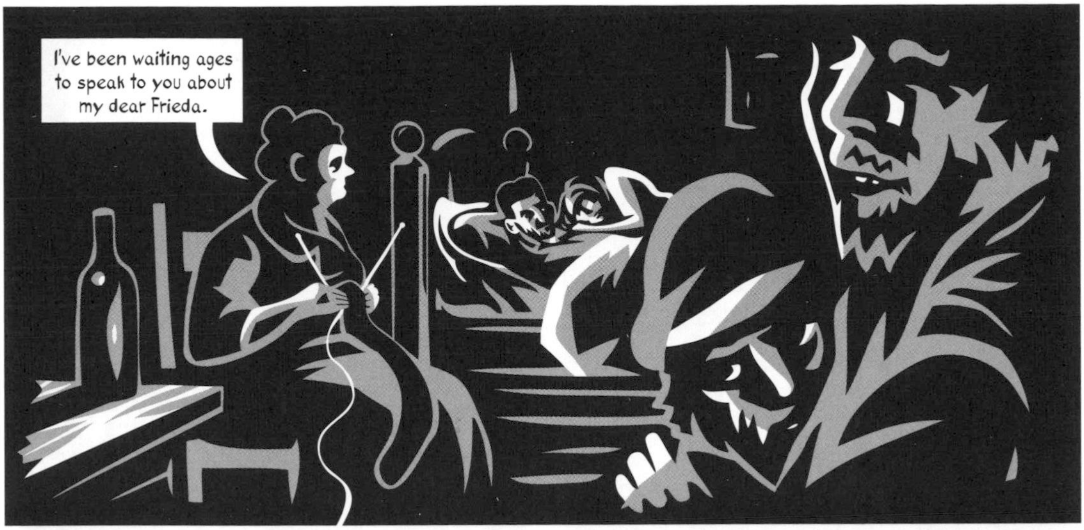
I've been waiting ages to speak to you about my dear Frieda.

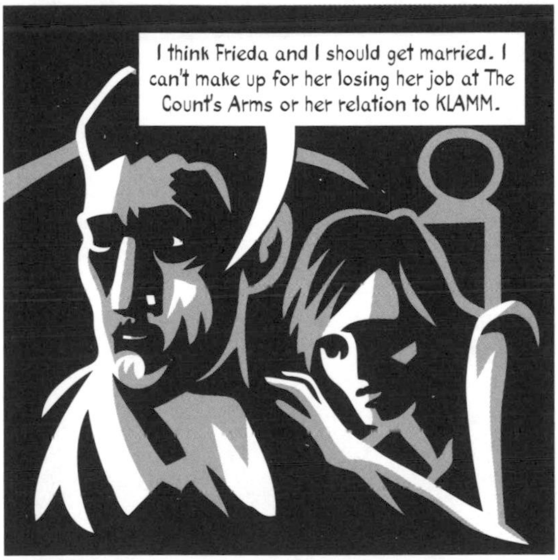
I think Frieda and I should get married. I can't make up for her losing her job at The Count's Arms or her relation to KLAMM.

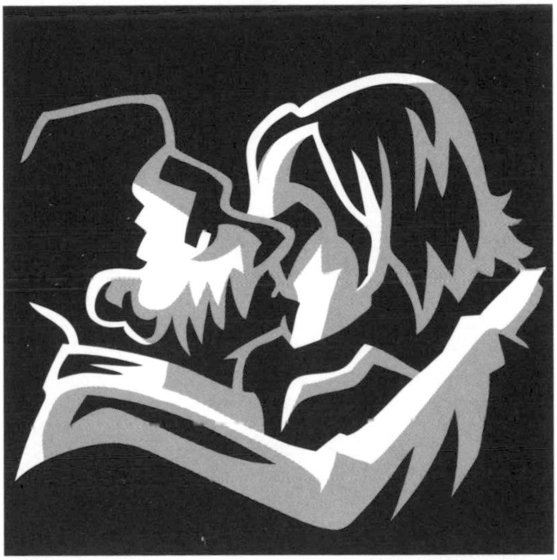

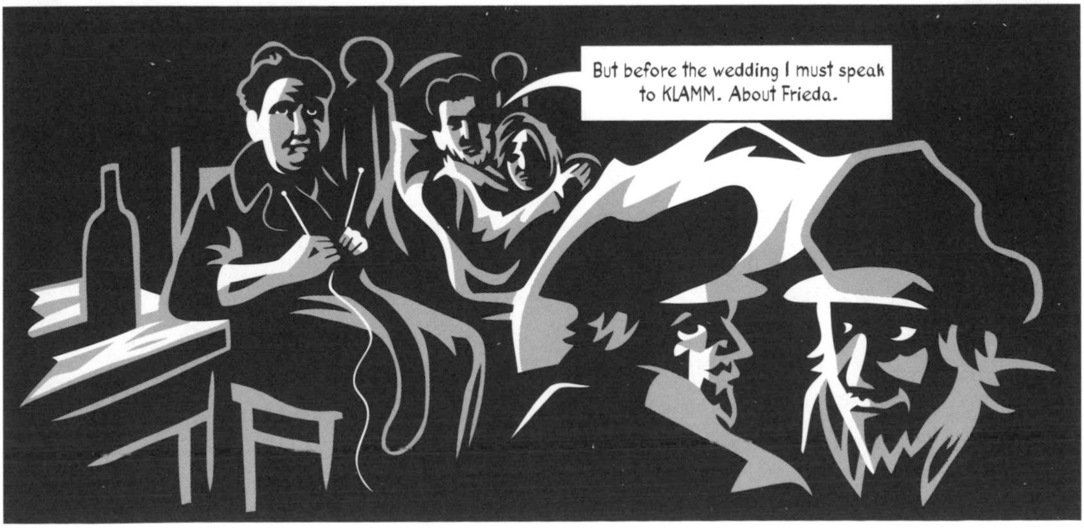
But before the wedding I must speak to KLAMM. About Frieda.

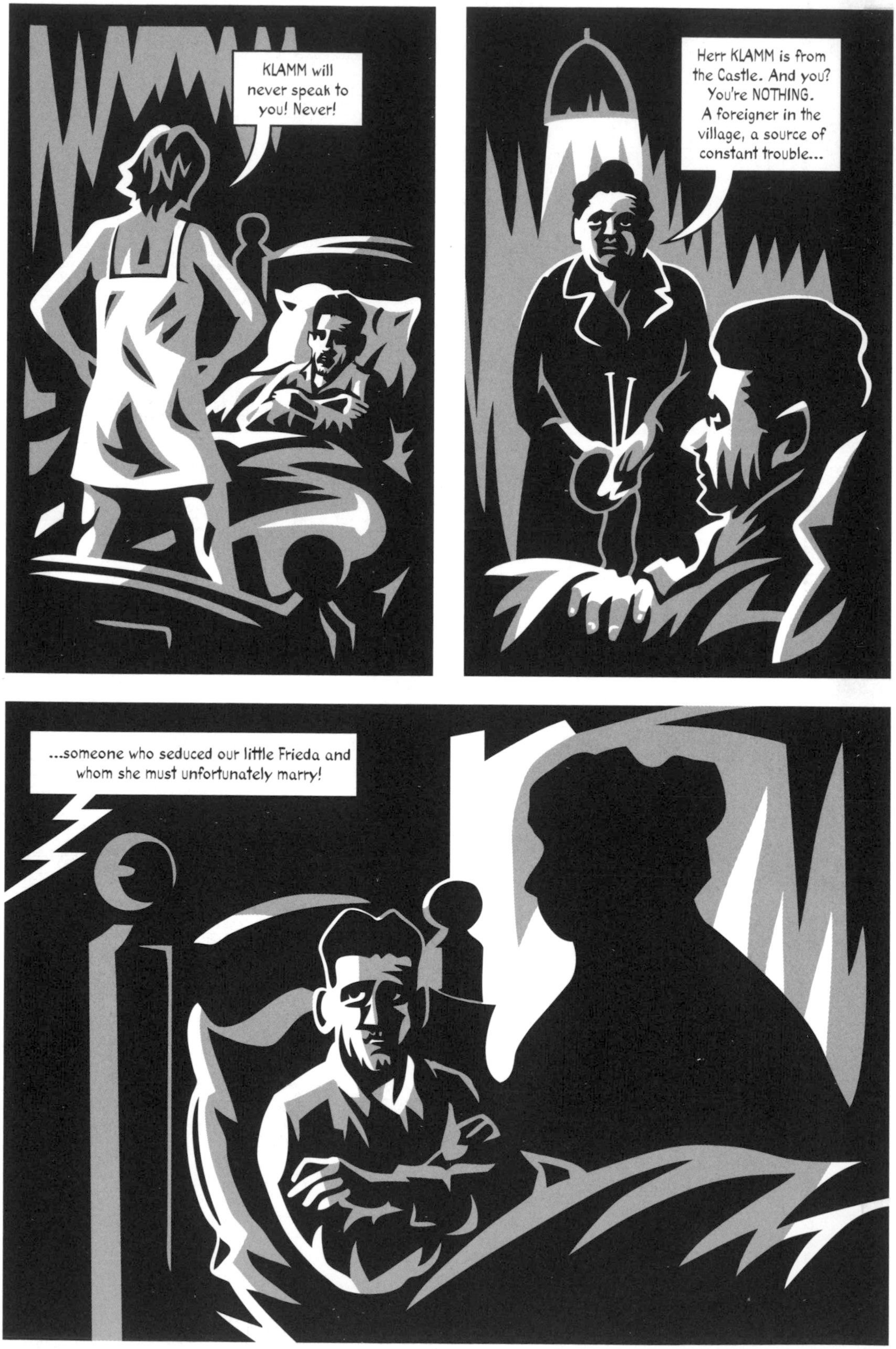
KLAMM will never speak to you! Never!
Herr KLAMM is from the Castle. And you? You're NOTHING. A foreigner in the village, a source of constant trouble...
...someone who seduced our little Frieda and whom she must unfortunately marry!

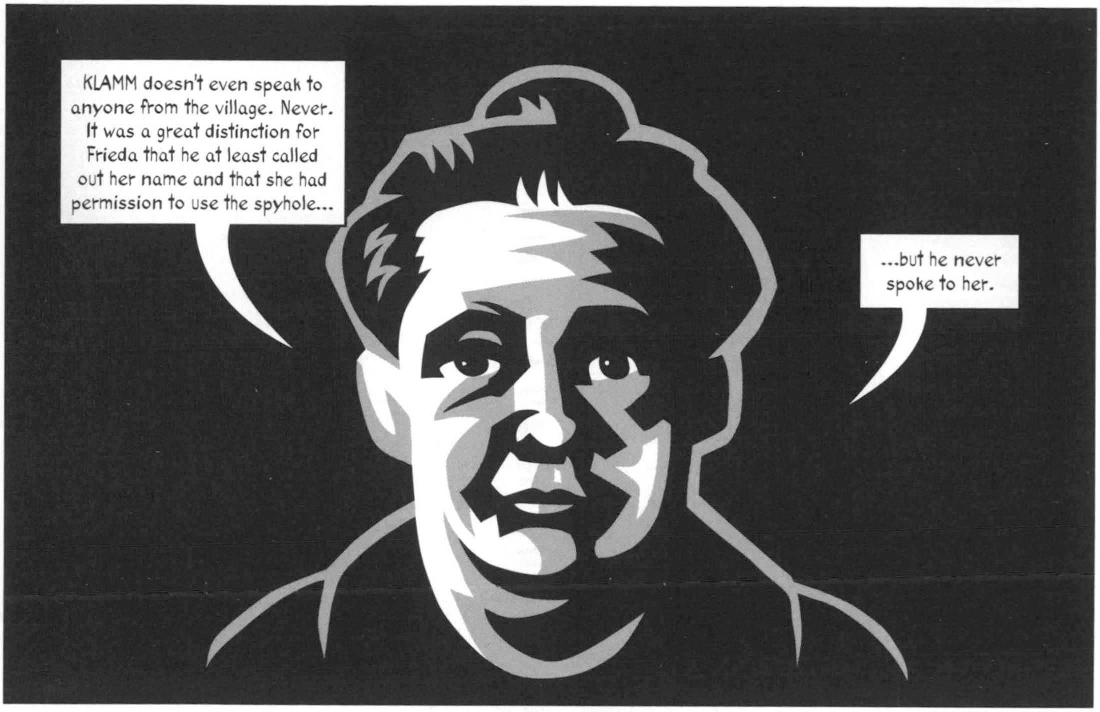
KLAMM doesn't even speak to anyone from the village. Never. It was a great distinction for Frieda that he at least called out her name and that she had permission to use the spyhole...
...but he never spoke to her.

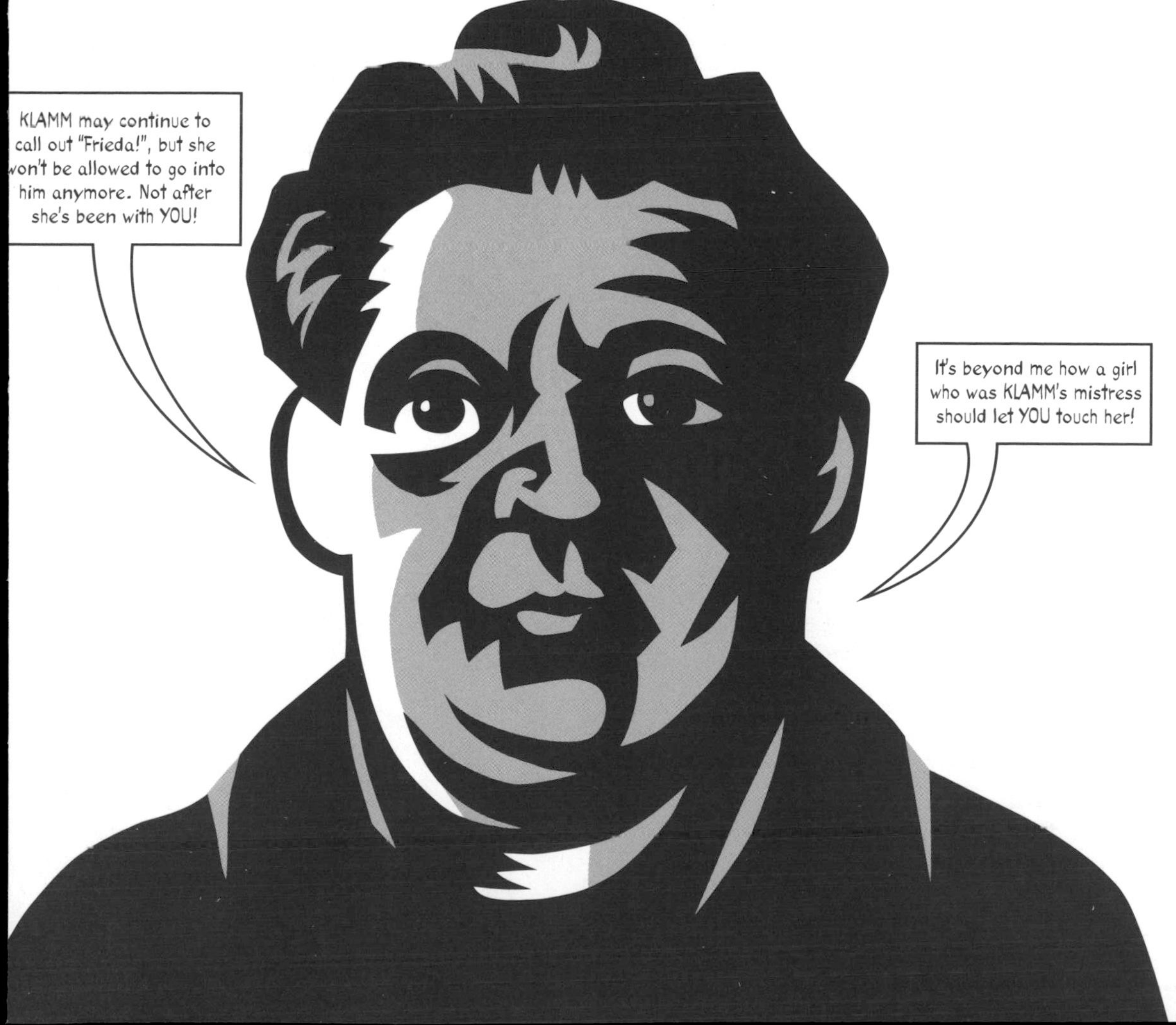
KLAMM may continue to call out "Frieda!", but she won't be allowed to go into him anymore. Not after she's been with YOU!
It's beyond me how a girl who was KLAMM's mistress should let YOU touch her!

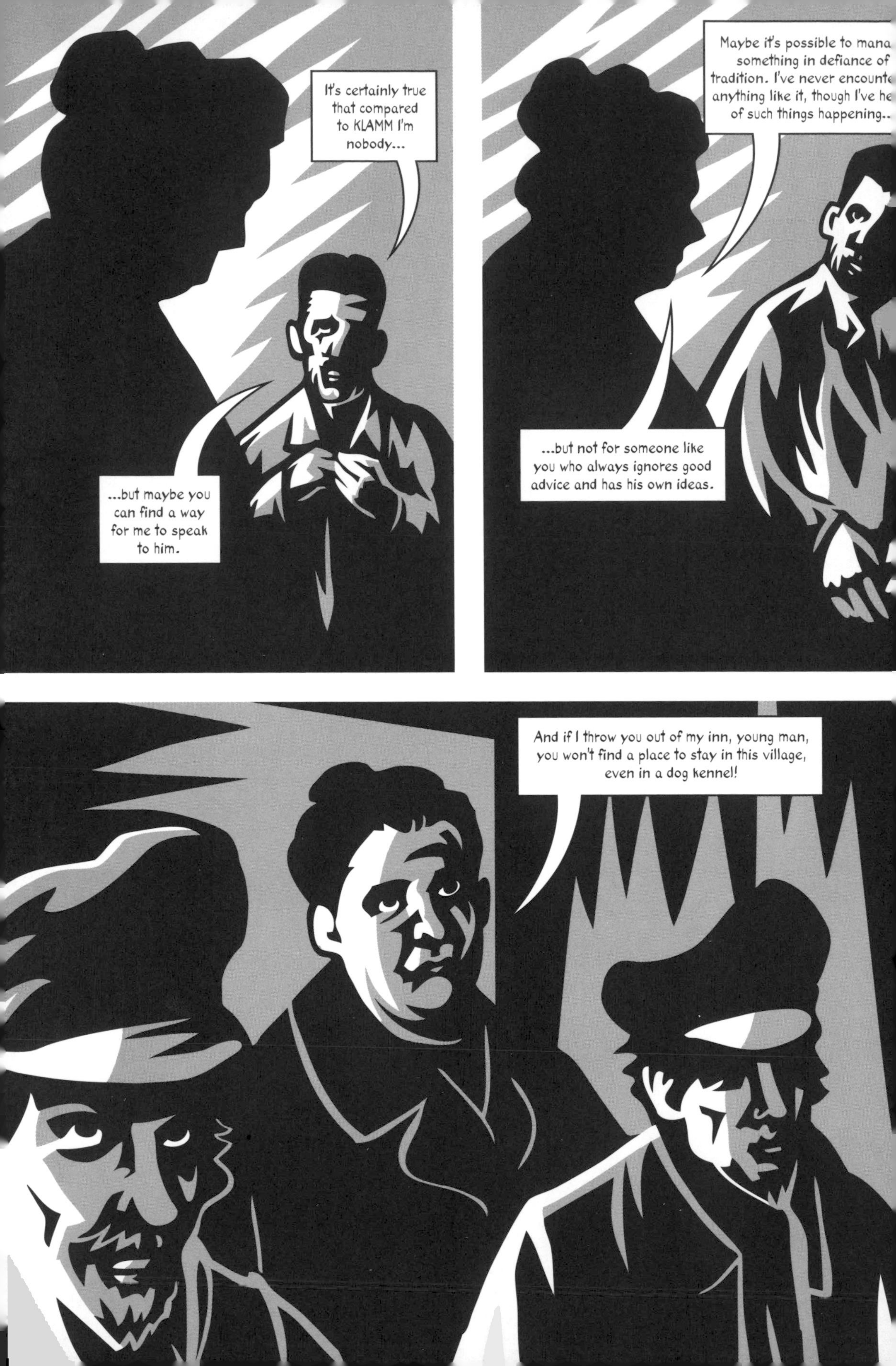
It's certainly true that compared to KLAMM I'm nobody...
...but maybe you can find a way for me to speak to him.
Maybe it's possible to mana something in defiance of tradition. I've never encounte anything like it, though I've he of such things happening..
...but not for someone like you who always ignores good advice and has his own ideas.
And if I throw you out of my inn, young man, you won't find a place to stay in this village, even in a dog kennel!

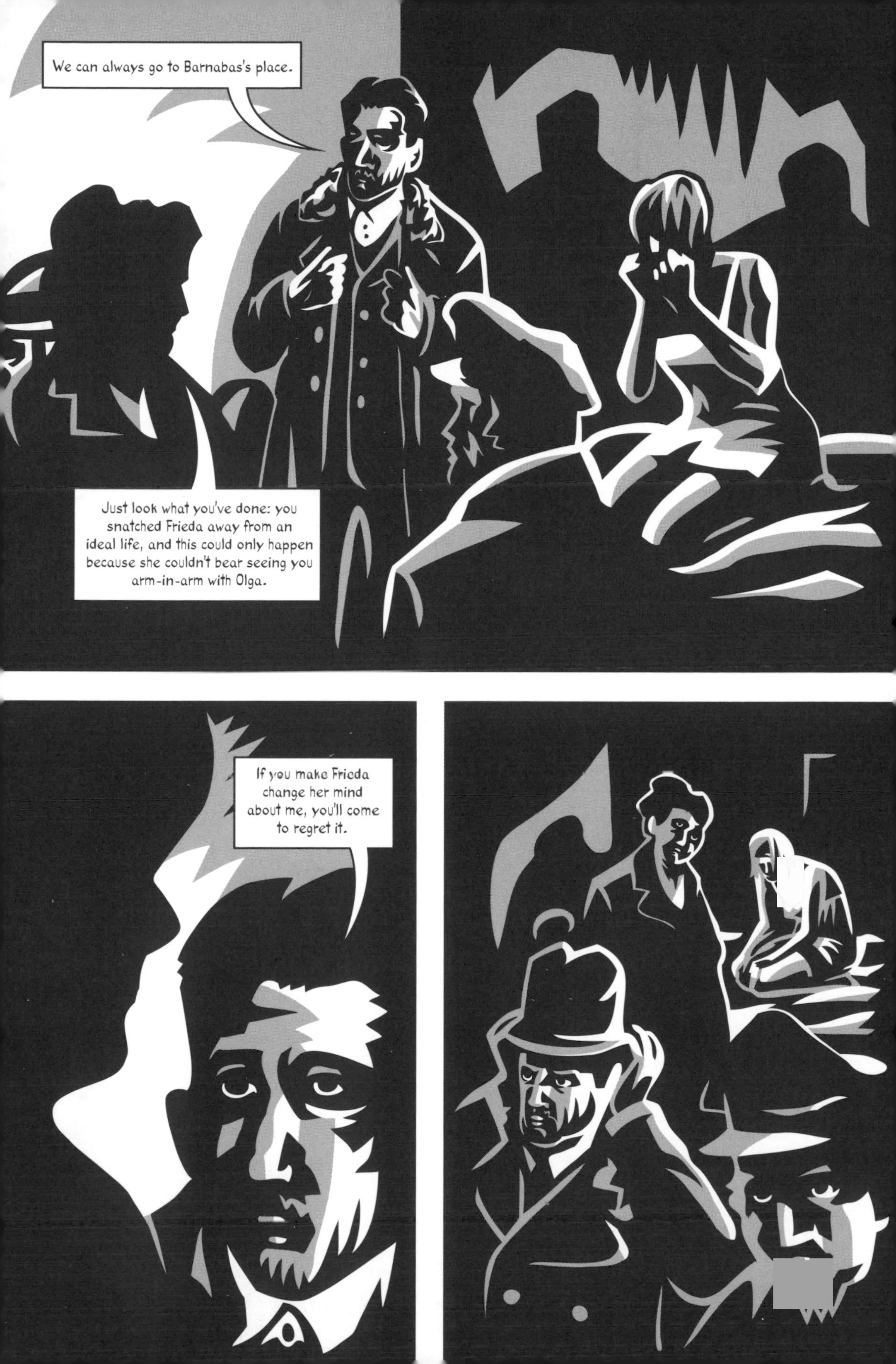
We can always go to Barnabas's place.
Just look what you've done: you snatched Frieda away from an ideal life, and this could only happen because she couldn't bear seeing you arm-in-arm with Olga.
If you make Frieda change her mind about me, you'll come to regret it.

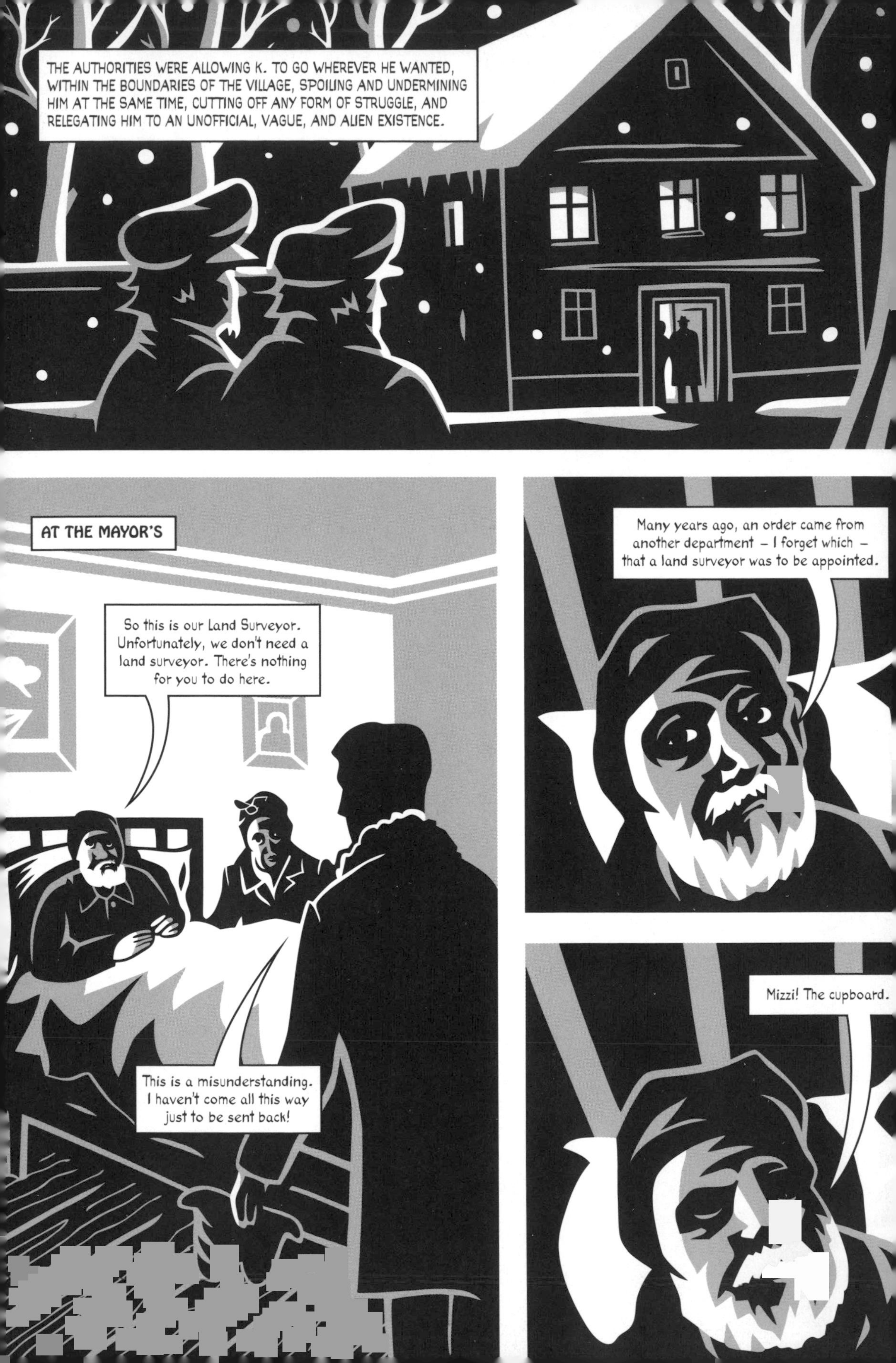
THE AUTHORITIES WERE ALLOWING K. TO GO WHEREVER HE WANTED, WITHIN THE BOUNDARIES OF THE VILLAGE, SPOILING AND UNDERMINING HIM AT THE SAME TIME, CUTTING OFF ANY FORM OF STRUGGLE, AND RELEGATING HIM TO AN UNOFFICIAL, VAGUE, AND ALIEN EXISTENCE.
AT THE MAYOR'S
So this is our Land Surveyor. Unfortunately, we don't need a land surveyor. There's nothing for you to do here.
This is a misunderstanding. I haven't come all this way just to be sent back!
Many years ago, an order came from another department – I forget which – that a land surveyor was to be appointed.
Mizzi! The cupboard.

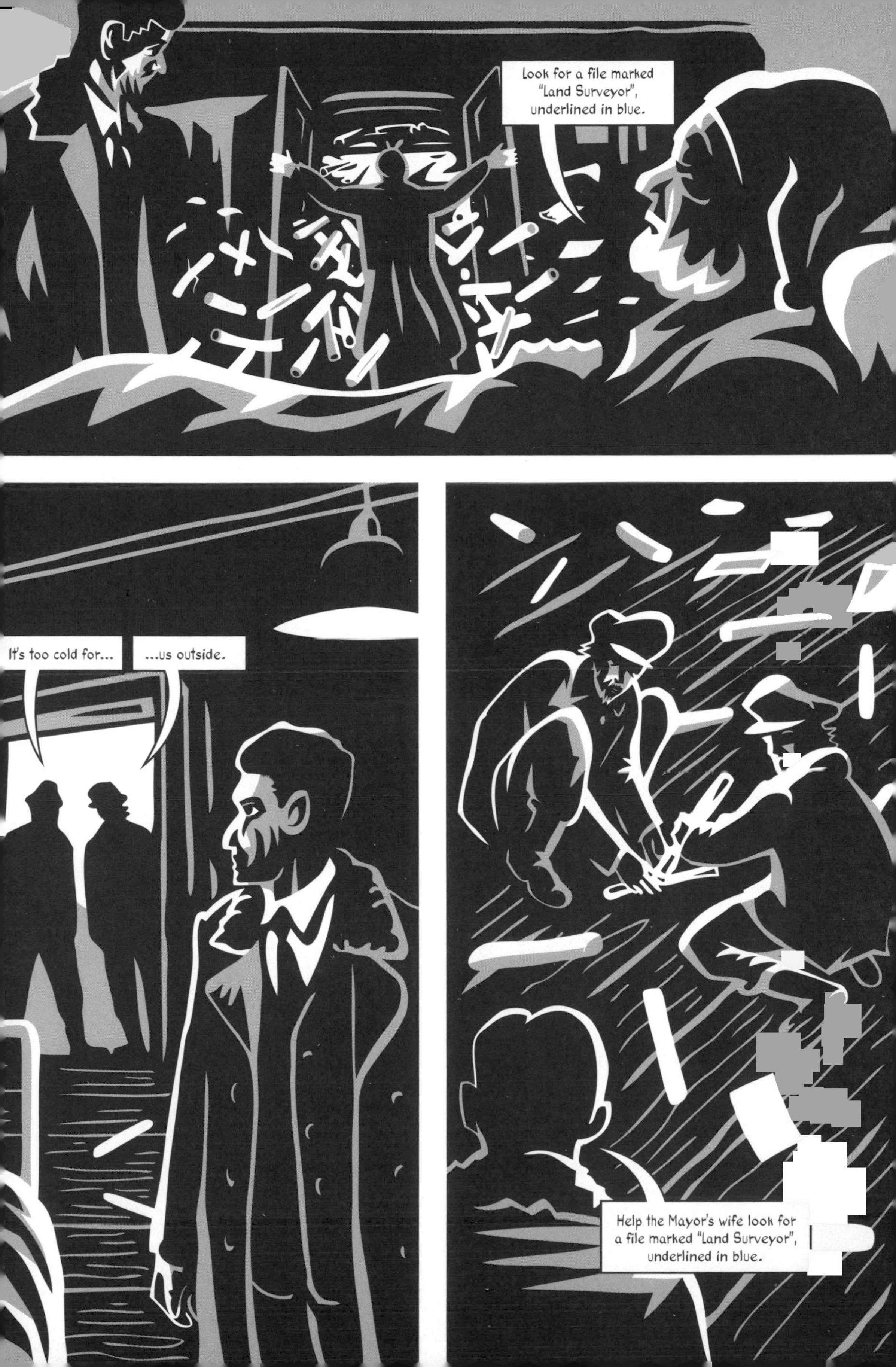
Look for a file marked "Land Surveyor", underlined in blue.
It's too cold for...
...us outside.
Help the Mayor's wife look for a file marked "Land Surveyor", underlined in blue.

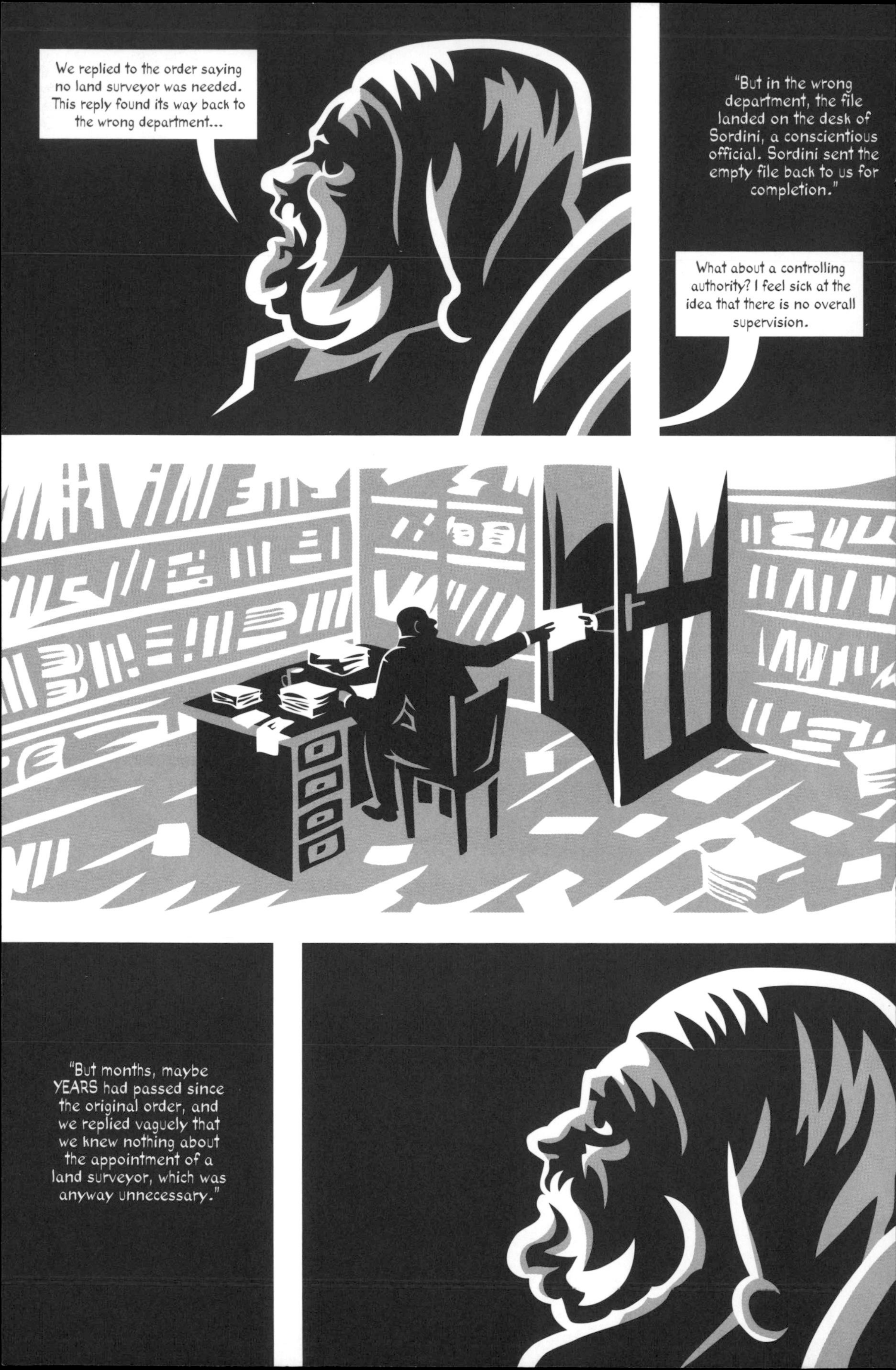
We replied to the order saying no land surveyor was needed. This reply found its way back to the wrong department...
"But in the wrong department, the file landed on the desk of Sordini, a conscientious official. Sordini sent the empty file back to us for completion."
What about a controlling authority? I feel sick at the idea that there is no overall supervision.
"But months, maybe YEARS had passed since the original order, and we replied vaguely that we knew nothing about the appointment of a land surveyor, which was anyway unnecessary."

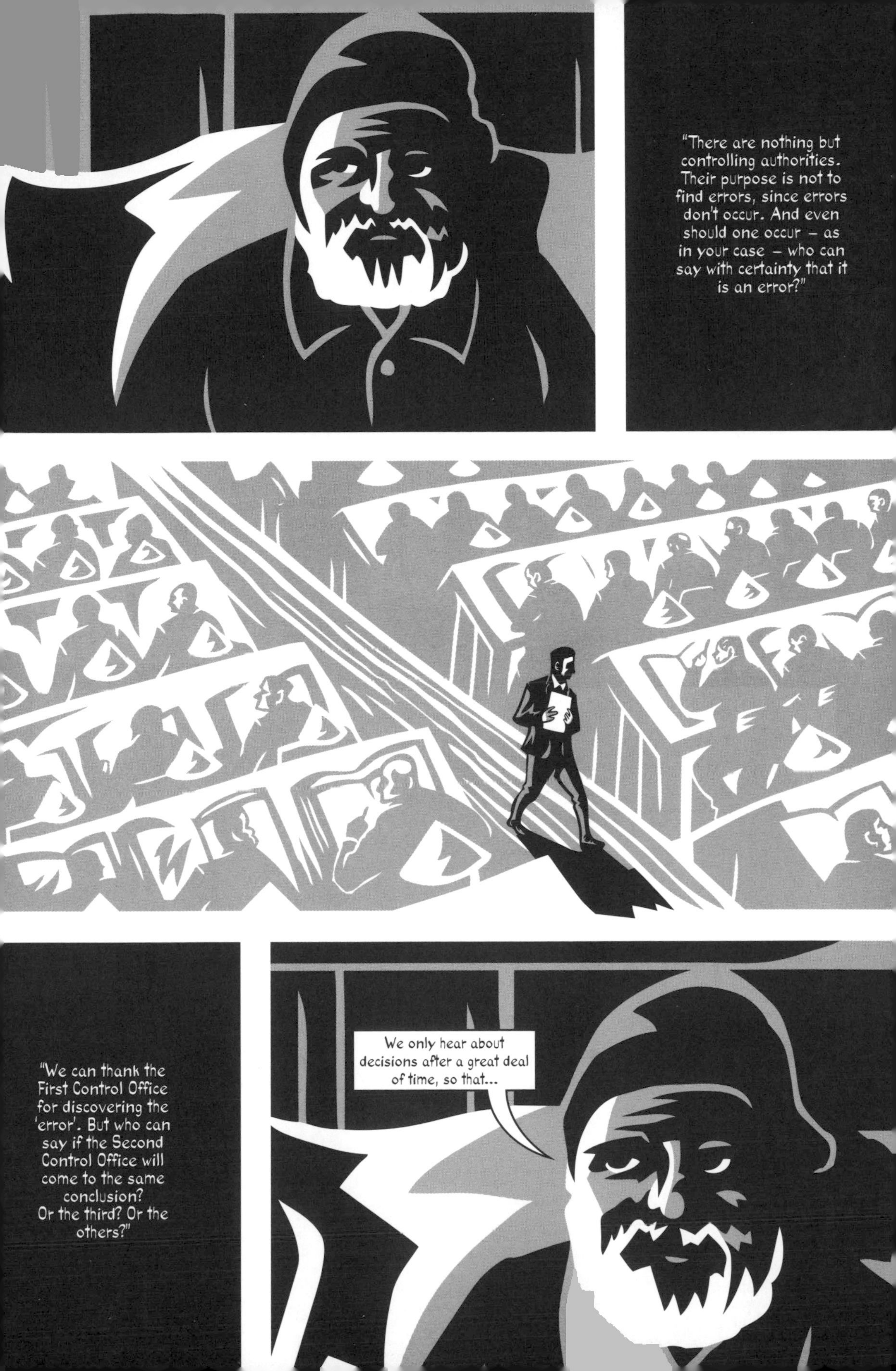
"There are nothing but controlling authorities. Their purpose is not to find errors, since errors don't occur. And even should one occur – as in your case – who can say with certainty that it is an error?"
"We can thank the First Control Office for discovering the 'error'. But who can say if the Second Control Office will come to the same conclusion? Or the third? Or the others?"
We only hear about decisions after a great deal of time, so that...

"...an affair which has been decided long ago is still heatedly dicussed. I don't know if such a decision has been made in your case: some things suggest yes, others suggest no."

"I do know this: a Control Office discovered that a request for a land surveyor had been made many years ago, and an enquiry had been sent to me, to which I replied that no land surveyor was needed, and the matter was closed."

So imagine my disappointment when, after a happy end to the whole business, YOU suddenly turn up, and it looks as if it's about to start up all over again!

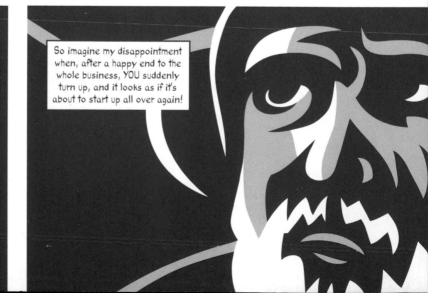

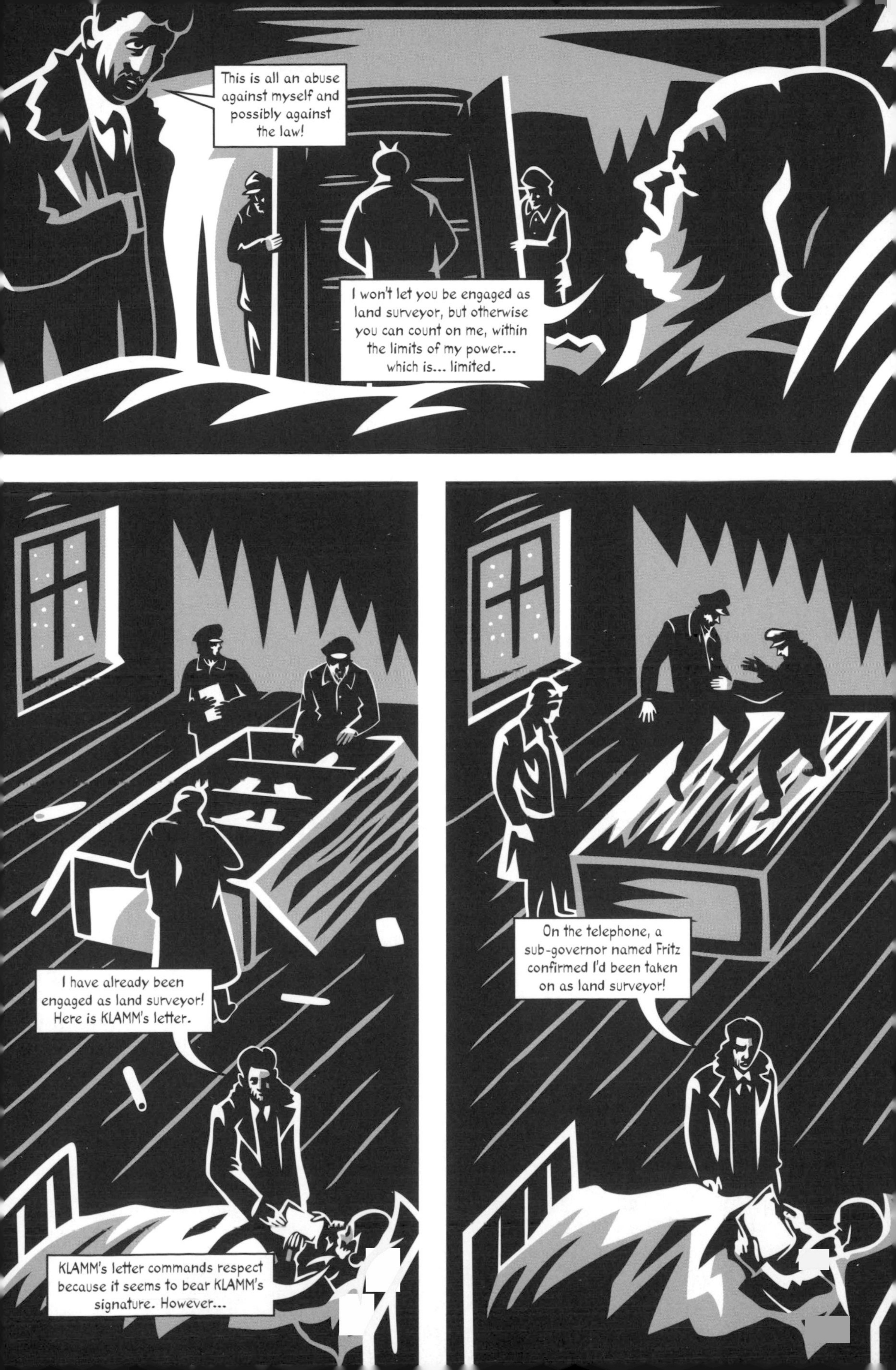
This is all an abuse against myself and possibly against the law!
I won't let you be engaged as land surveyor, but otherwise you can count on me, within the limits of my power... which is... limited.
I have already been engaged as land surveyor! Here is KLAMM's letter.
KLAMM's letter commands respect because it seems to bear KLAMM's signature. However...
On the telephone, a sub-governor named Fritz confirmed I'd been taken on as land surveyor!

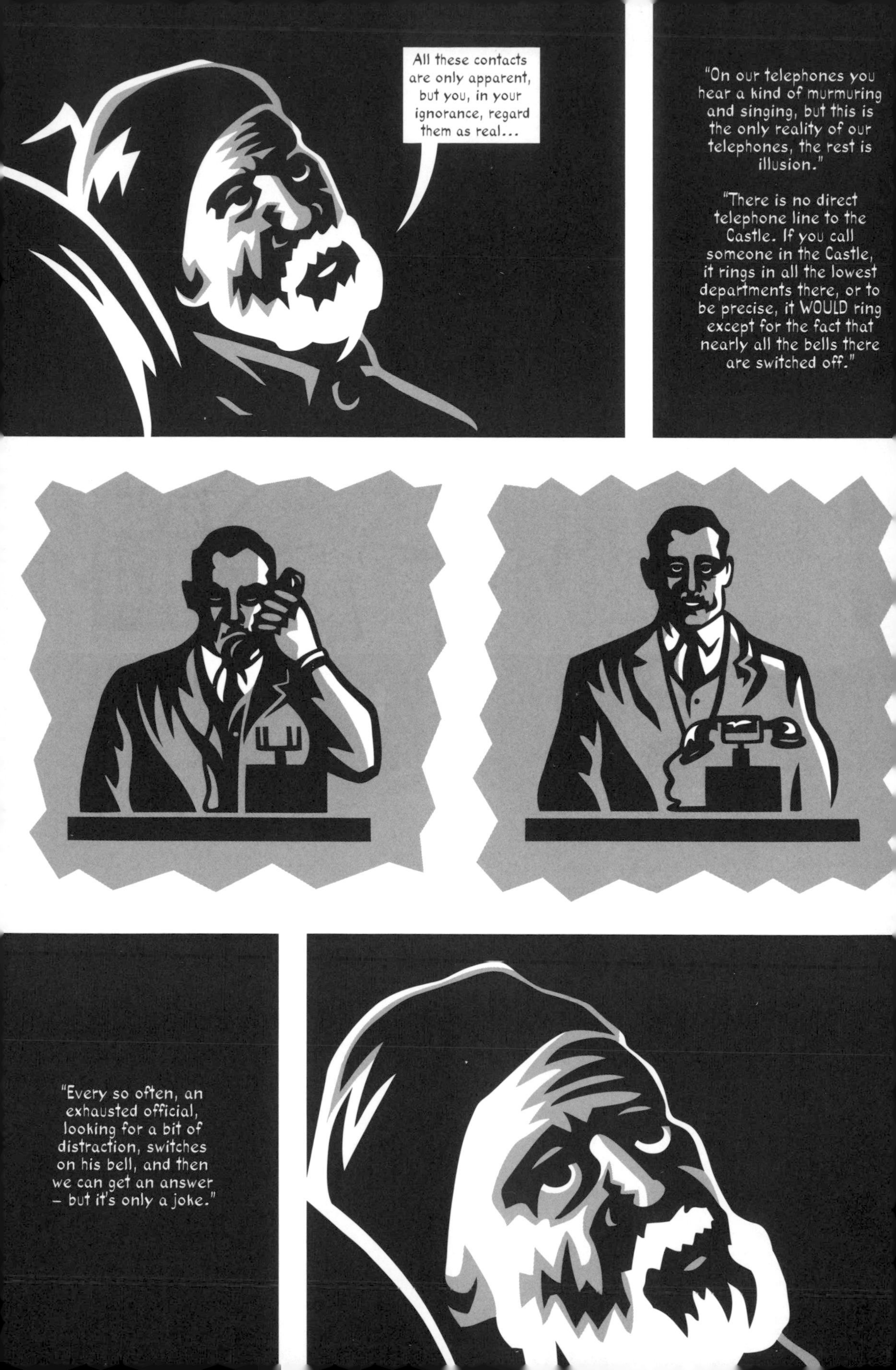
All these contacts are only apparent, but you, in your ignorance, regard them as real...
"On our telephones you hear a kind of murmuring and singing, but this is the only reality of our telephones, the rest is illusion."
"There is no direct telephone line to the Castle. If you call someone in the Castle, it rings in all the lowest departments there, or to be precise, it WOULD ring except for the fact that nearly all the bells there are switched off."
"Every so often, an exhausted official, looking for a bit of distraction, switches on his bell, and then we can get an answer – but it's only a joke."

So everything is unclear, including my being thrown out?
No one is keeping you here. But it doesn't mean you are being "thrown out".
If a decision is made, I will send for you.
I want no favours from the Castle, only my rights.
What's keeping me here? The long journey, the hopes I had after being taken on, my lack of funds, the impossibility of finding another job back home, and last but not least, Frieda.

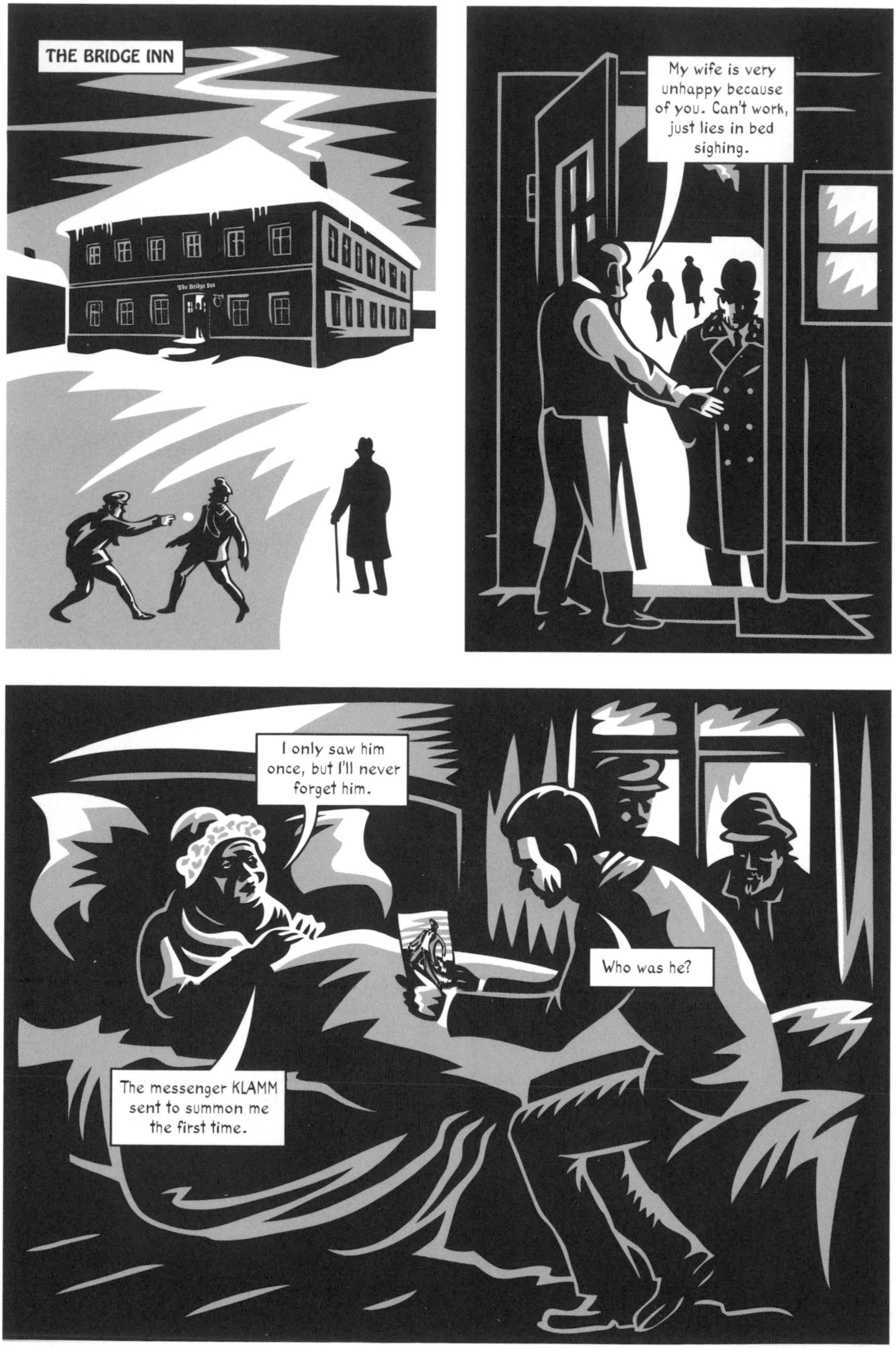
THE BRIDGE INN
My wife is very unhappy because of you. Can't work, just lies in bed sighing.
I only saw him once, but I'll never forget him.
Who was he?
The messenger KLAMM sent to summon me the first time.

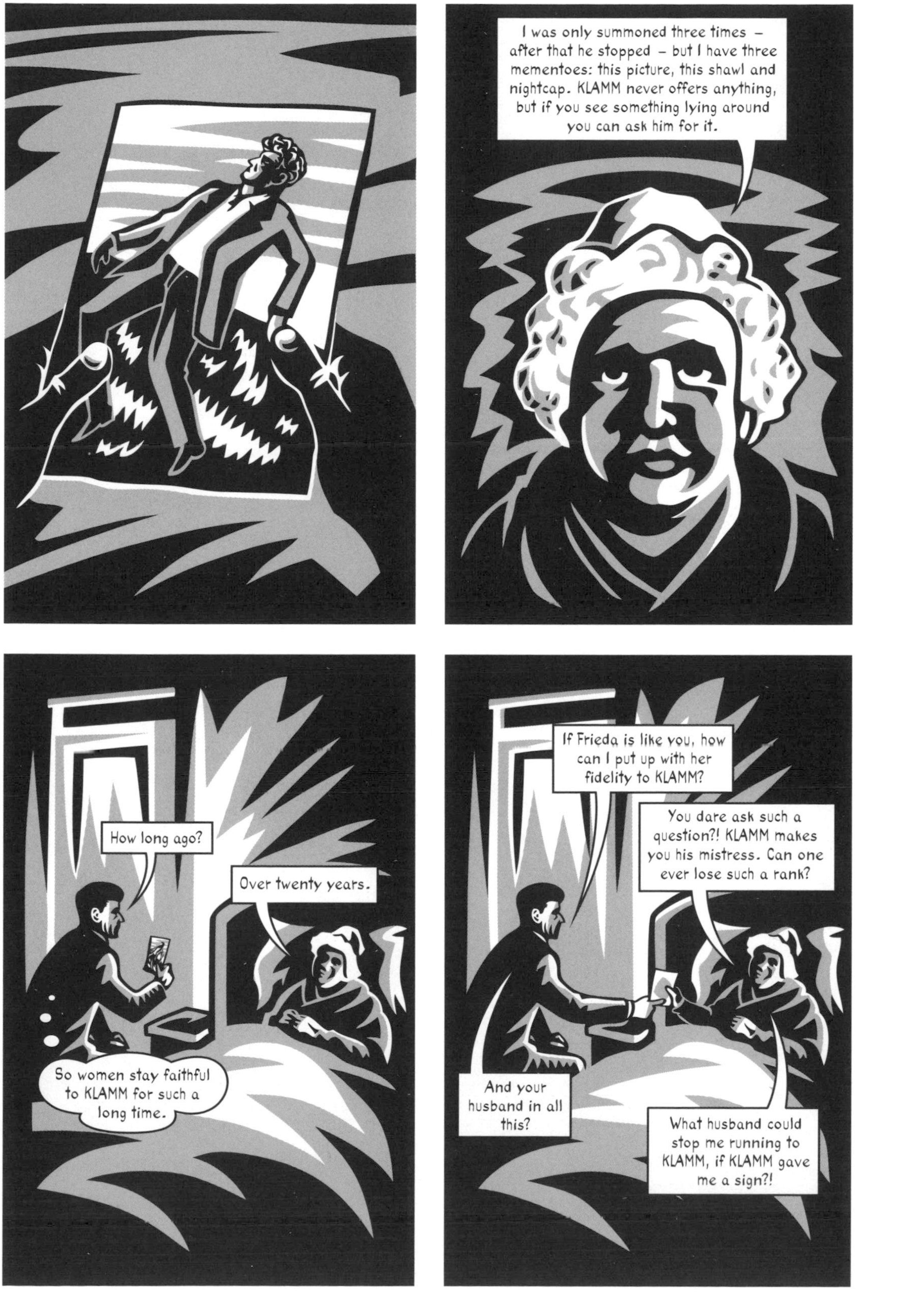
I was only summoned three times – after that he stopped – but I have three mementoes: this picture, this shawl and nightcap. KLAMM never offers anything, but if you see something lying around you can ask him for it.
How long ago?
Over twenty years.
So women stay faithful to KLAMM for such a long time.
If Frieda is like you, how can I put up with her fidelity to KLAMM?
You dare ask such a question?! KLAMM makes you his mistress. Can one ever lose such a rank?
And your husband in all this?
What husband could stop me running to KLAMM, if KLAMM gave me a sign?!

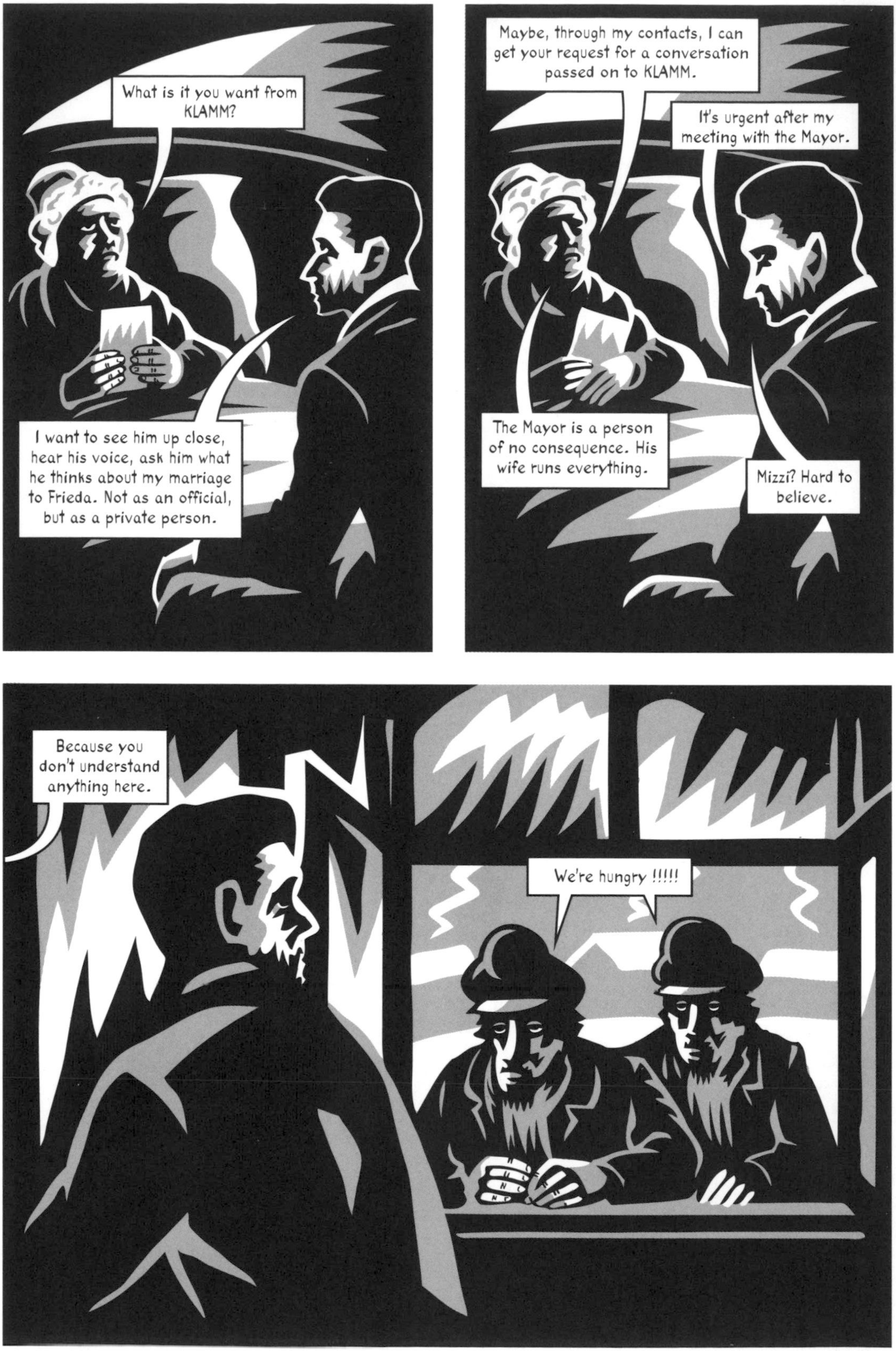
What is it you want from KLAMM?
I want to see him up close, hear his voice, ask him what he thinks about my marriage to Frieda. Not as an official, but as a private person.
Maybe, through my contacts, I can get your request for a conversation passed on to KLAMM.
It's urgent after my meeting with the Mayor.
The Mayor is a person of no consequence. His wife runs everything.
Mizzi? Hard to believe.
Because you don't understand anything here.
We're hungry !!!!!

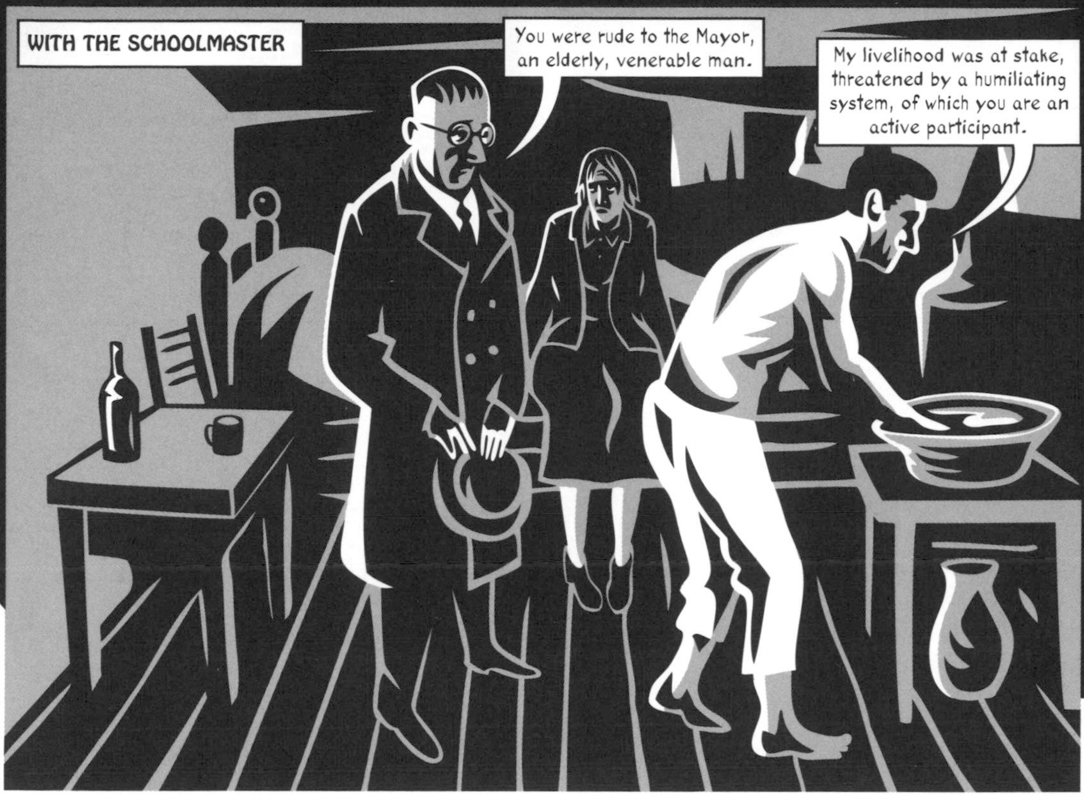
WITH THE SCHOOLMASTER
You were rude to the Mayor, an elderly, venerable man.
My livelihood was at stake, threatened by a humiliating system, of which you are an active participant.

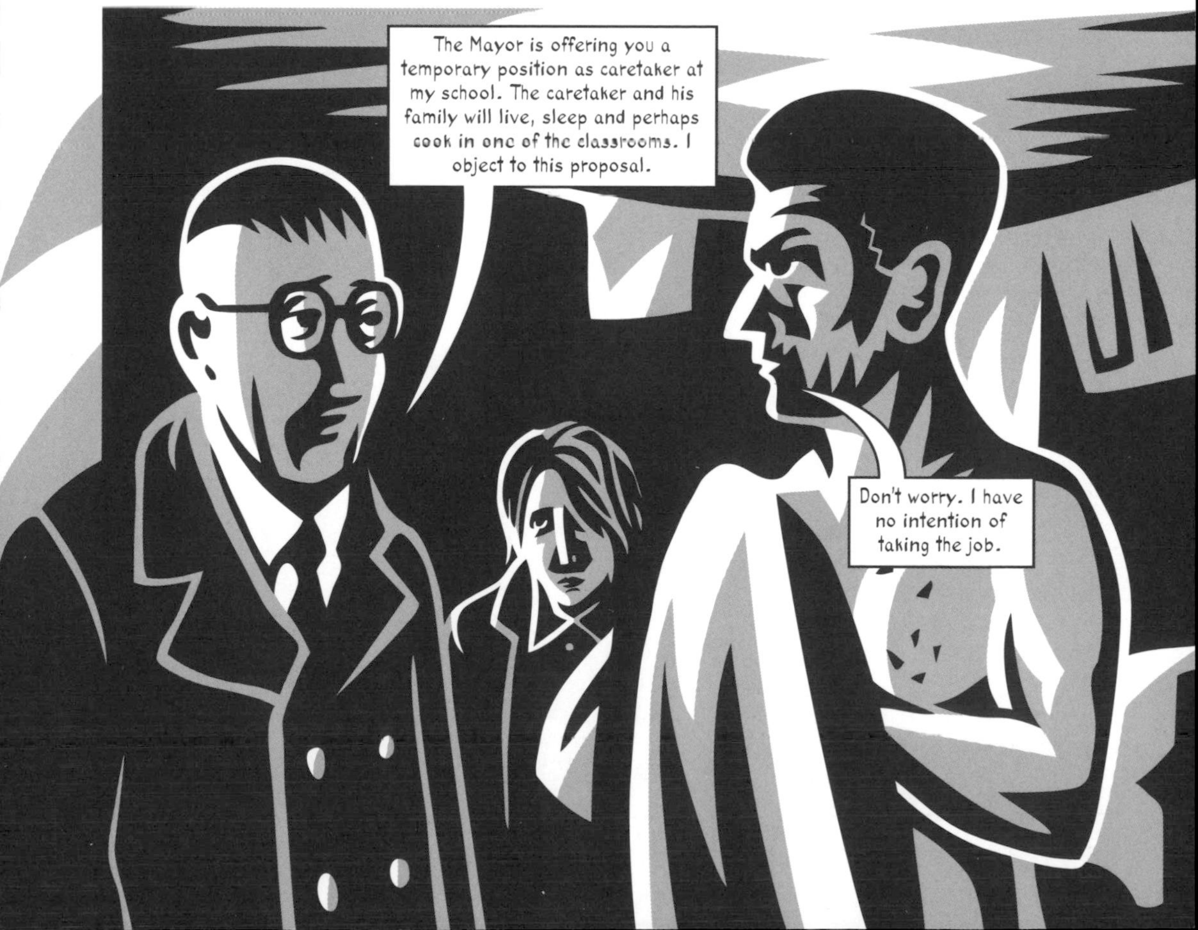
The Mayor is offering you a temporary position as caretaker at my school. The caretaker and his family will live, sleep and perhaps cook in one of the classrooms. I object to this proposal.
Don't worry. I have no intention of taking the job.

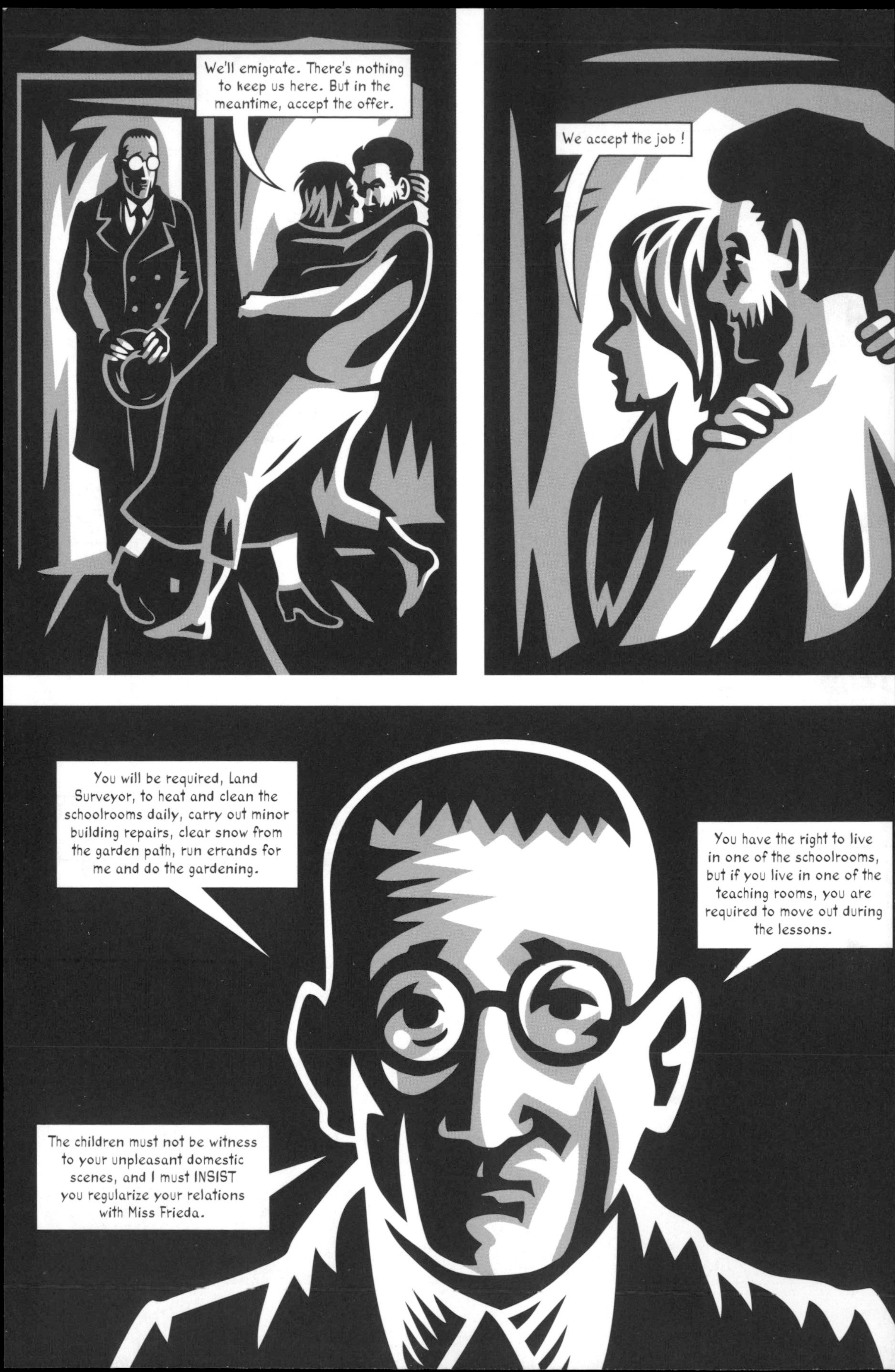
We'll emigrate. There's nothing to keep us here. But in the meantime, accept the offer.
We accept the job !
You will be required, Land Surveyor, to heat and clean the schoolrooms daily, carry out minor building repairs, clear snow from the garden path, run errands for me and do the gardening.
You have the right to live in one of the schoolrooms, but if you live in one of the teaching rooms, you are required to move out during the lessons.
The children must not be witness to your unpleasant domestic scenes, and I must INSIST you regularize your relations with Miss Frieda.

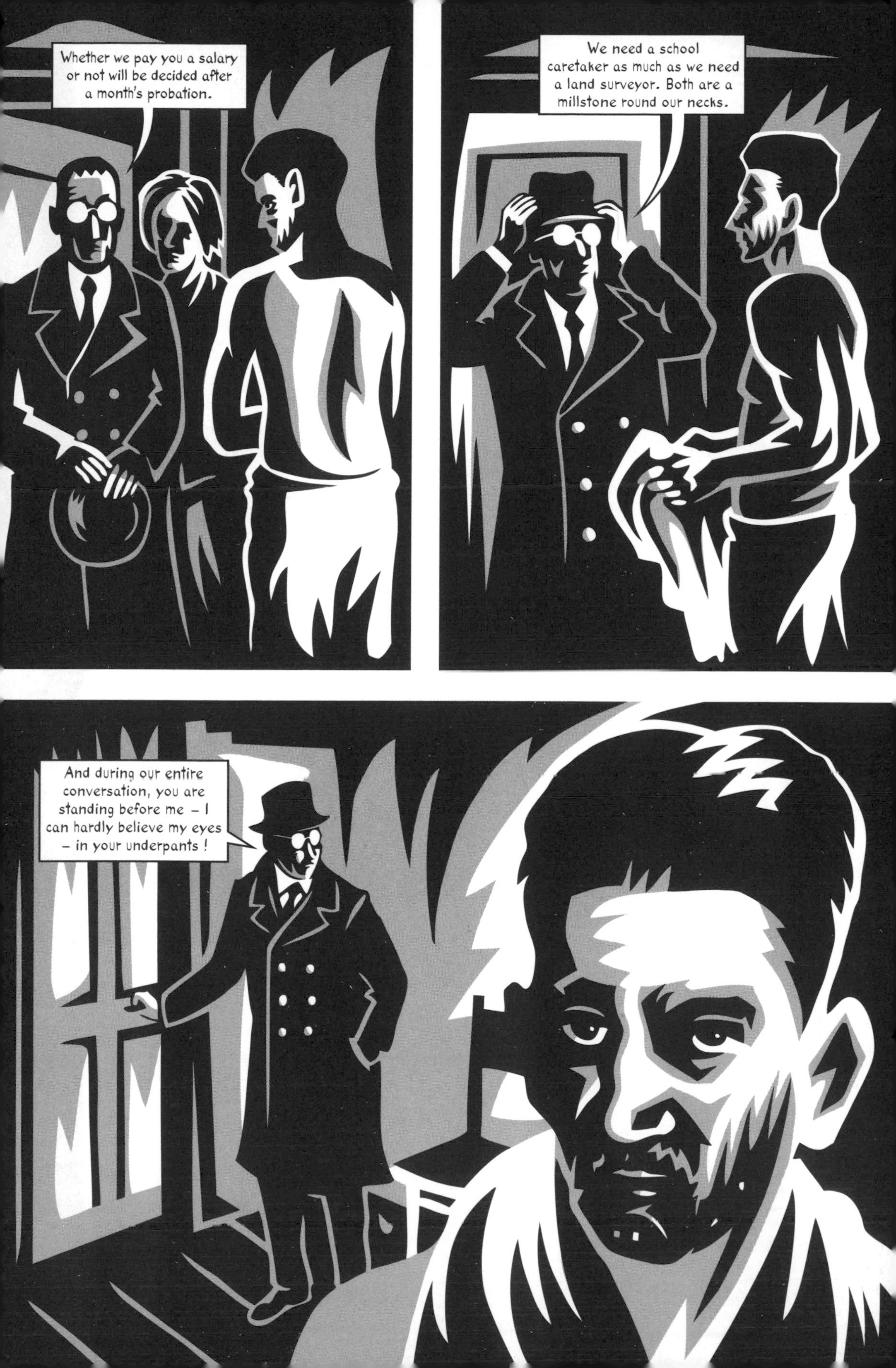
Whether we pay you a salary or not will be decided after a month's probation.
We need a school caretaker as much as we need a land surveyor. Both are a millstone round our necks.
And during our entire conversation, you are standing before me – I can hardly believe my eyes – in your underpants !

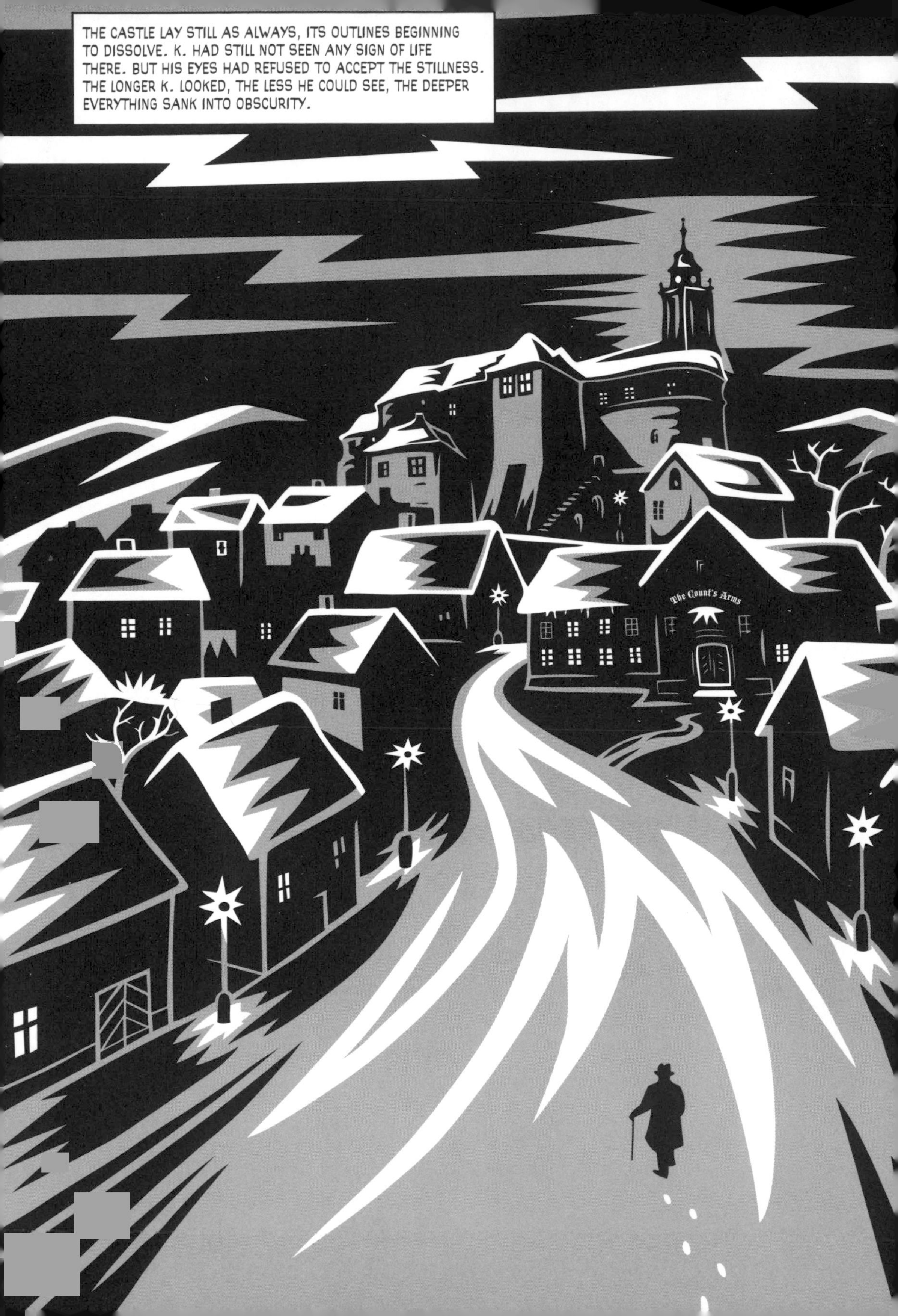
THE CASTLE LAY STILL AS ALWAYS, ITS OUTLINES BEGINNING TO DISSOLVE. K. HAD STILL NOT SEEN ANY SIGN OF LIFE THERE. BUT HIS EYES HAD REFUSED TO ACCEPT THE STILLNESS. THE LONGER K. LOOKED, THE LESS HE COULD SEE, THE DEEPER EVERYTHING SANK INTO OBSCURITY.
The Count's Arms

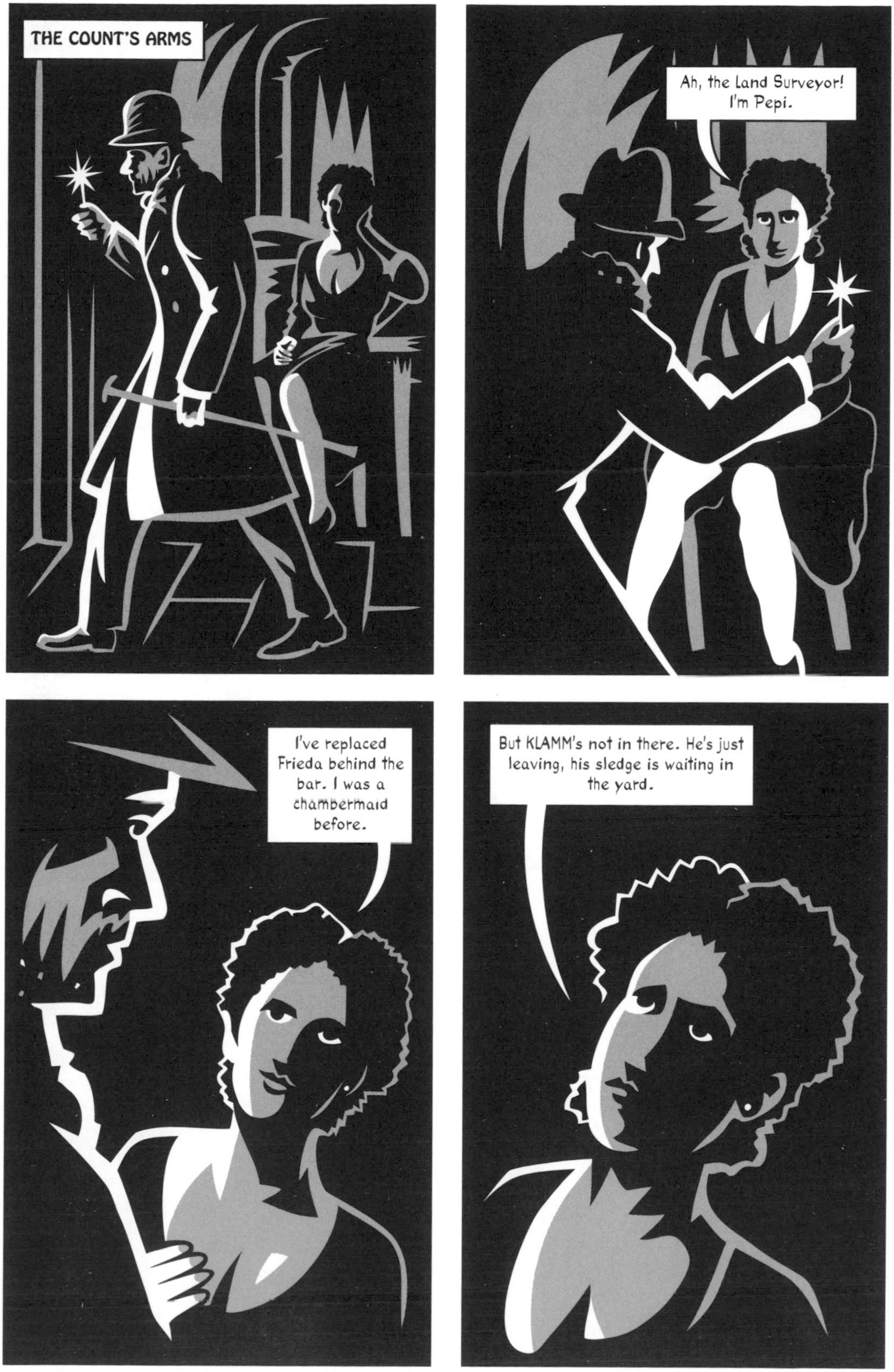
THE COUNT'S ARMS
Ah, the Land Surveyor! I'm Pepi.
I've replaced Frieda behind the bar. I was a chambermaid before.
But KLAMM's not in there. He's just leaving, his sledge is waiting in the yard.

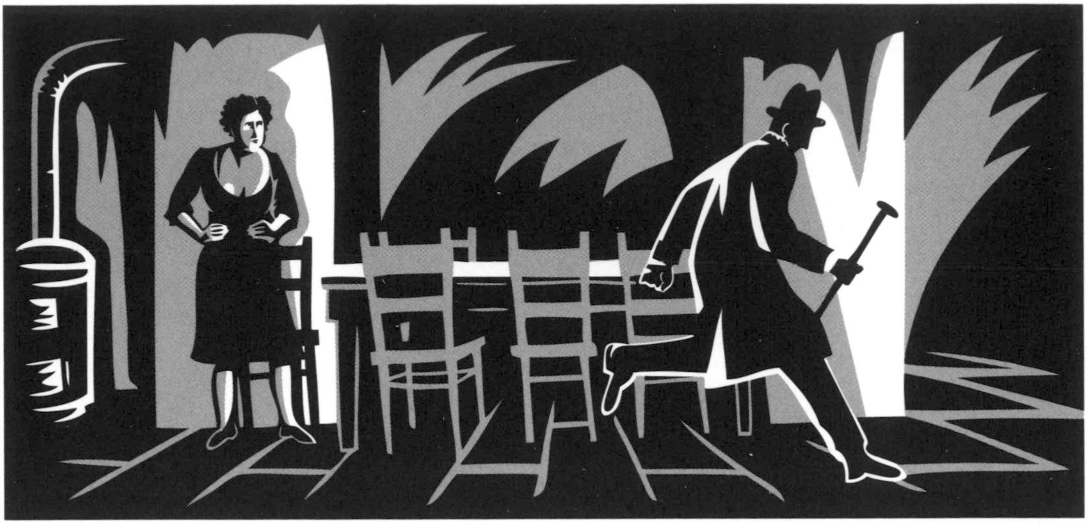

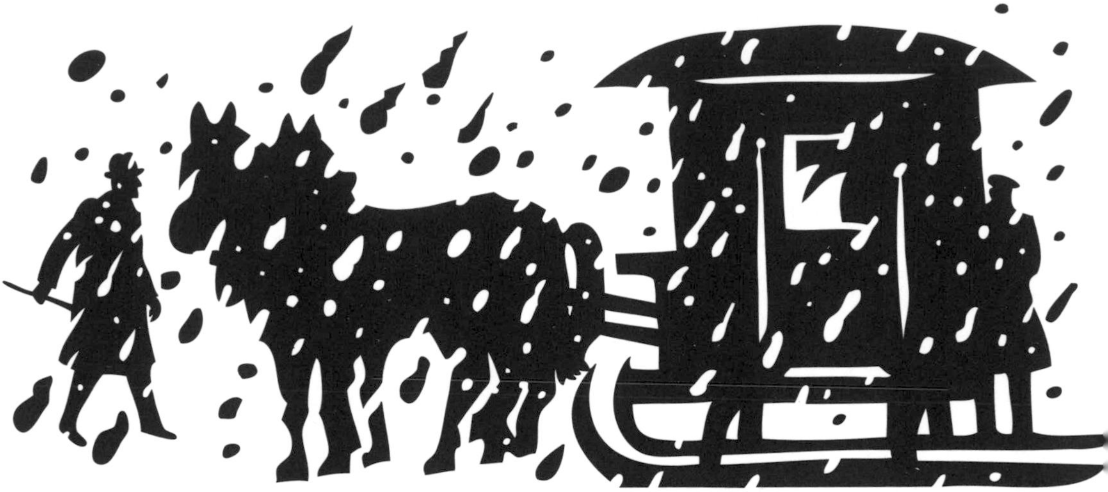

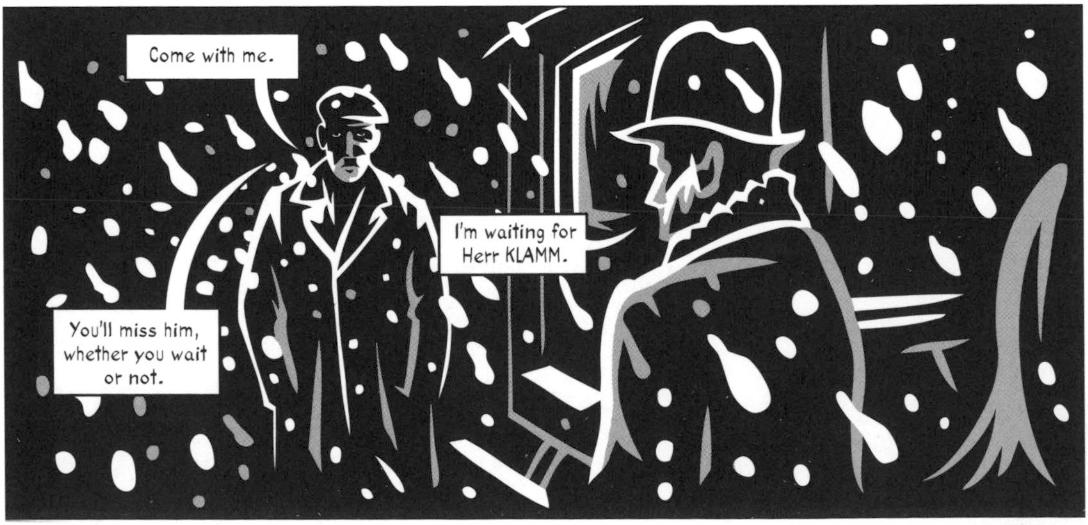
Come with me.
I'm waiting for Herr KLAMM.
You'll miss him, whether you wait or not.

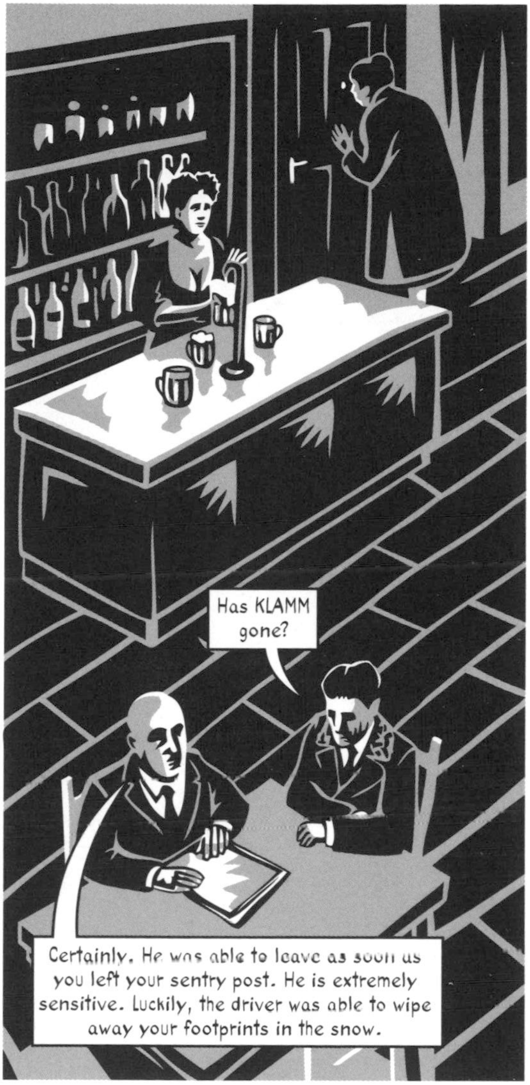
Has KLAMM gone?
Certainly. He was able to leave as soon as you left your sentry post. He is extremely sensitive. Luckily, the driver was able to wipe away your footprints in the snow.

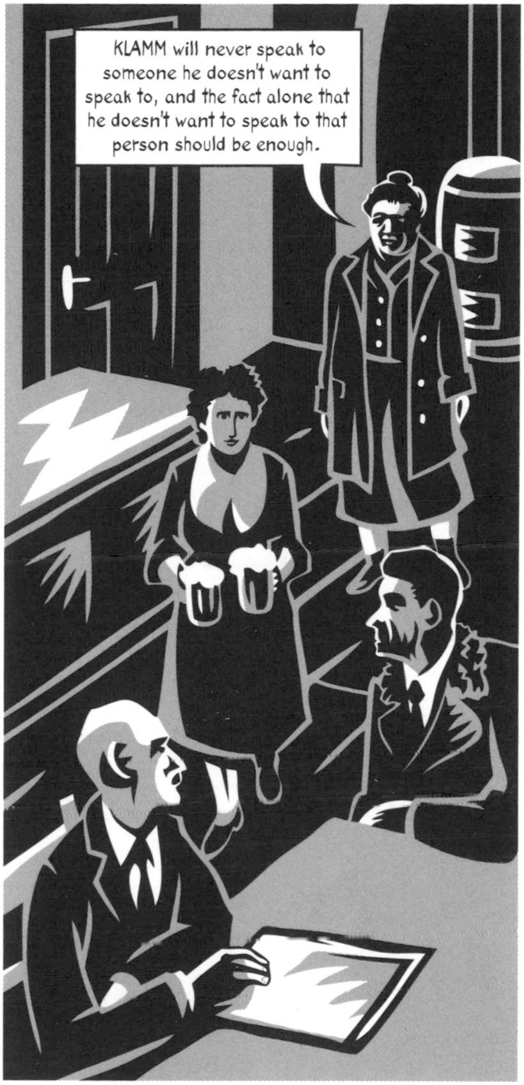
KLAMM will never speak to someone he doesn't want to speak to, and the fact alone that he doesn't want to speak to that person should be enough.

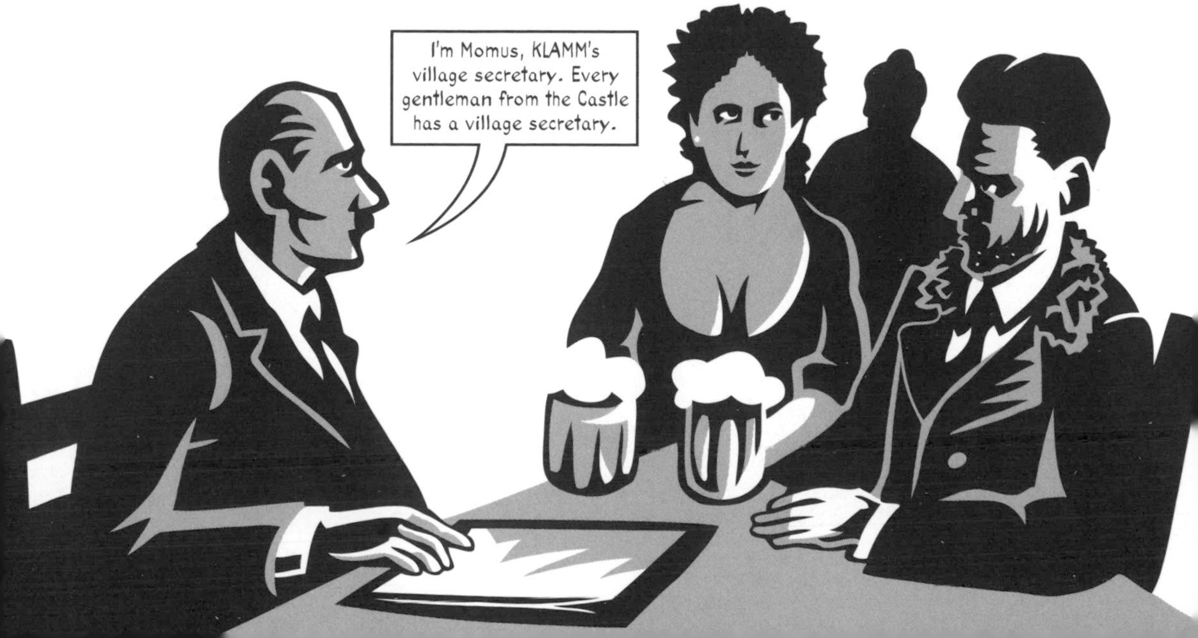
I'm Momus, KLAMM's village secretary. Every gentleman from the Castle has a village secretary.

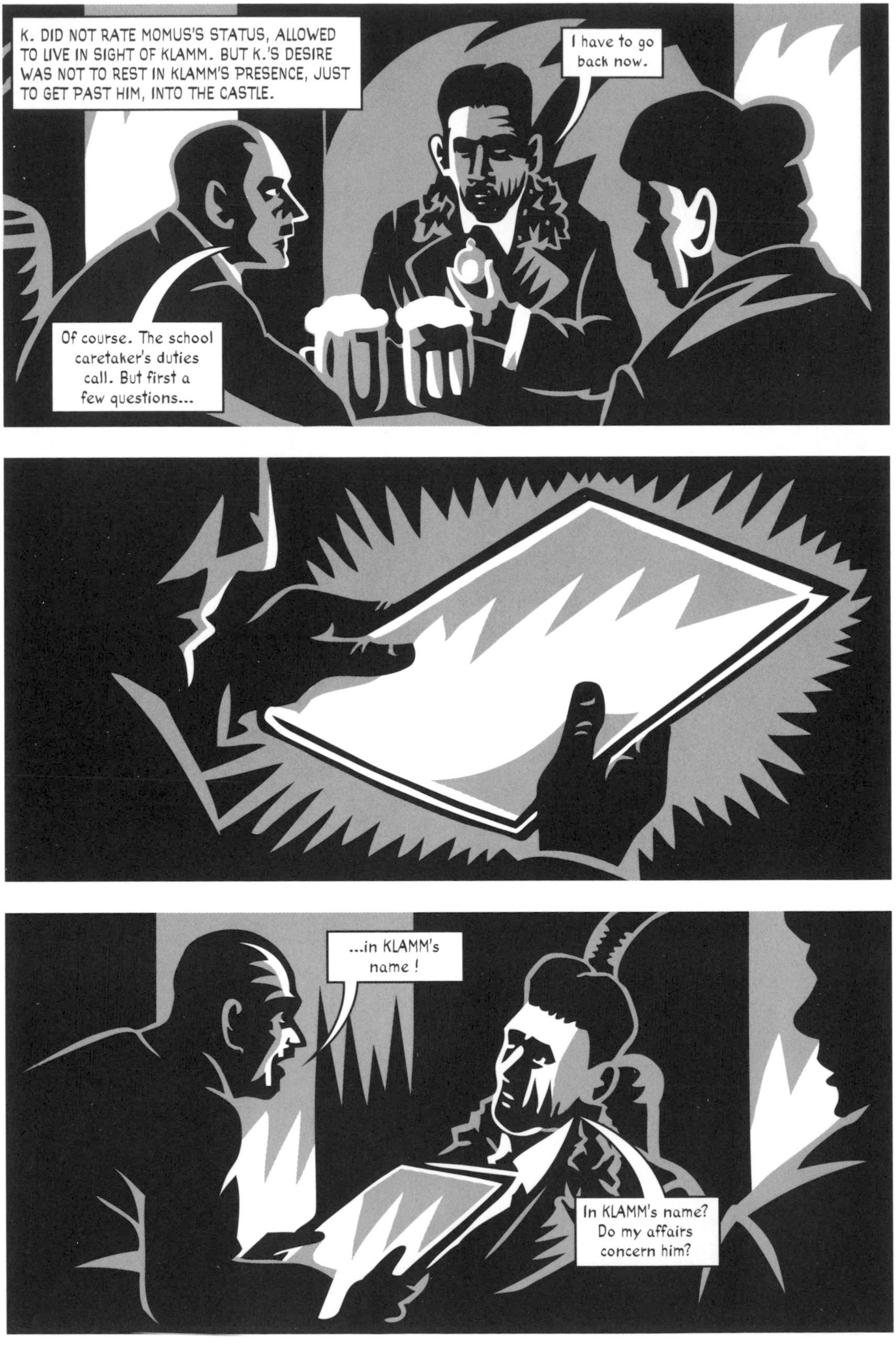
K. DID NOT RATE MOMUS'S STATUS, ALLOWED TO LIVE IN SIGHT OF KLAMM. BUT K.'S DESIRE WAS NOT TO REST IN KLAMM'S PRESENCE, JUST TO GET PAST HIM, INTO THE CASTLE.
I have to go back now.
Of course. The school caretaker's duties call. But first a few questions...
...in KLAMM's name!
In KLAMM's name? Do my affairs concern him?

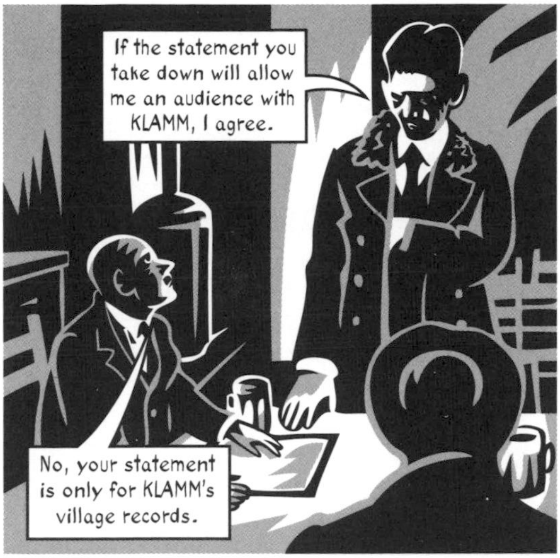
If the statement you take down will allow me an audience with KLAMM, I agree.
No, your statement is only for KLAMM's village records.

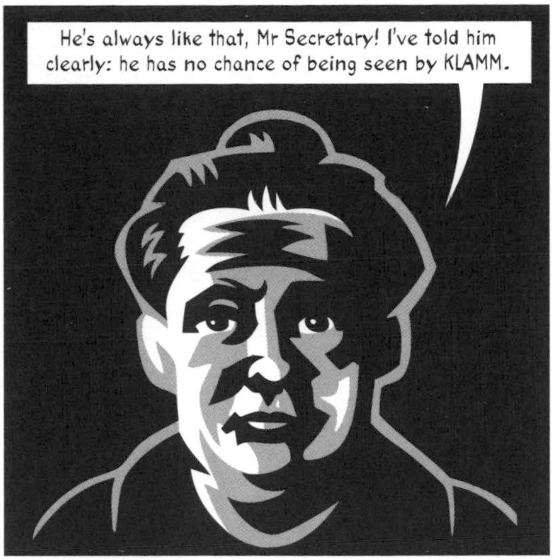
He's always like that, Mr Secretary! I've told him clearly: he has no chance of being seen by KLAMM.

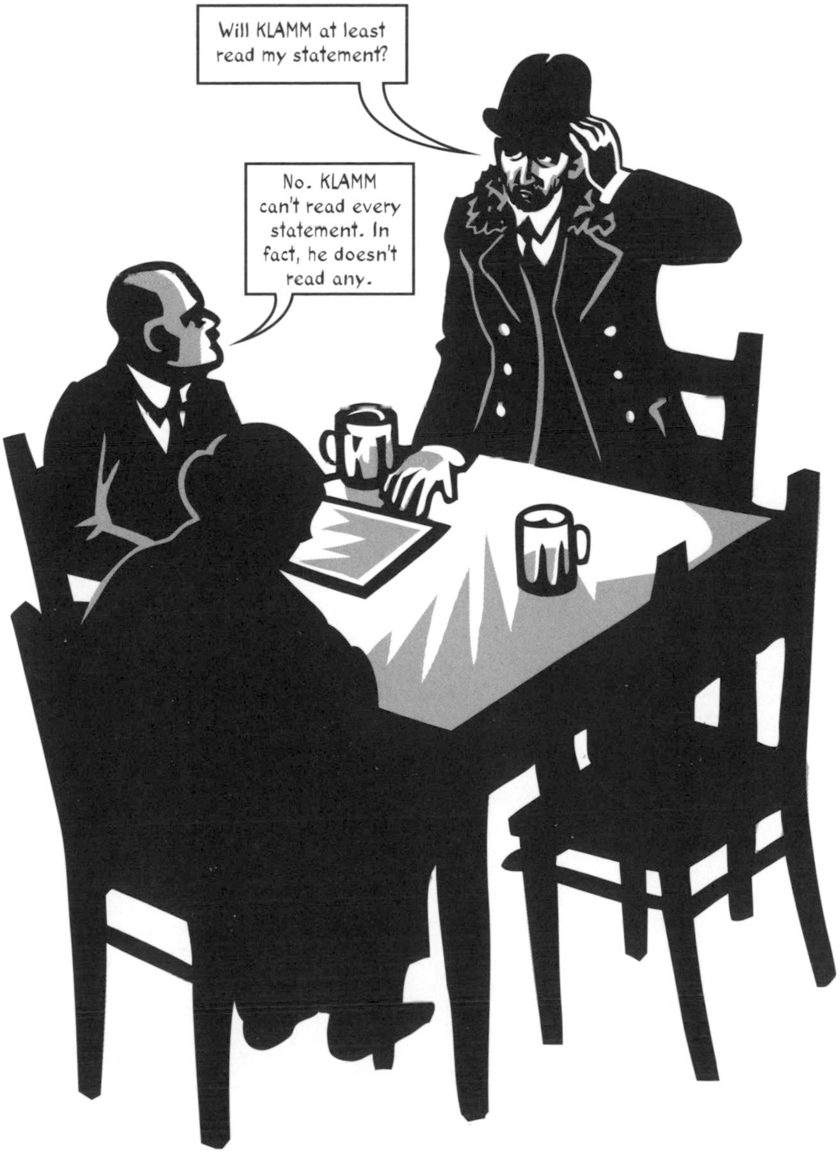
Will KLAMM at least read my statement?
No. KLAMM can't read every statement. In fact, he doesn't read any.

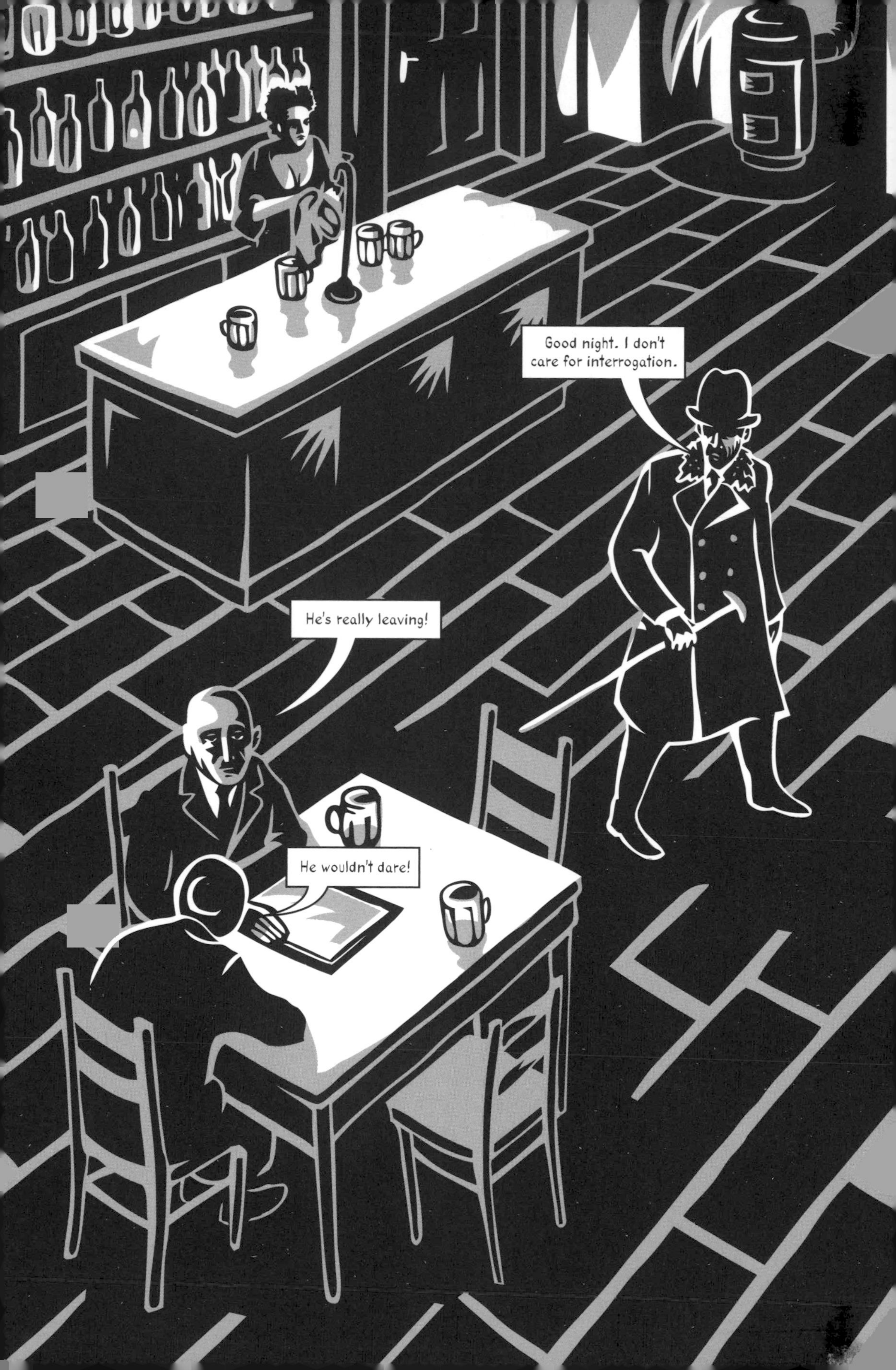
Good night. I don't care for interrogation.
He's really leaving!
He wouldn't dare!

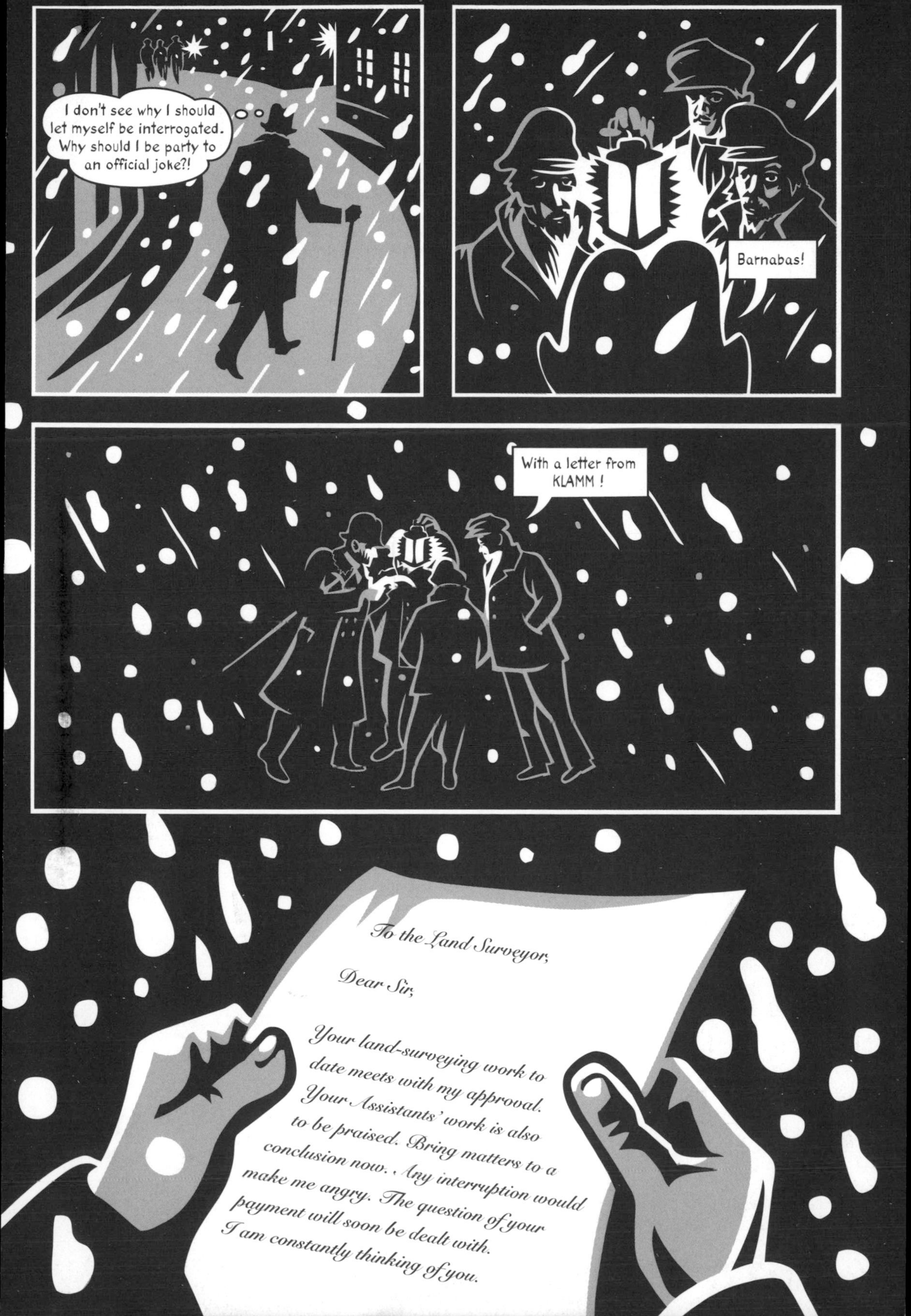
I don't see why I should let myself be interrogated. Why should I be party to an official joke?!
Barnabas!
With a letter from KLAMM !
To the Land Surveyor,
Dear Sir,
Your land-surveying work to date meets with my approval. Your Assistants' work is also to be praised. Bring matters to a conclusion now. Any interruption would make me angry. The question of your payment will soon be dealt with. I am constantly thinking of you.

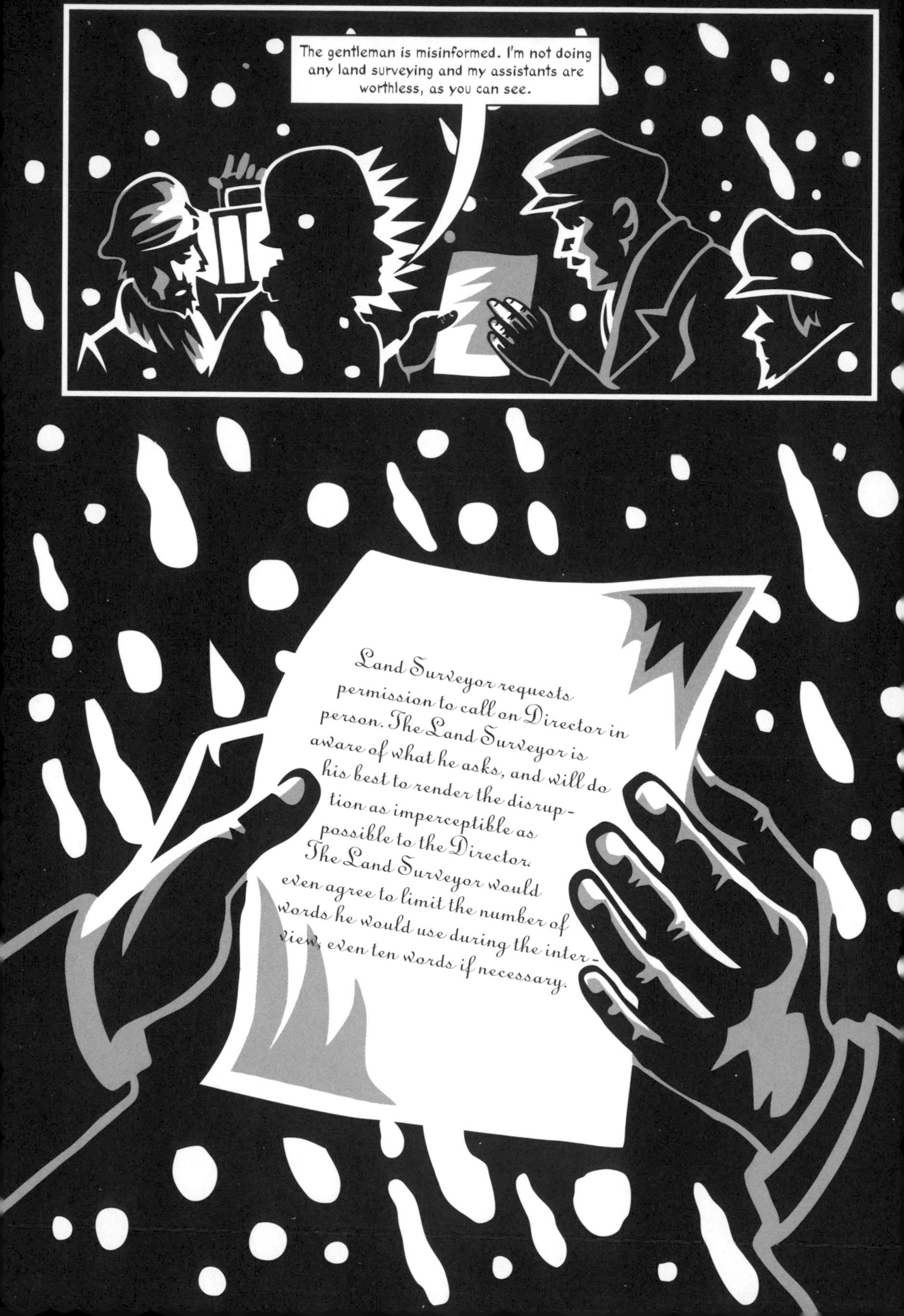
The gentleman is misinformed. I'm not doing any land surveying and my assistants are worthless, as you can see.
Land Surveyor requests permission to call on Director in person. The Land Surveyor is aware of what he asks, and will do his best to render the disruption as imperceptible as possible to the Director. The Land Surveyor would even agree to limit the number of words he would use during the interview, even ten words if necessary.

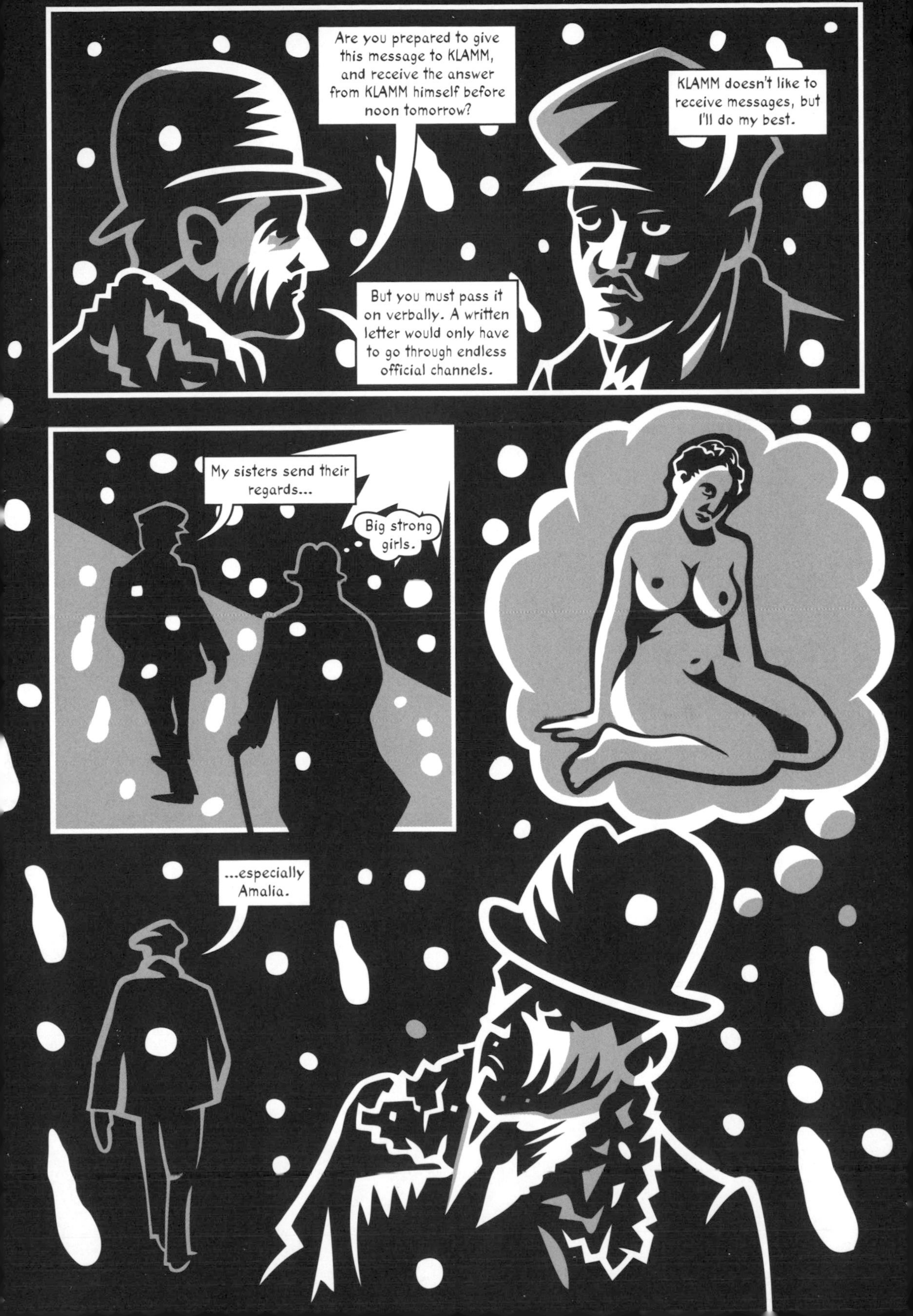
Are you prepared to give this message to KLAMM, and receive the answer from KLAMM himself before noon tomorrow?
KLAMM doesn't like to receive messages, but I'll do my best.
But you must pass it on verbally. A written letter would only have to go through endless official channels.
My sisters send their regards...
Big strong girls.
...especially Amalia.

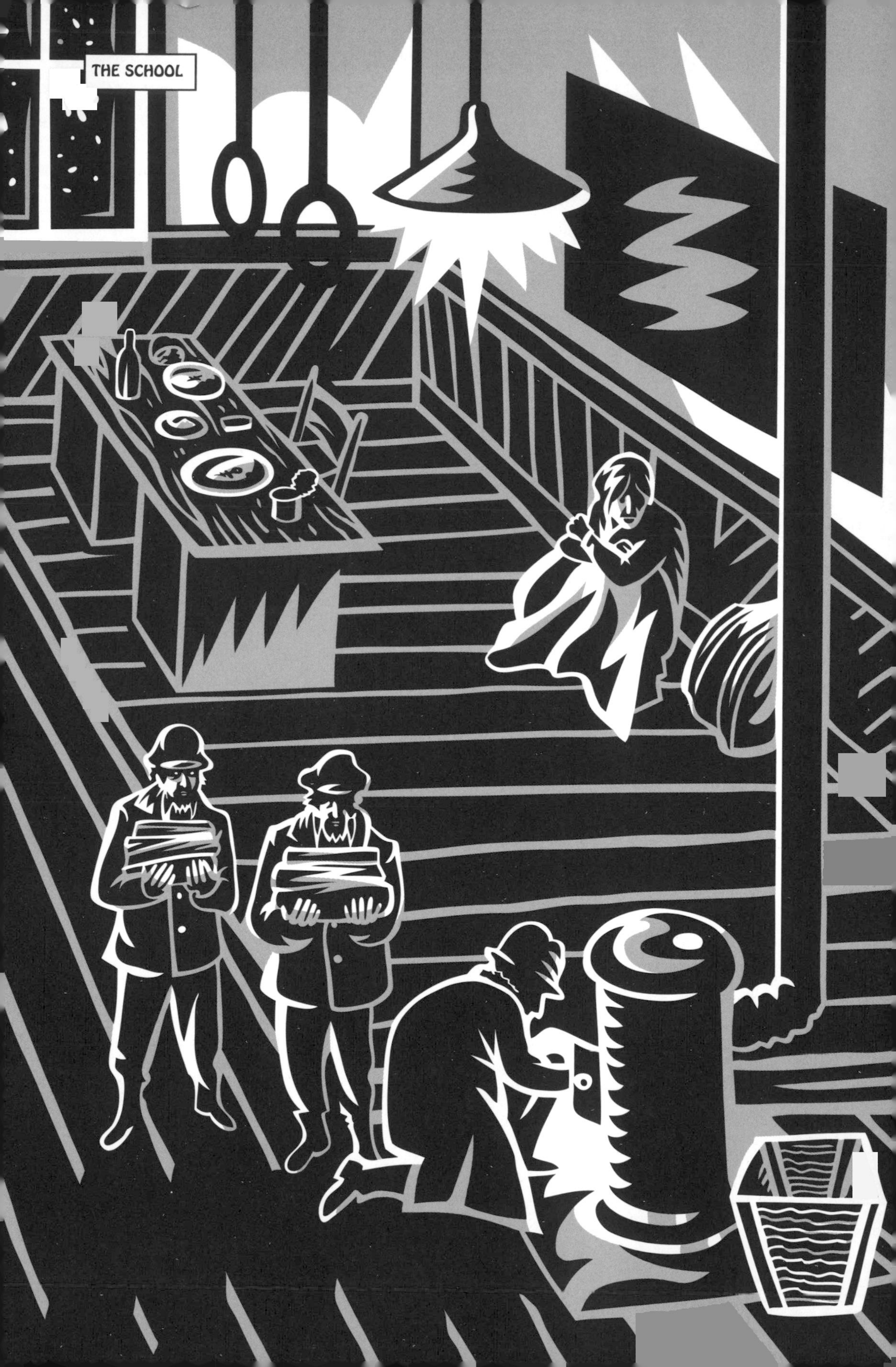
THE SCHOOL

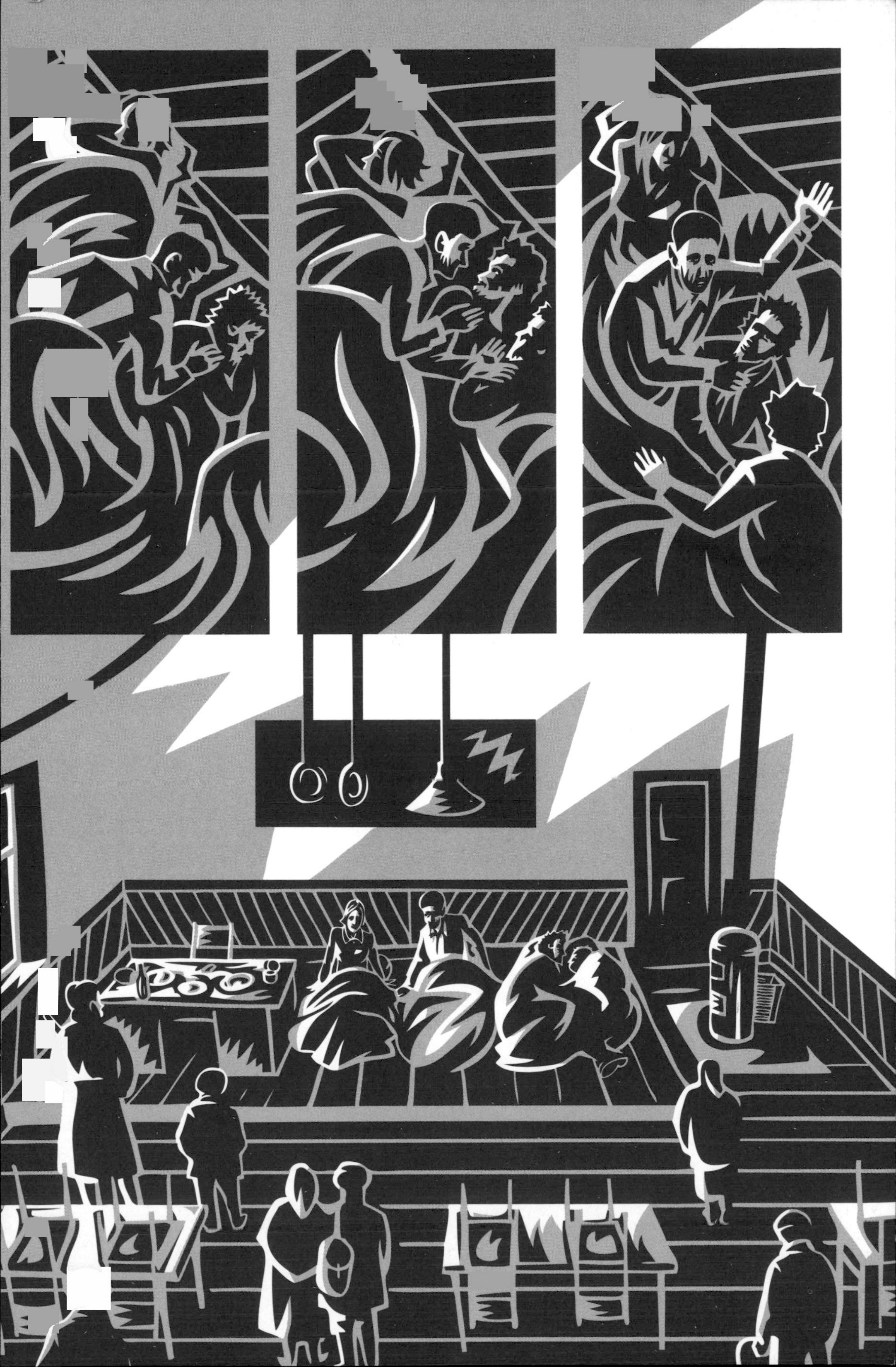

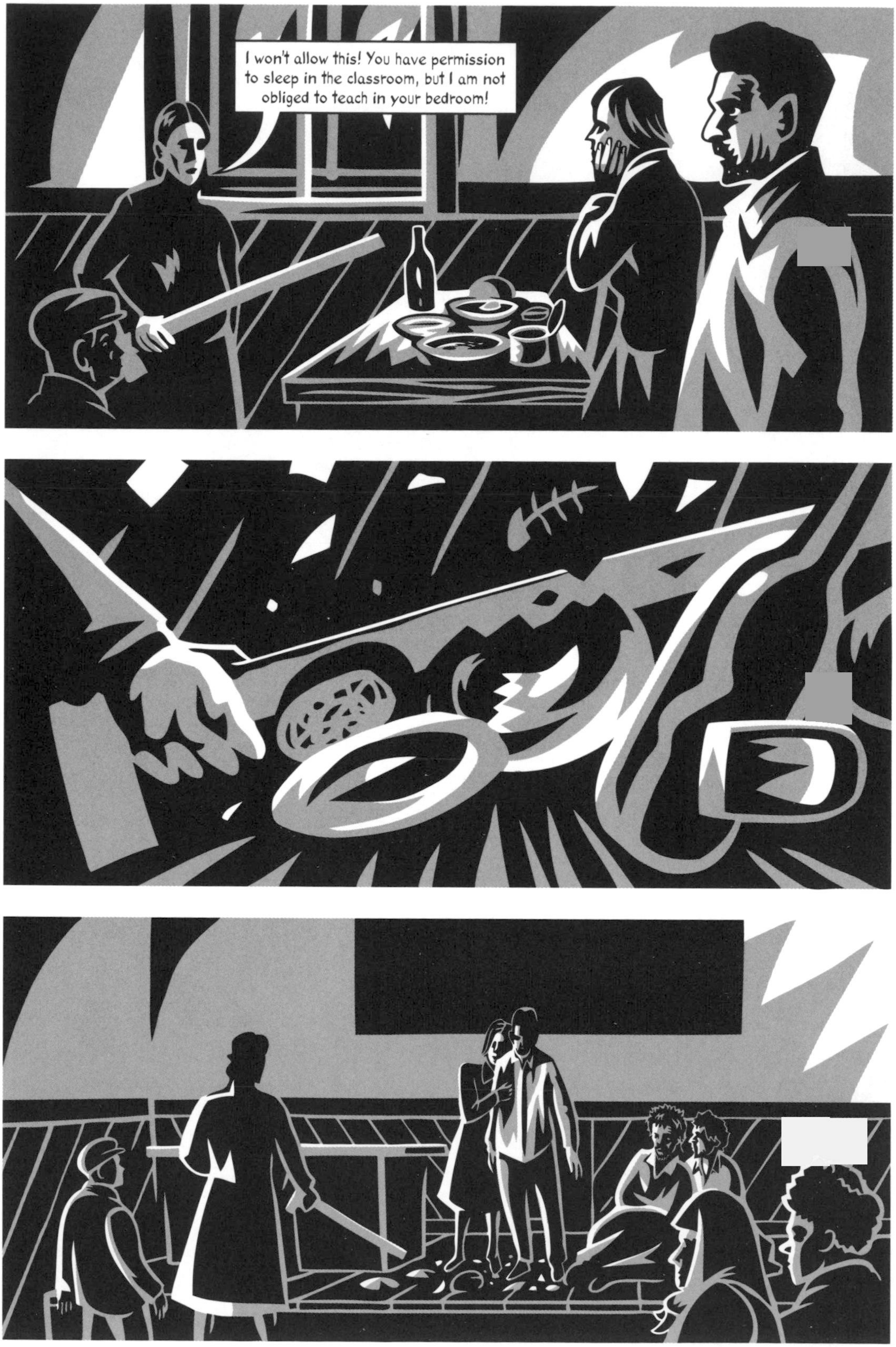
I won't allow this! You have permission to sleep in the classroom, but I am not obliged to teach in your bedroom!

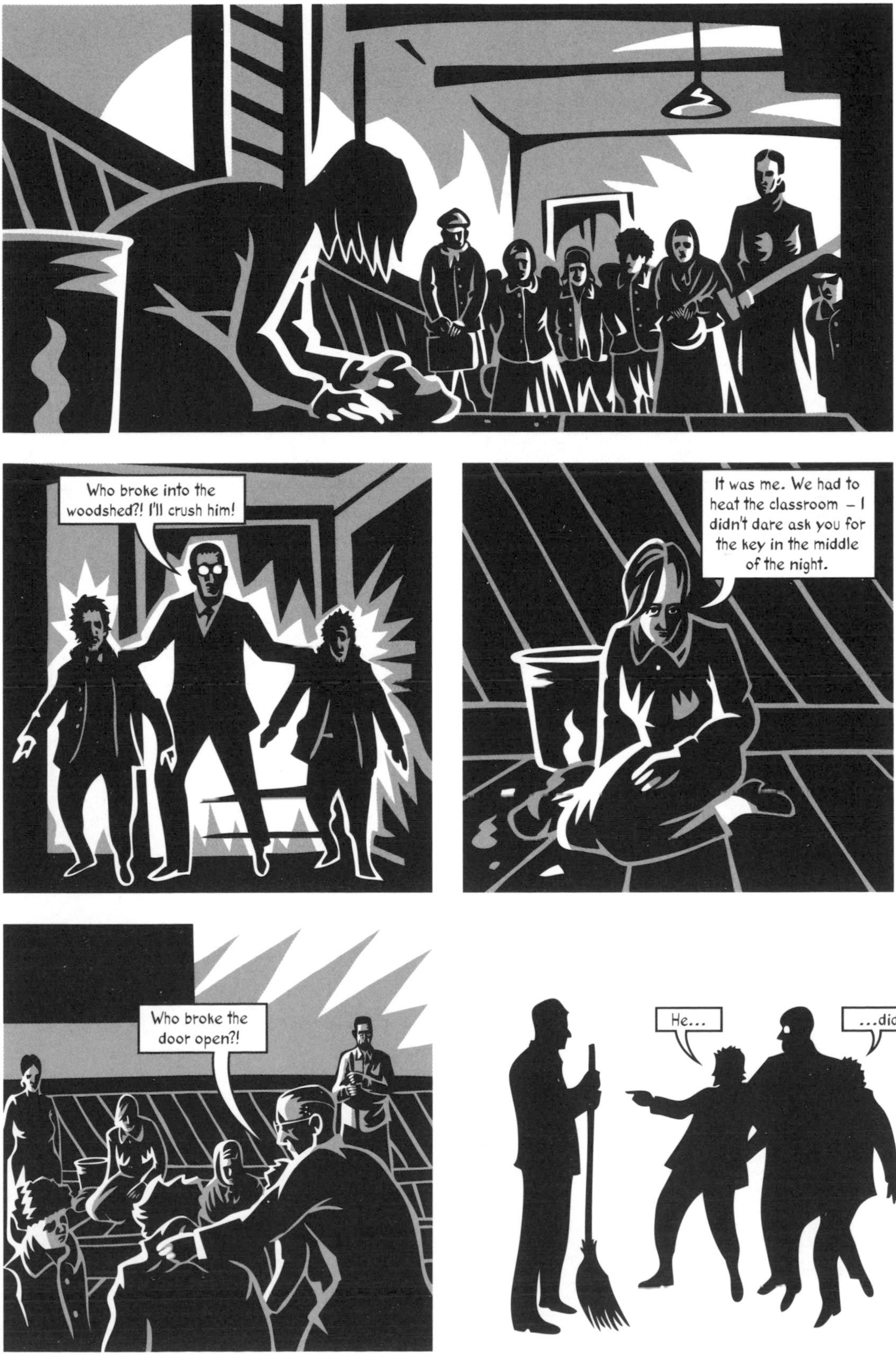
Who broke into the woodshed?! I'll crush him!
It was me. We had to heat the classroom – I didn't dare ask you for the key in the middle of the night.
Who broke the door open?!
He...
...did!

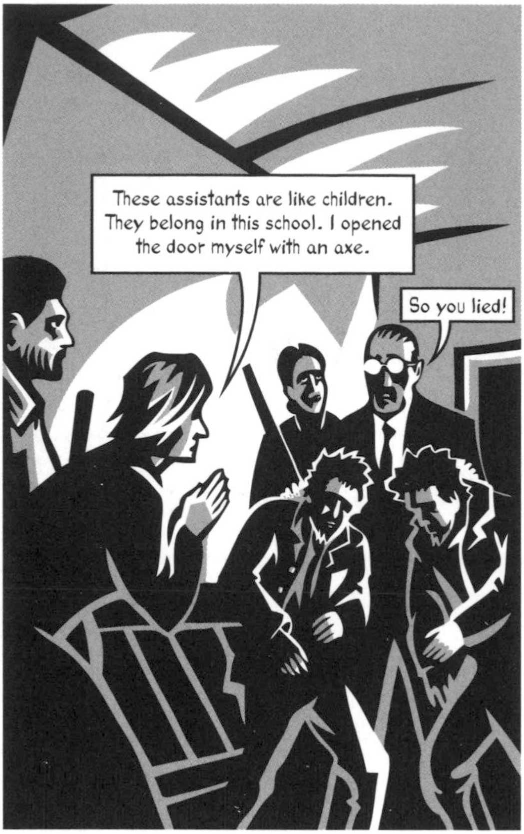
These assistants are like children. They belong in this school. I opened the door myself with an axe.
So you lied!

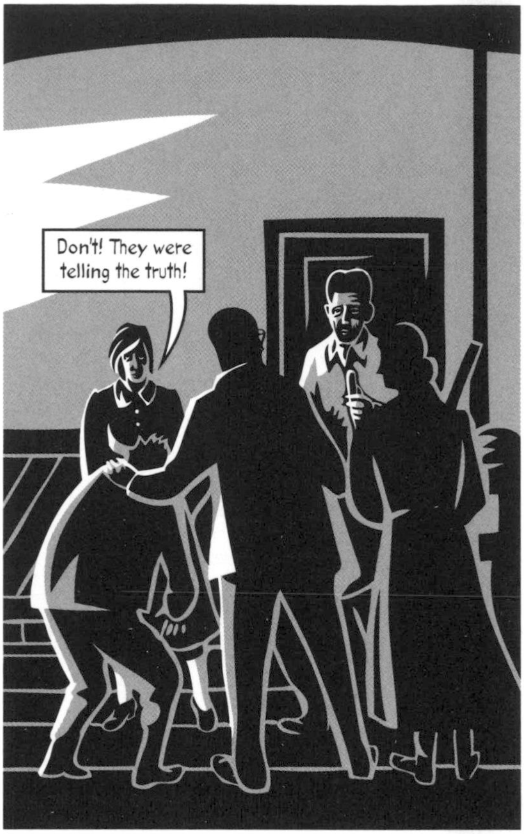
Don't! They were telling the truth!

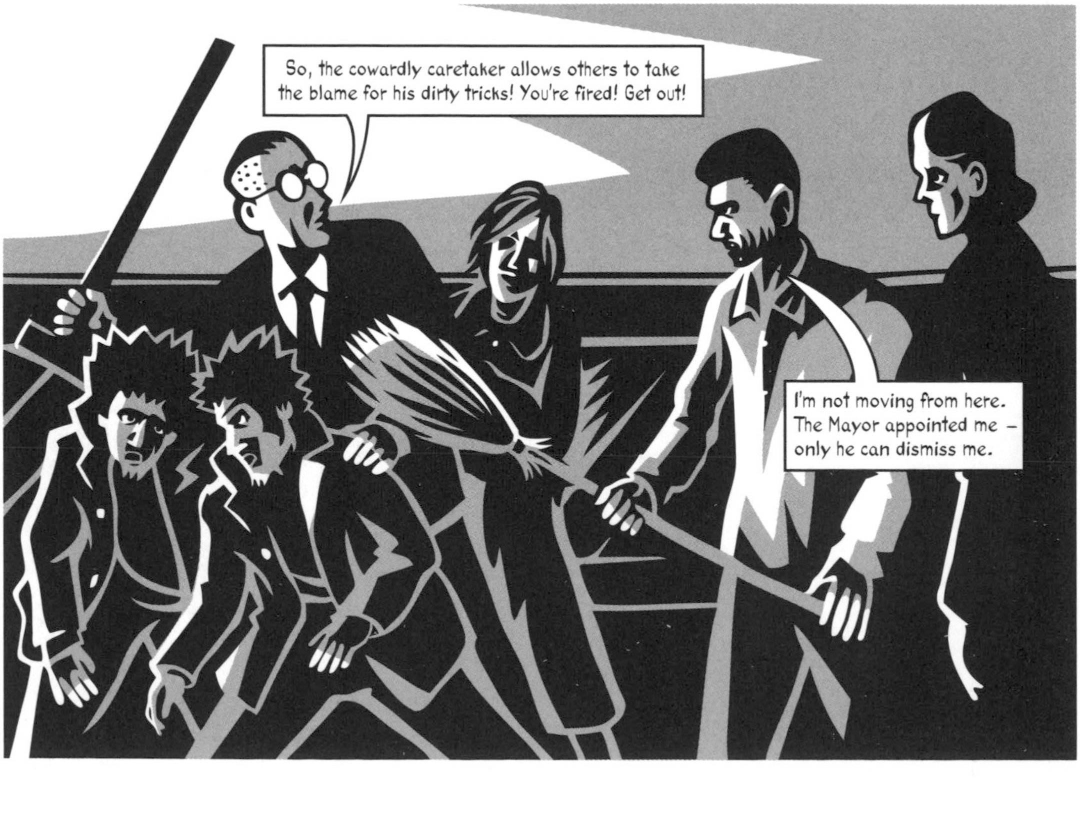
So, the cowardly caretaker allows others to take the blame for his dirty tricks! You're fired! Get out!
I'm not moving from here. The Mayor appointed me – only he can dismiss me.

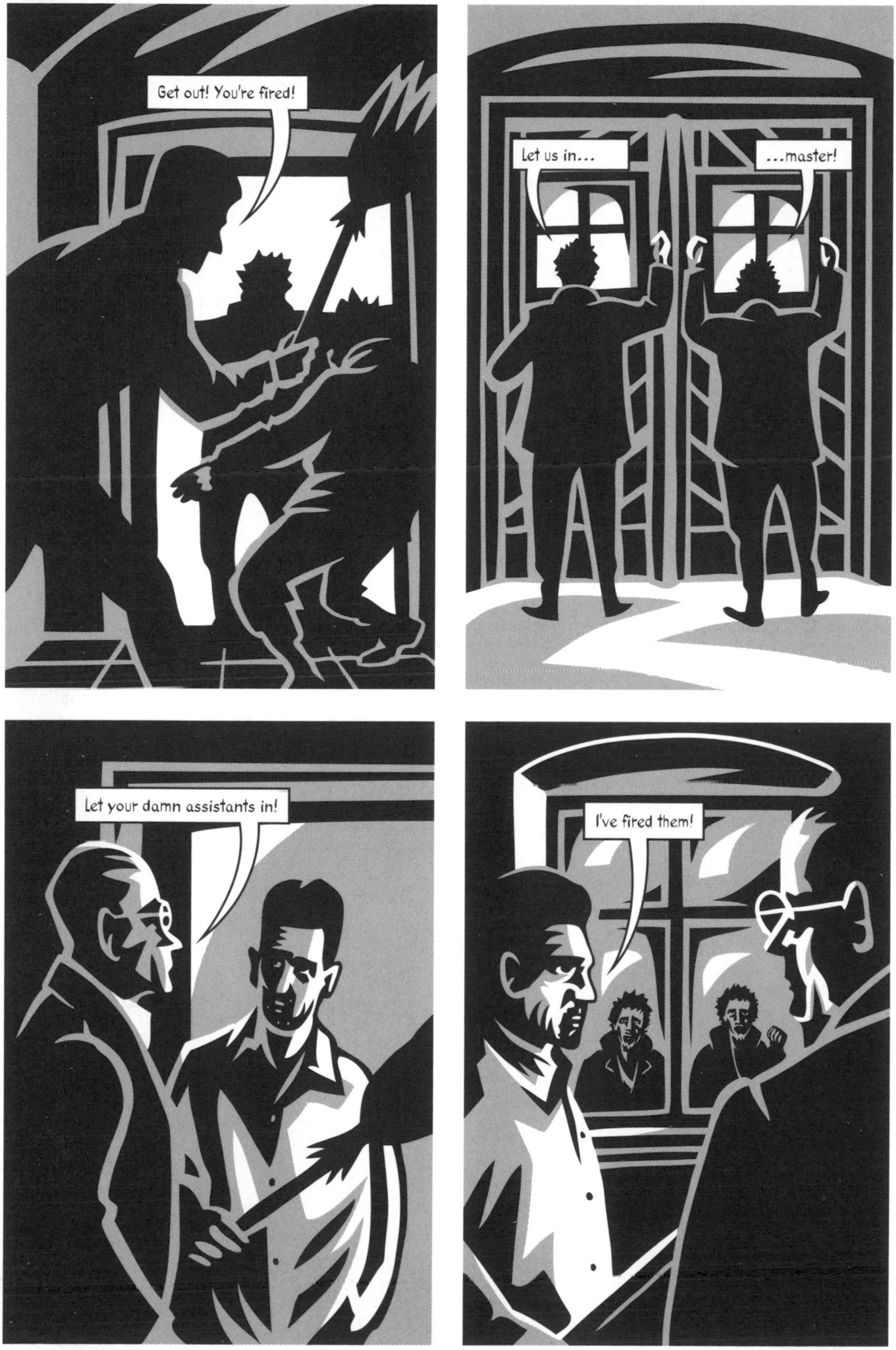
Get out! You're fired!
Let us in...
...master!
Let your damn assistants in!
I've fired them!

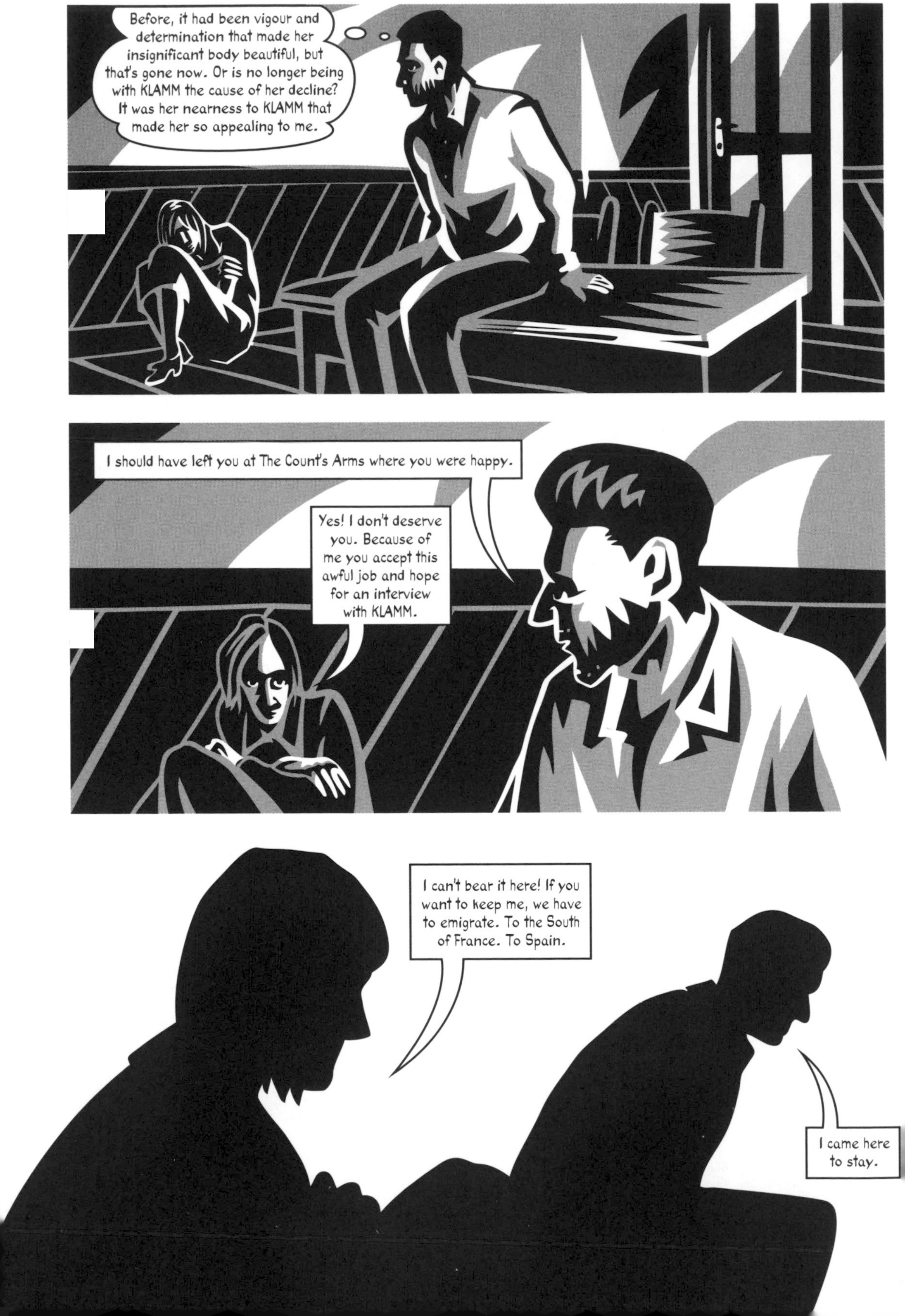

Before, it had been vigour and determination that made her insignificant body beautiful, but that's gone now. Or is no longer being with KLAMM the cause of her decline? It was her nearness to KLAMM that made her so appealing to me.
I should have left you at The Count's Arms where you were happy.
Yes! I don't deserve you. Because of me you accept this awful job and hope for an interview with KLAMM.
I can't bear it here! If you want to keep me, we have to emigrate. To the South of France. To Spain.
I came here to stay.

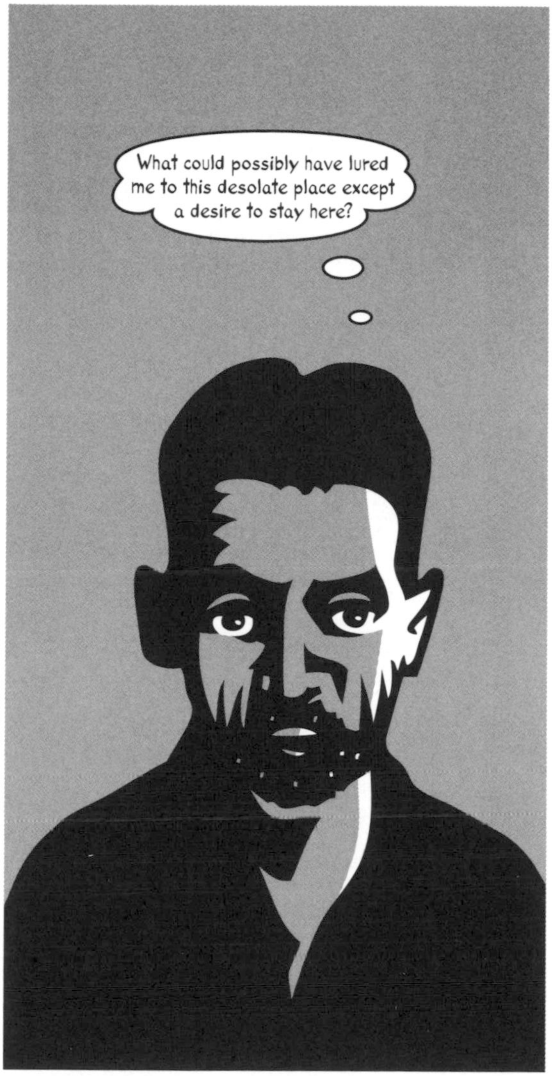
What could possibly have lured me to this desolate place except a desire to stay here?

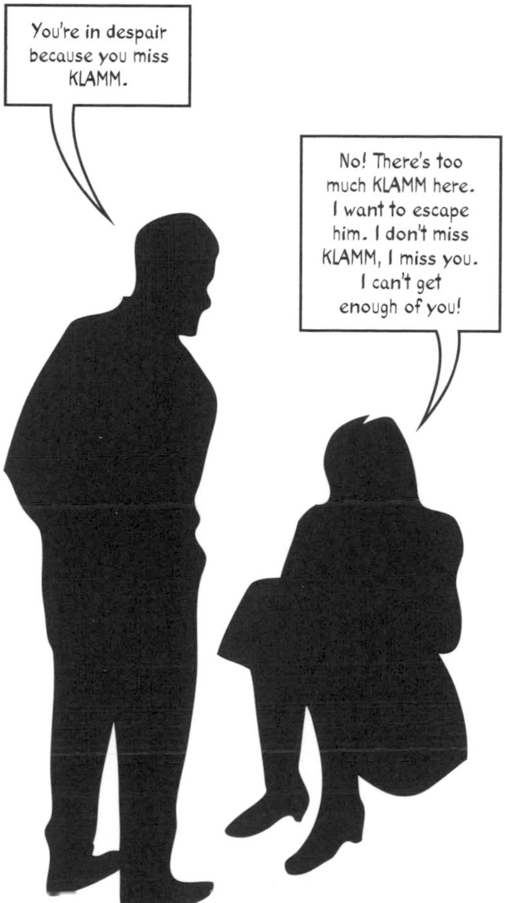
You're in despair because you miss KLAMM.
No! There's too much KLAMM here. I want to escape him. I don't miss KLAMM, I miss you. I can't get enough of you!

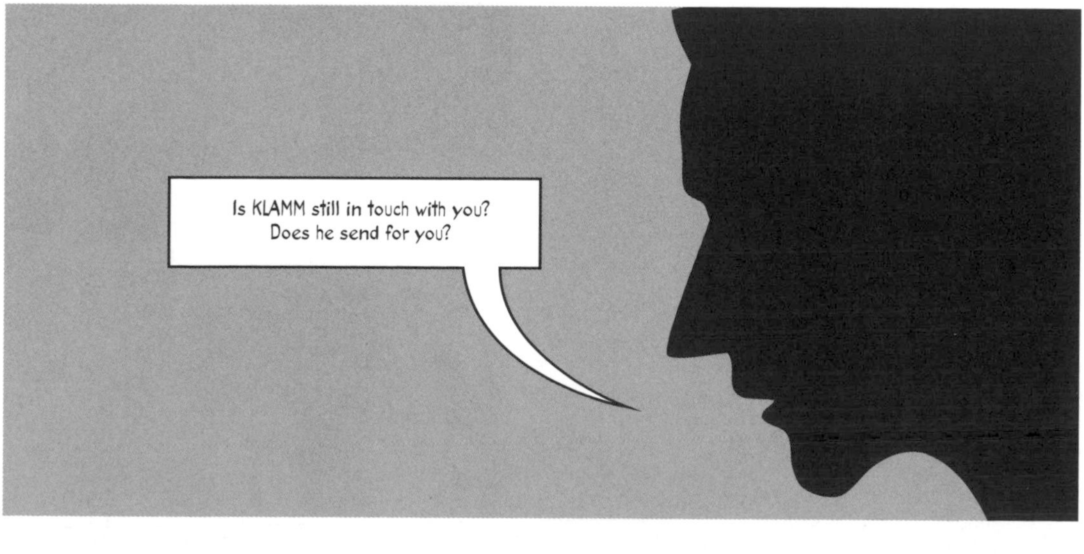
Is KLAMM still in touch with you? Does he send for you?

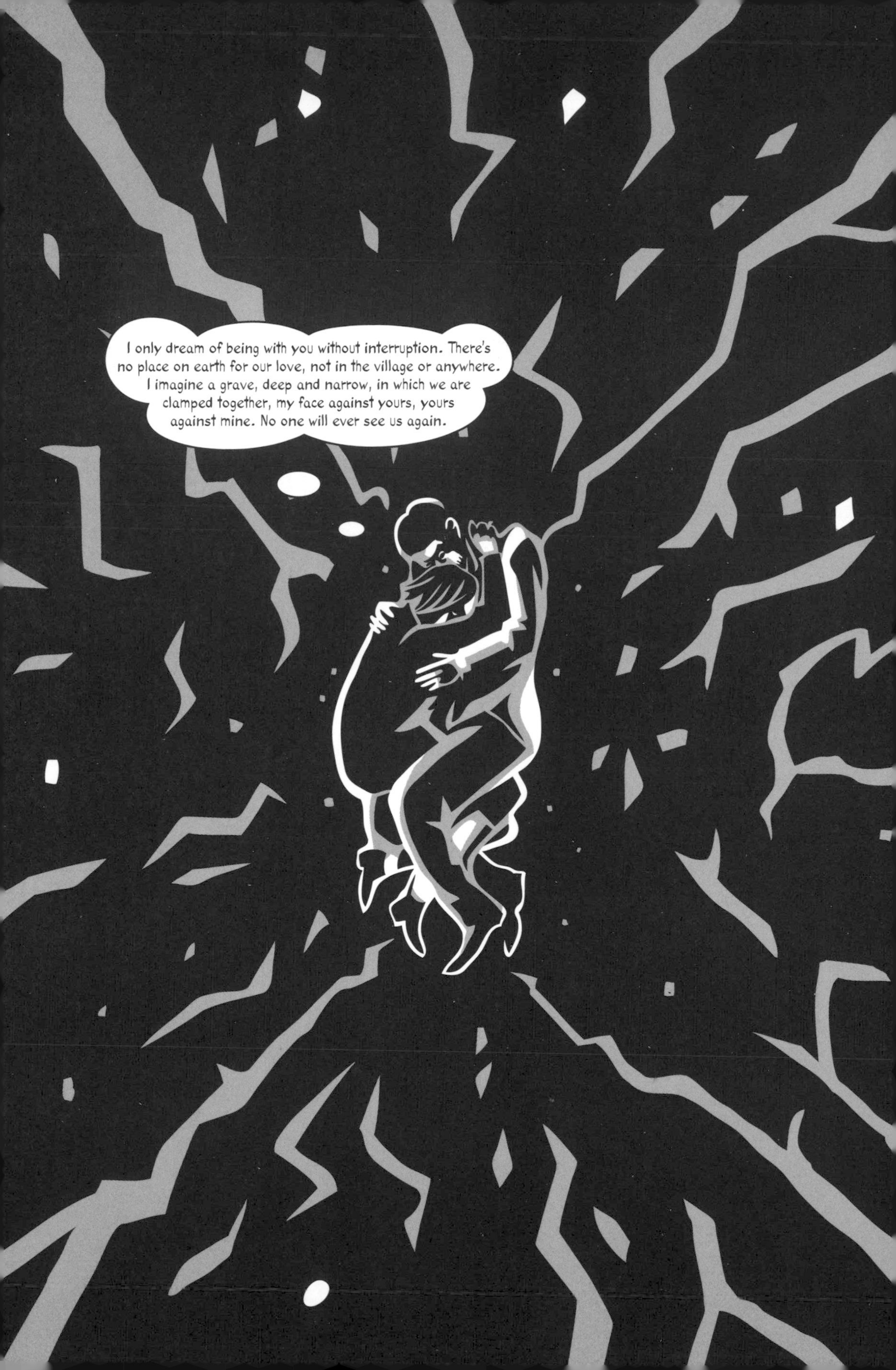
I only dream of being with you without interruption. There's no place on earth for our love, not in the village or anywhere. I imagine a grave, deep and narrow, in which we are clamped together, my face against yours, yours against mine. No one will ever see us again.

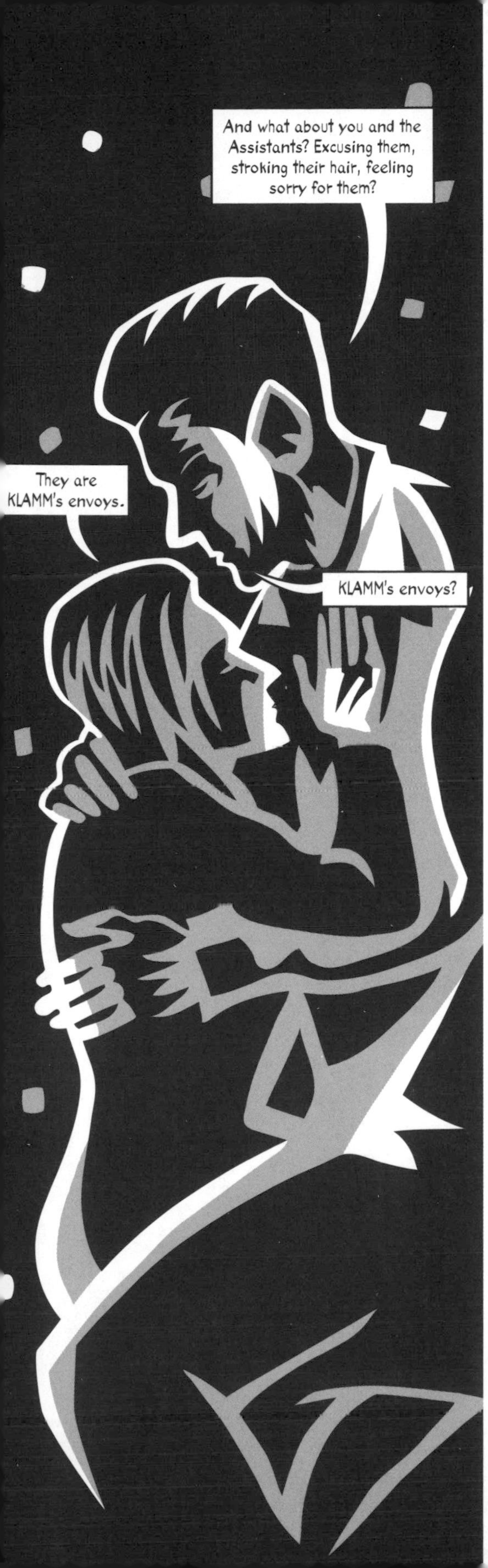
And what about you and the Assistants? Excusing them, stroking their hair, feeling sorry for them?
They are KLAMM's envoys.
KLAMM's envoys?

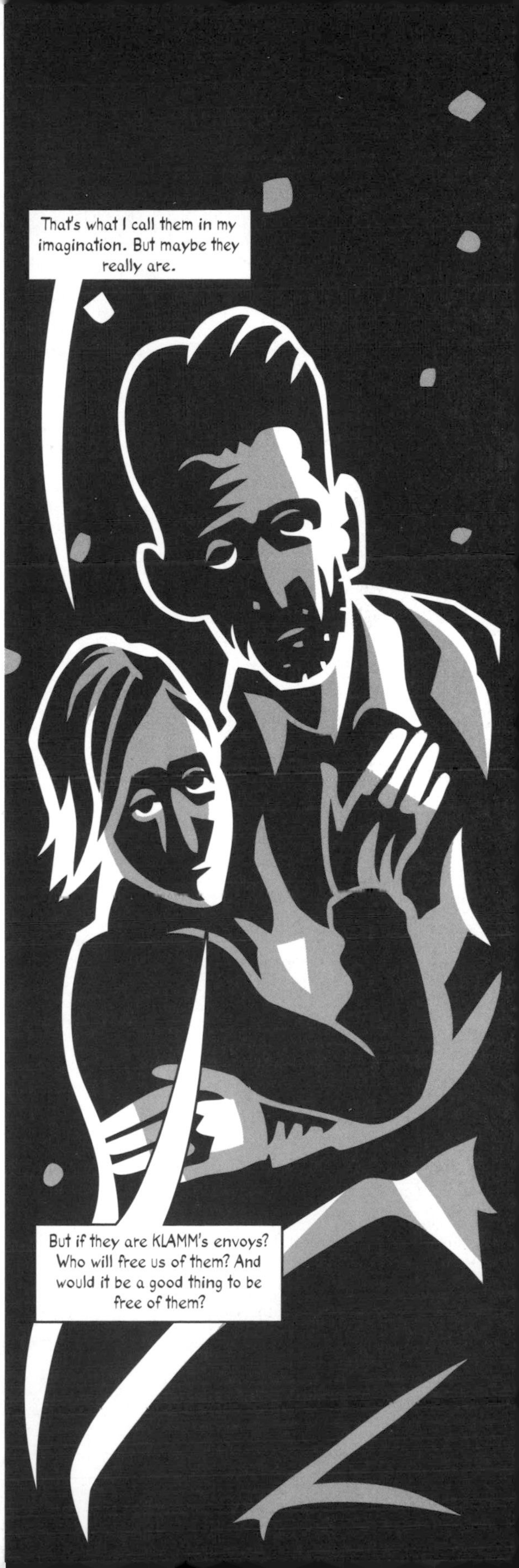
That's what I call them in my imagination. But maybe they really are.
But if they are KLAMM's envoys? Who will free us of them? And would it be a good thing to be free of them?

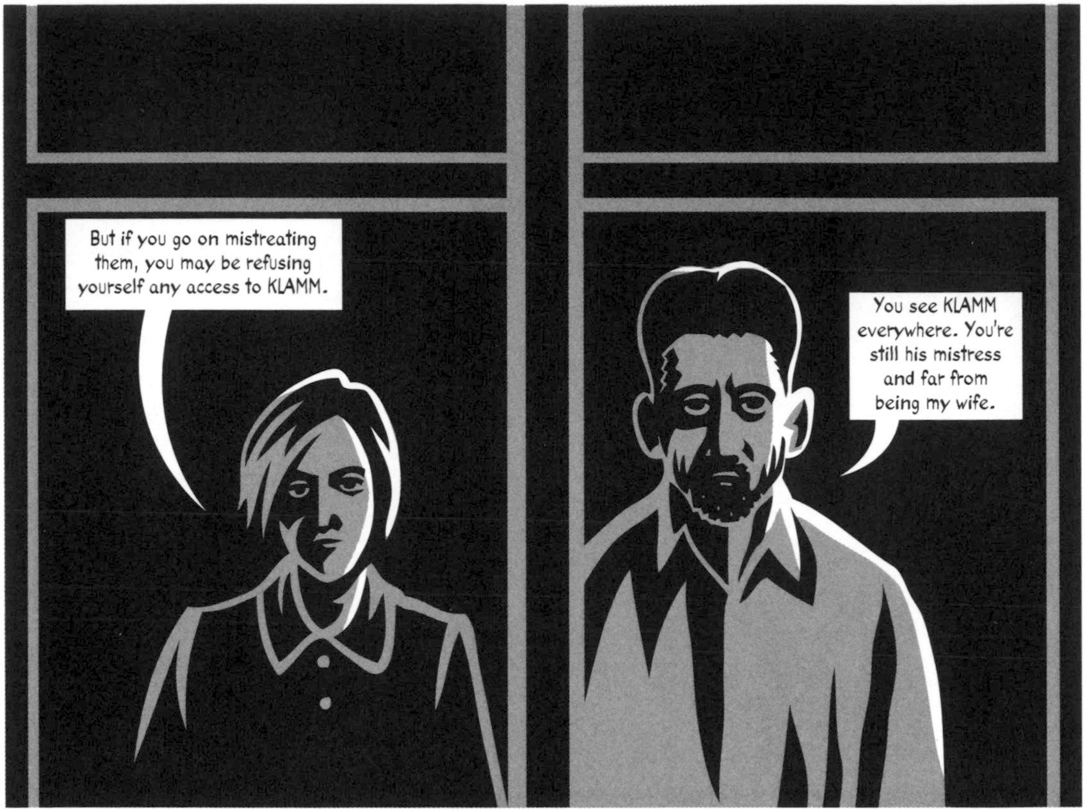
But if you go on mistreating them, you may be refusing yourself any access to KLAMM.
You see KLAMM everywhere. You're still his mistress and far from being my wife.

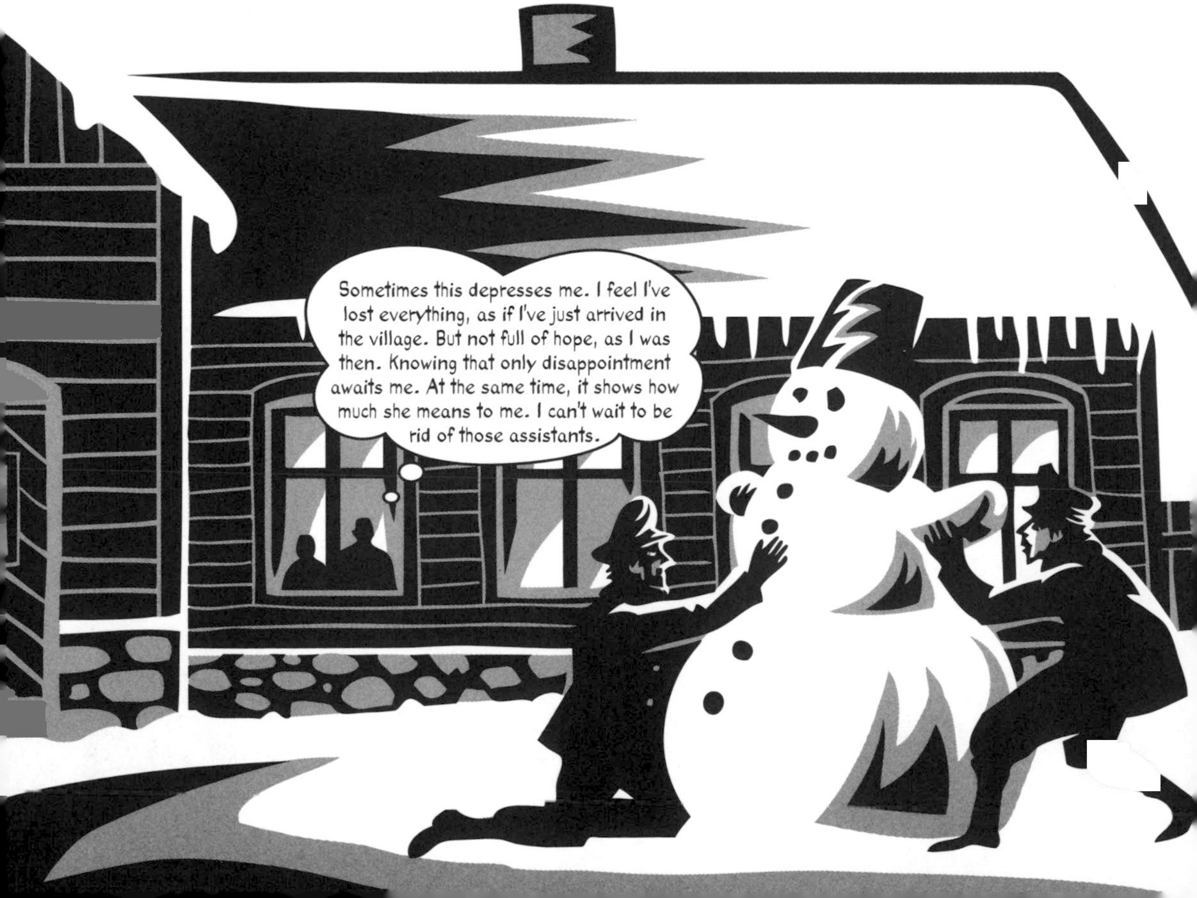
Sometimes this depresses me. I feel I've lost everything, as if I've just arrived in the village. But not full of hope, as I was then. Knowing that only disappointment awaits me. At the same time, it shows how much she means to me. I can't wait to be rid of those assistants.

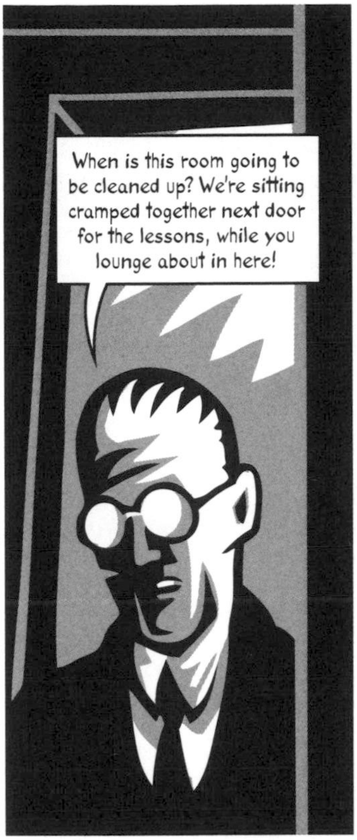
When is this room going to be cleaned up? We're sitting cramped together next door for the lessons, while you lounge about in here!

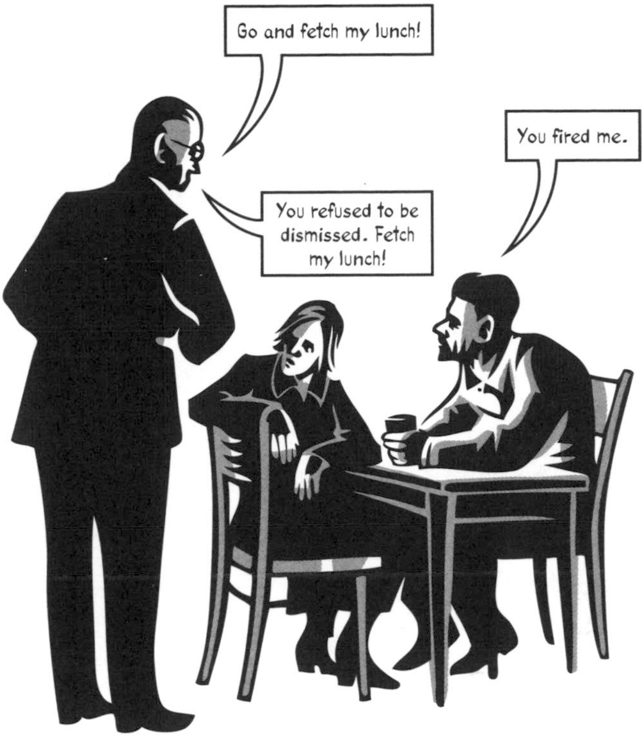
Go and fetch my lunch!
You fired me.
You refused to be dismissed. Fetch my lunch!

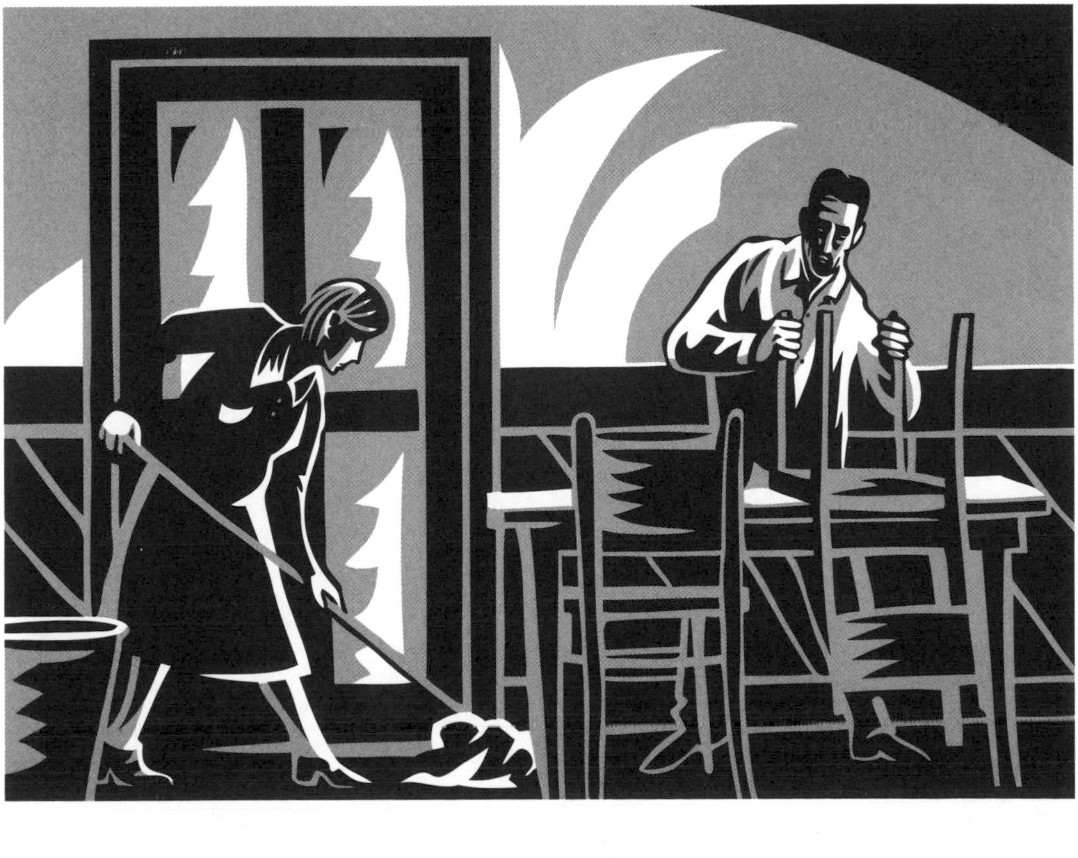

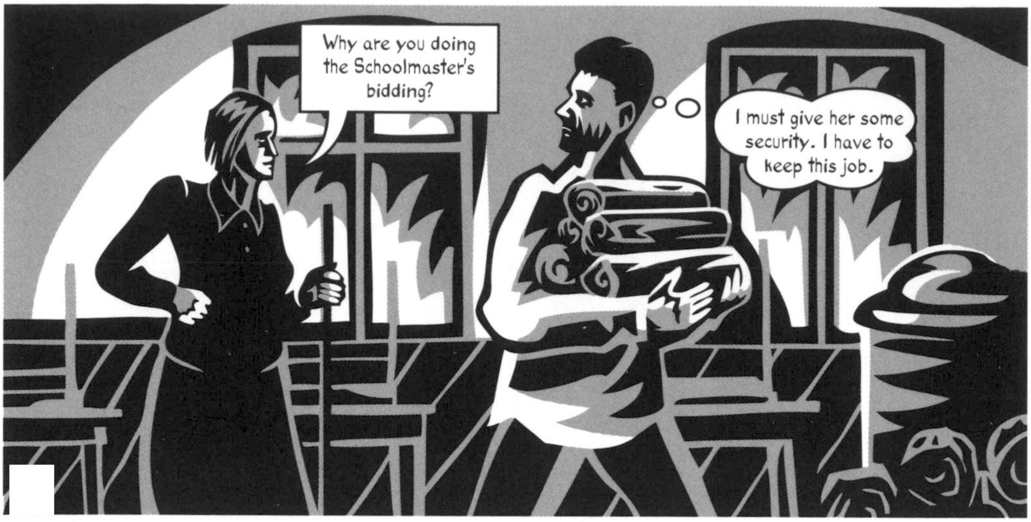
Why are you doing the Schoolmaster's bidding?
I must give her some security. I have to keep this job.

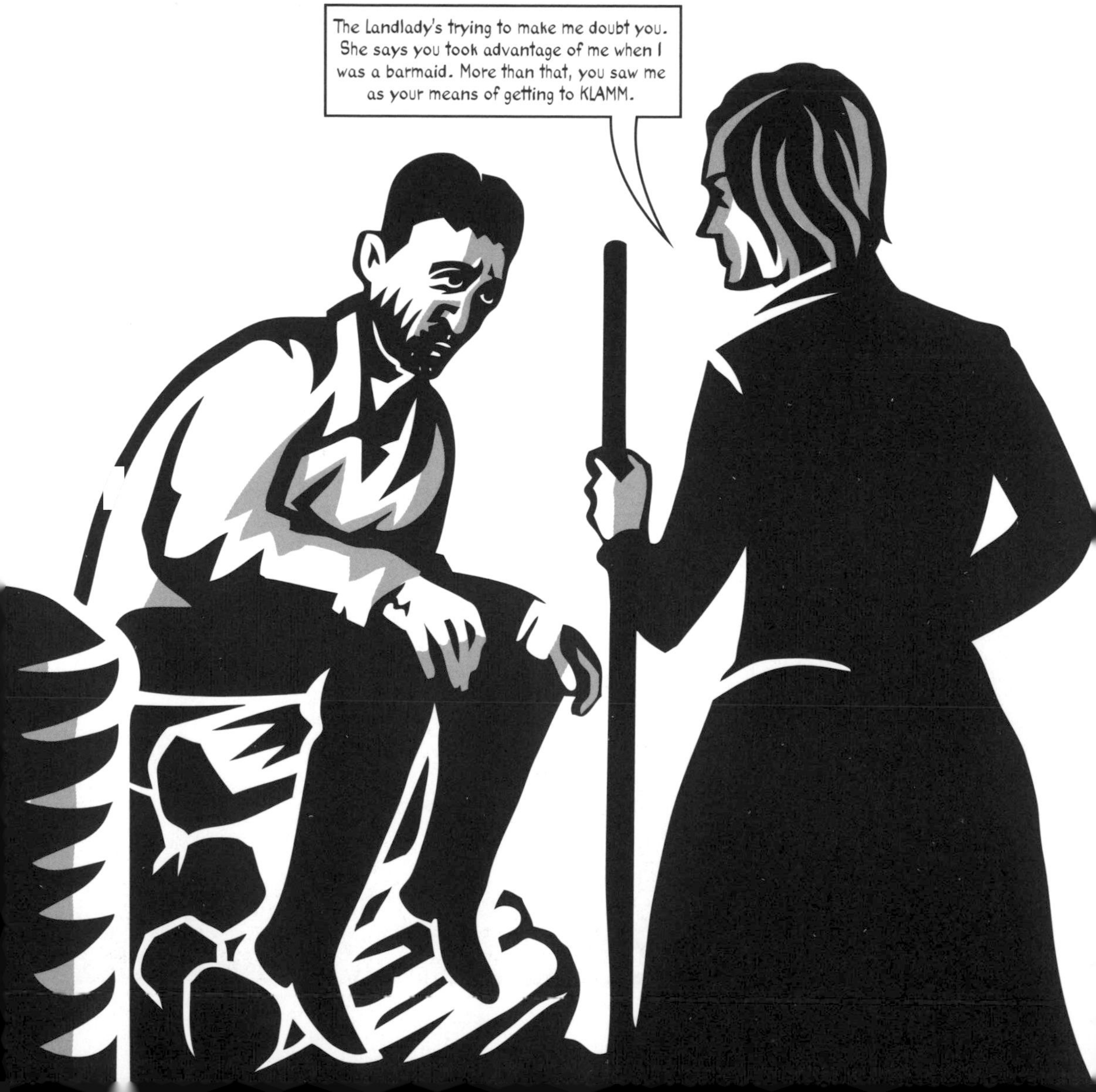
The Landlady's trying to make me doubt you. She says you took advantage of me when I was a barmaid. More than that, you saw me as your means of getting to KLAMM.

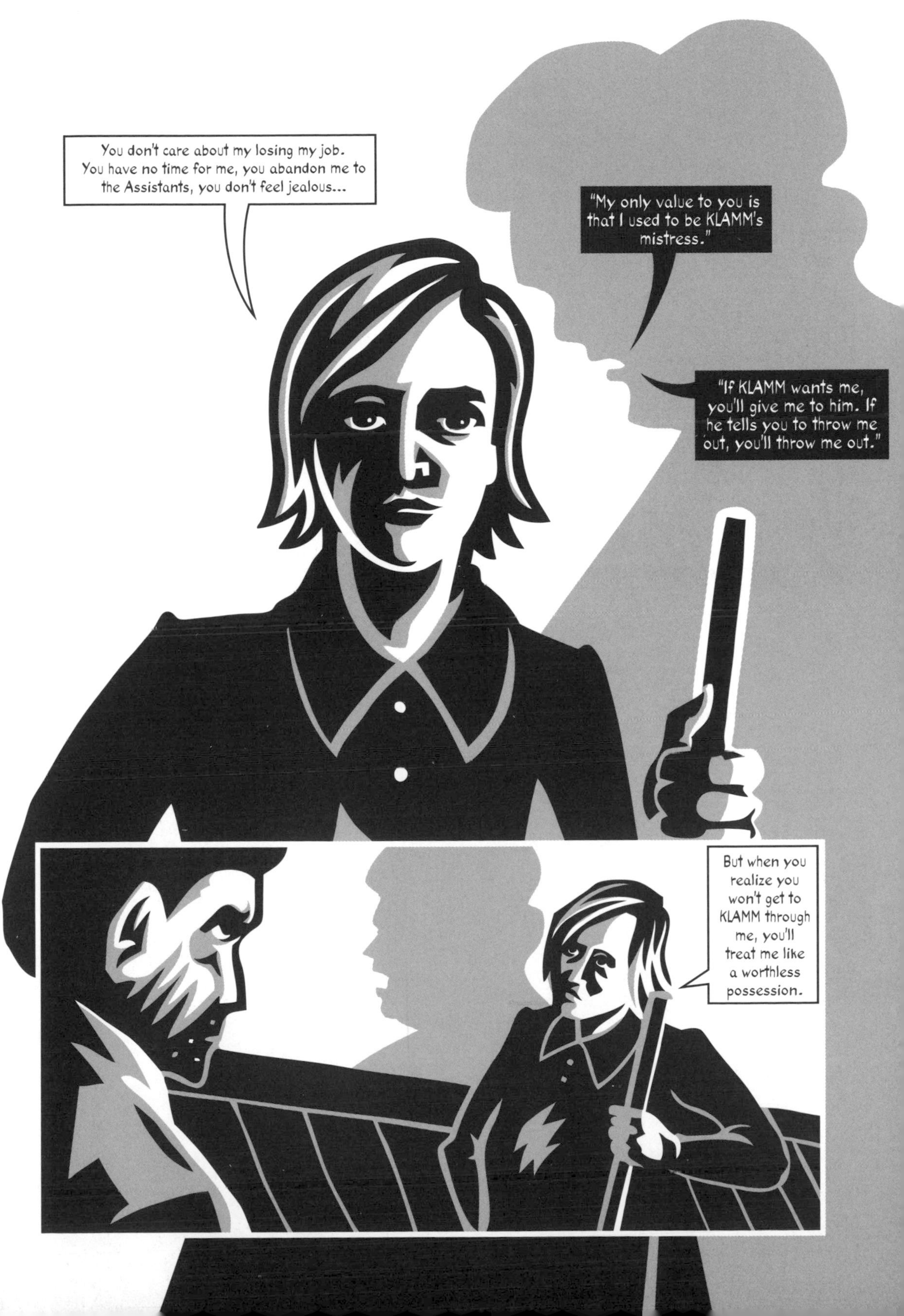

You don't care about my losing my job. You have no time for me, you abandon me to the Assistants, you don't feel jealous...
"My only value to you is that I used to be KLAMM's mistress."
"If KLAMM wants me, you'll give me to him. If he tells you to throw me out, you'll throw me out."
But when you realize you won't get to KLAMM through me, you'll treat me like a worthless possession.

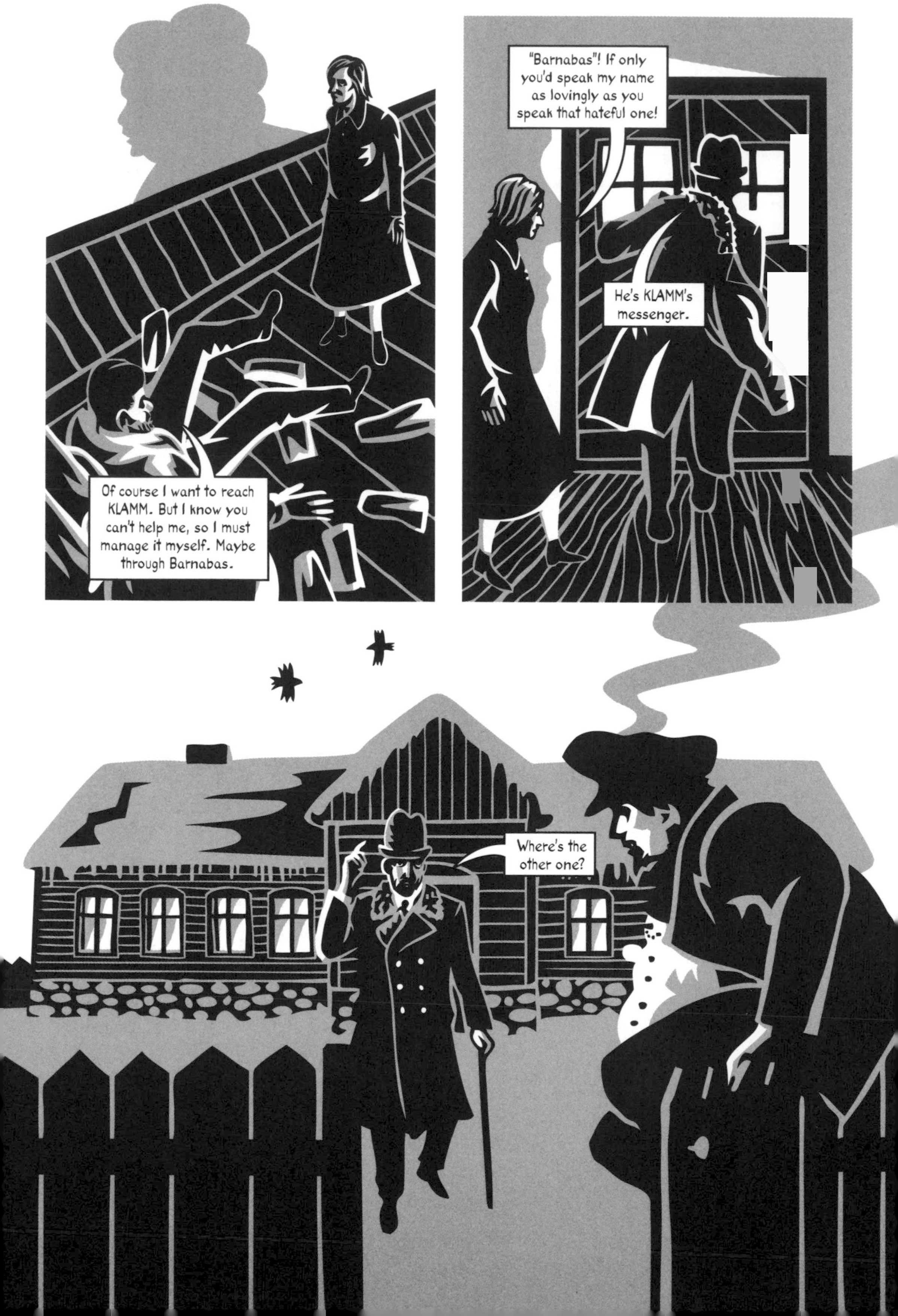
Of course I want to reach KLAMM. But I know you can't help me, so I must manage it myself. Maybe through Barnabas.
"Barnabas"! If only you'd speak my name as lovingly as you speak that hateful one!
He's KLAMM's messenger.
Where's the other one?

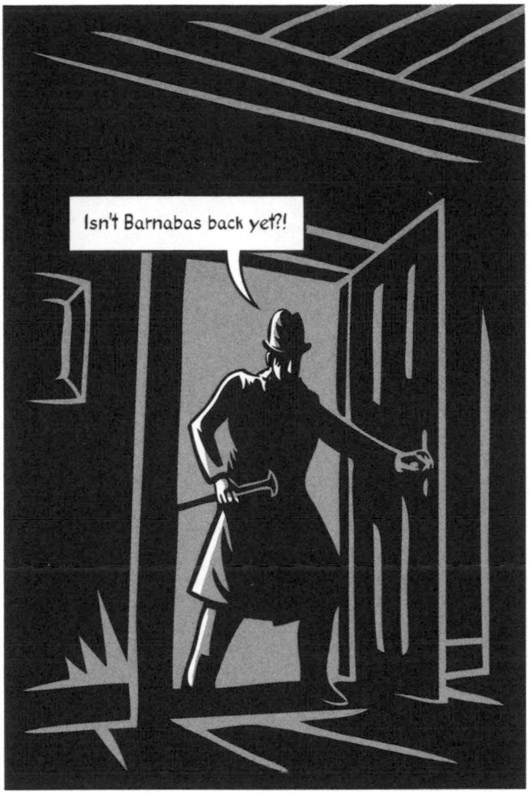
Isn't Barnabas back yet?!

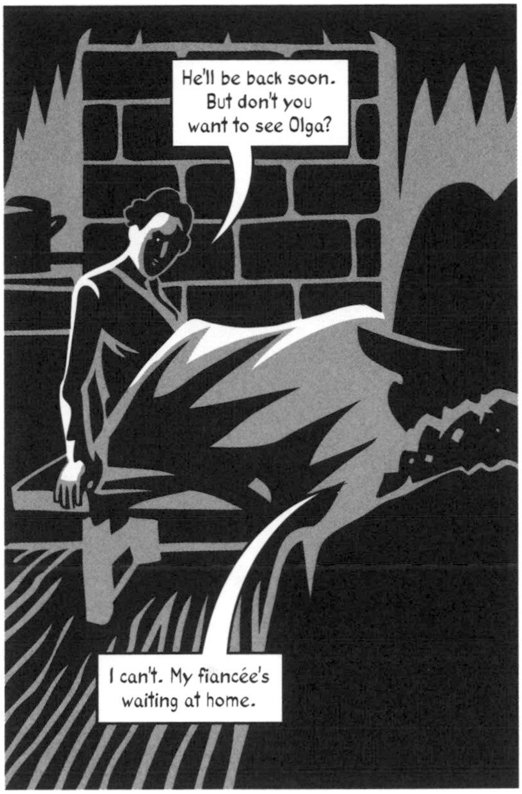
He'll be back soon. But don't you want to see Olga?
I can't. My fiancée's waiting at home.

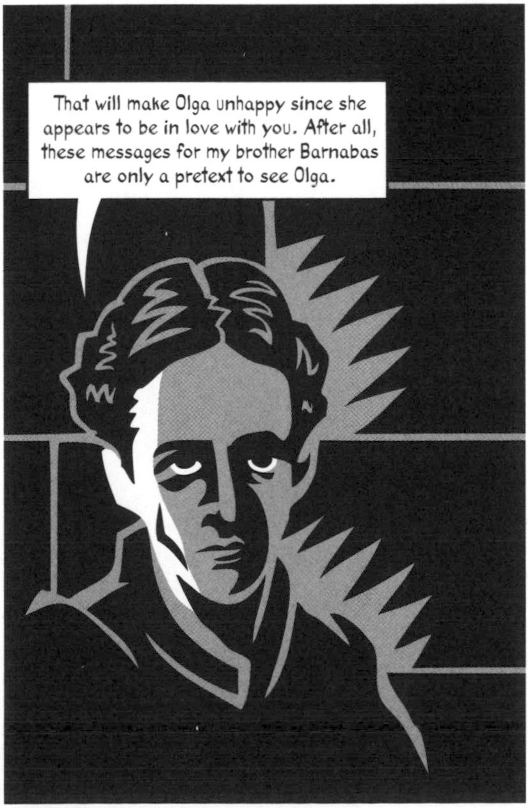
That will make Olga unhappy since she appears to be in love with you. After all, these messages for my brother Barnabas are only a pretext to see Olga.

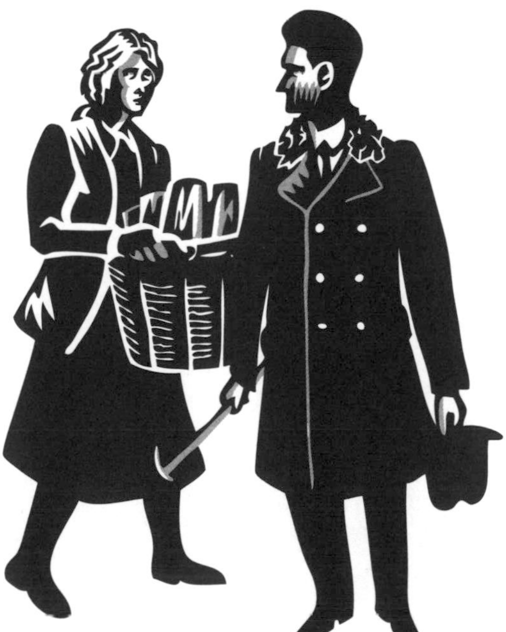

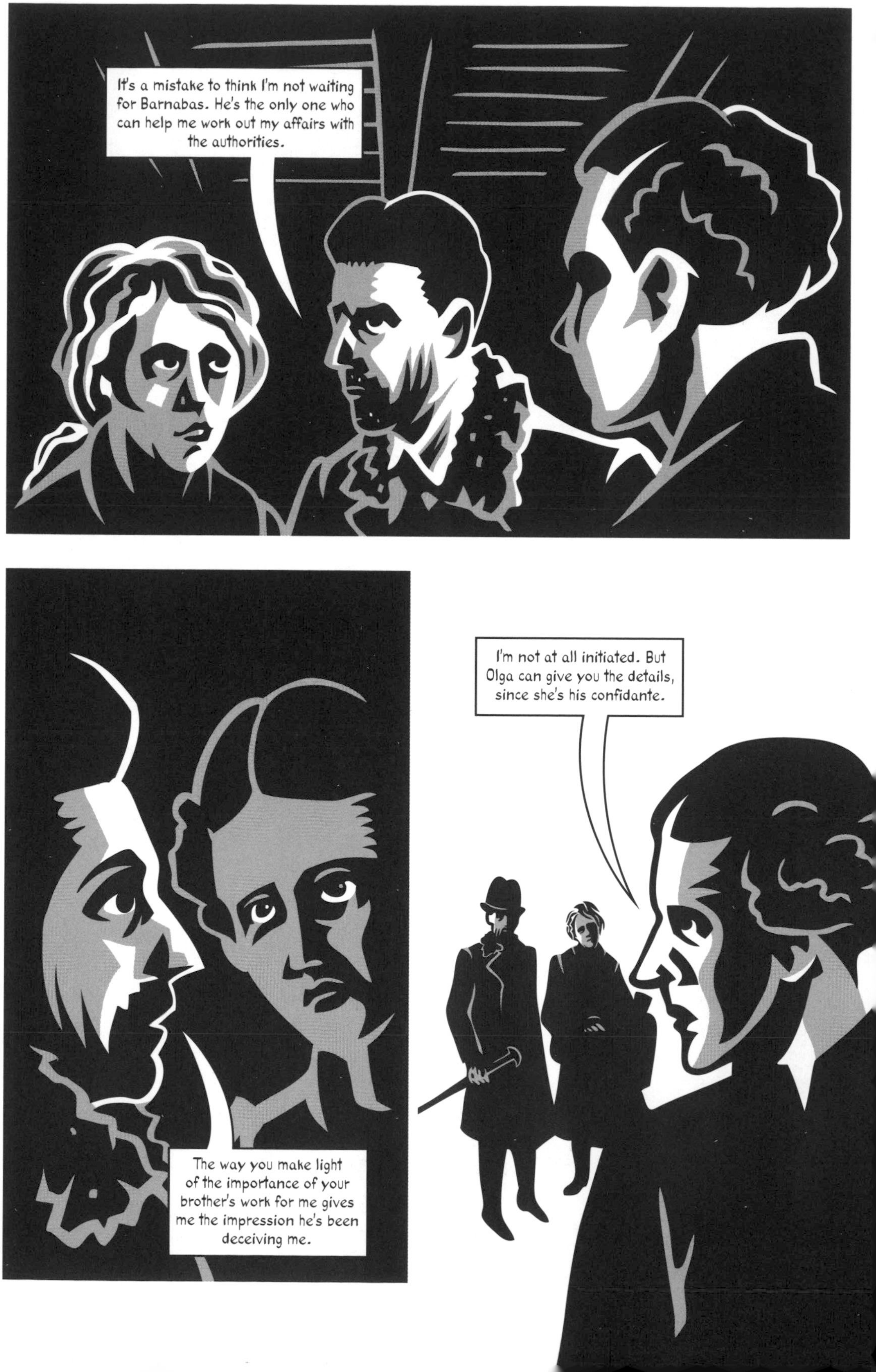
It's a mistake to think I'm not waiting for Barnabas. He's the only one who can help me work out my affairs with the authorities.
I'm not at all initiated. But Olga can give you the details, since she's his confidante.
The way you make light of the importance of your brother's work for me gives me the impression he's been deceiving me.

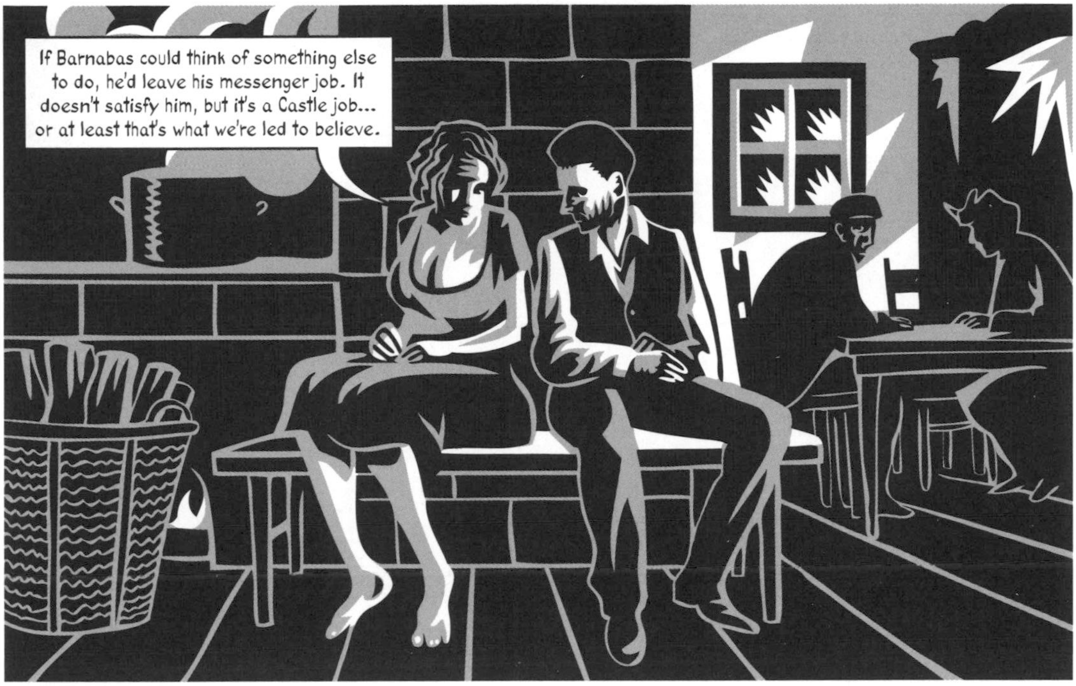
If Barnabas could think of something else to do, he'd leave his messenger job. It doesn't satisfy him, but it's a Castle job... or at least that's what we're led to believe.

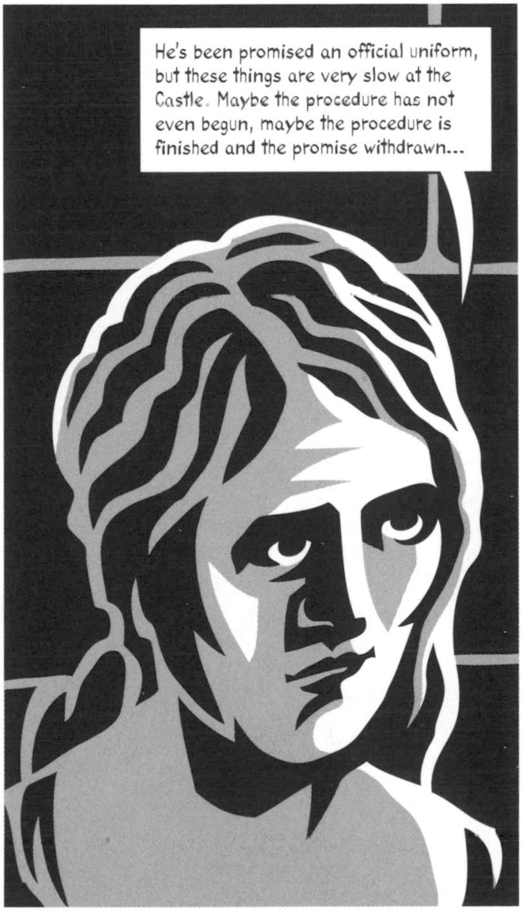
He's been promised an official uniform, but these things are very slow at the Castle. Maybe the procedure has not even begun, maybe the procedure is finished and the promise withdrawn...

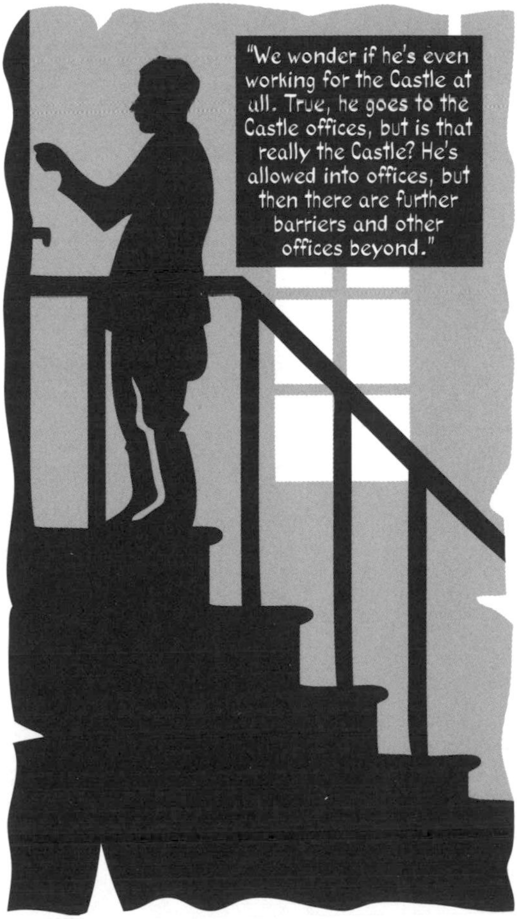
"We wonder if he's even working for the Castle at all. True, he goes to the Castle offices, but is that really the Castle? He's allowed into offices, but then there are further barriers and other offices beyond."

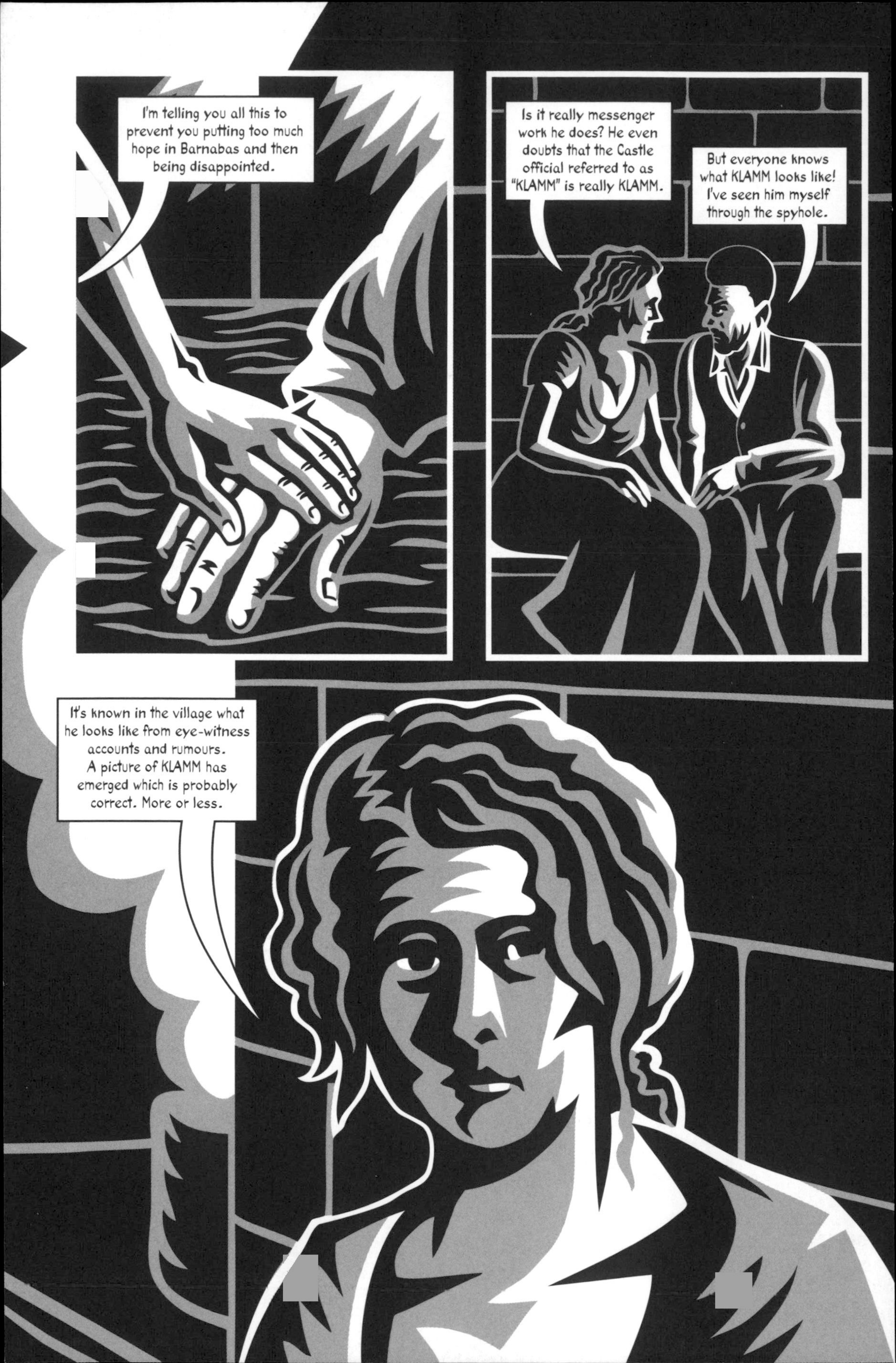
I'm telling you all this to prevent you putting too much hope in Barnabas and then being disappointed.
Is it really messenger work he does? He even doubts that the Castle official referred to as "KLAMM" is really KLAMM.
But everyone knows what KLAMM looks like! I've seen him myself through the spyhole.
It's known in the village what he looks like from eye-witness accounts and rumours. A picture of KLAMM has emerged which is probably correct. More or less.

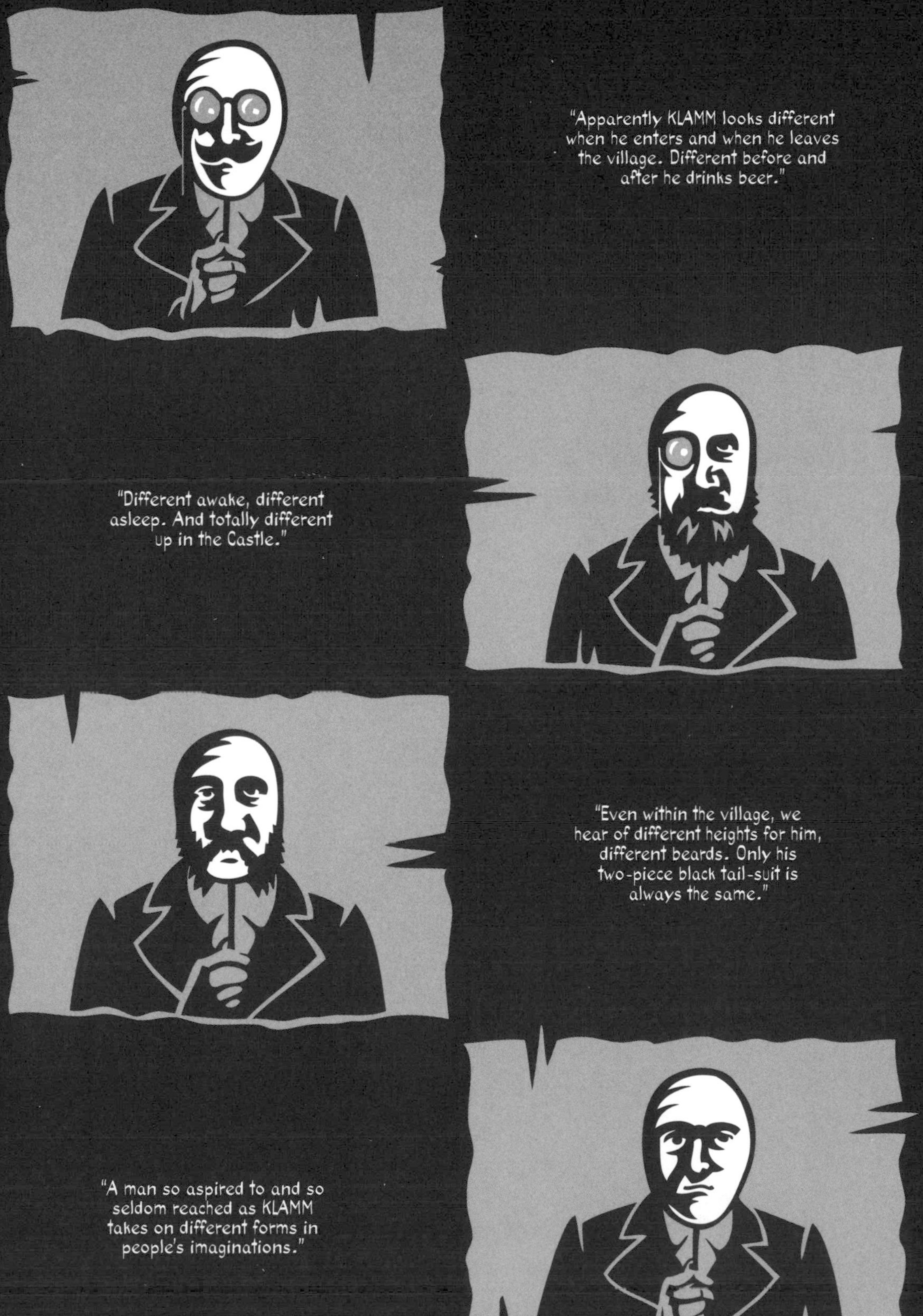
"Apparently KLAMM looks different when he enters and when he leaves the village. Different before and after he drinks beer."
"Different awake, different asleep. And totally different up in the Castle."
"Even within the village, we hear of different heights for him, different beards. Only his two-piece black tail-suit is always the same."
"A man so aspired to and so seldom reached as KLAMM takes on different forms in people's imaginations."

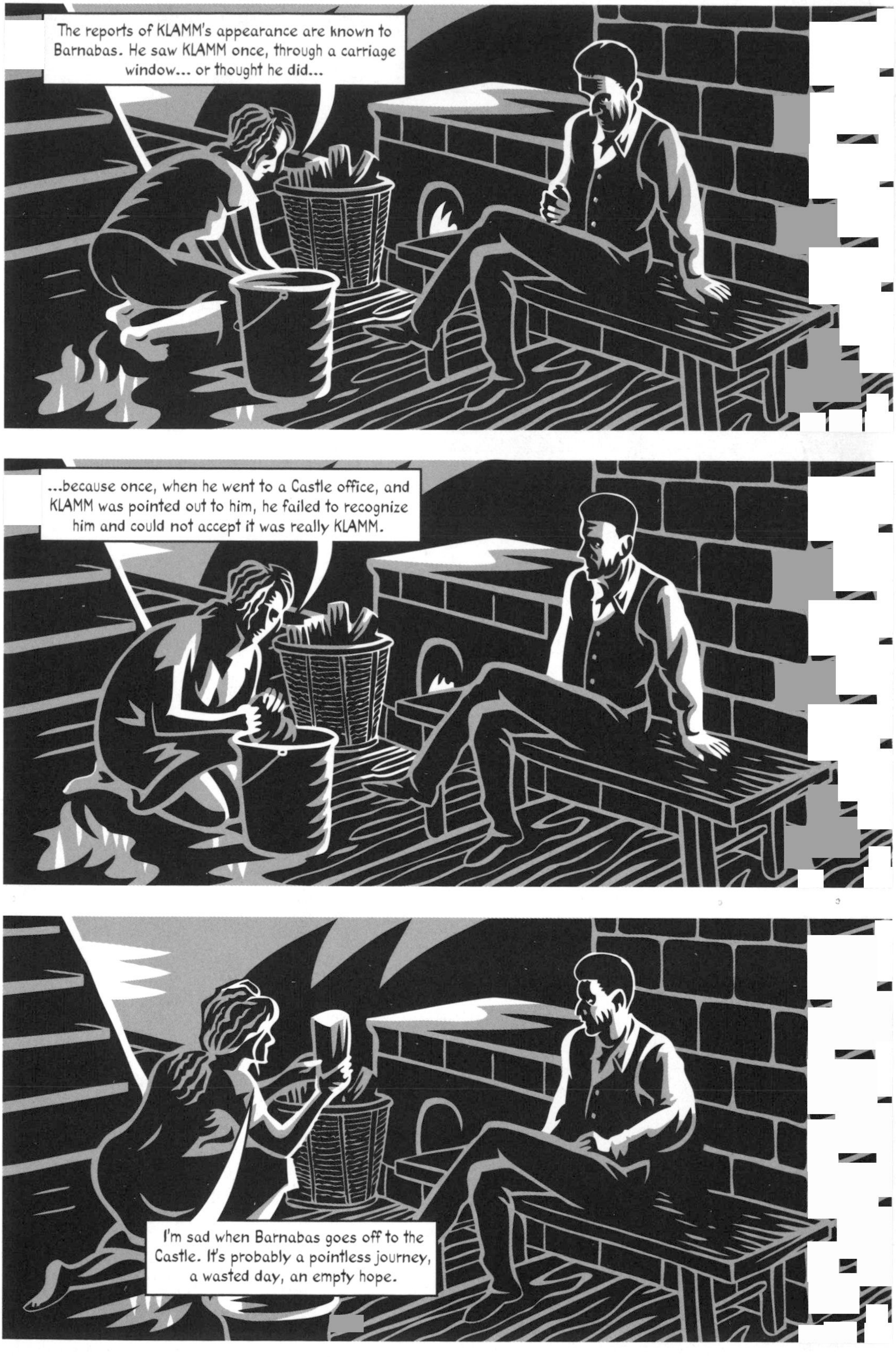

The reports of KLAMM's appearance are known to Barnabas. He saw KLAMM once, through a carriage window... or thought he did...
...because once, when he went to a Castle office, and KLAMM was pointed out to him, he failed to recognize him and could not accept it was really KLAMM.
I'm sad when Barnabas goes off to the Castle. It's probably a pointless journey, a wasted day, an empty hope.

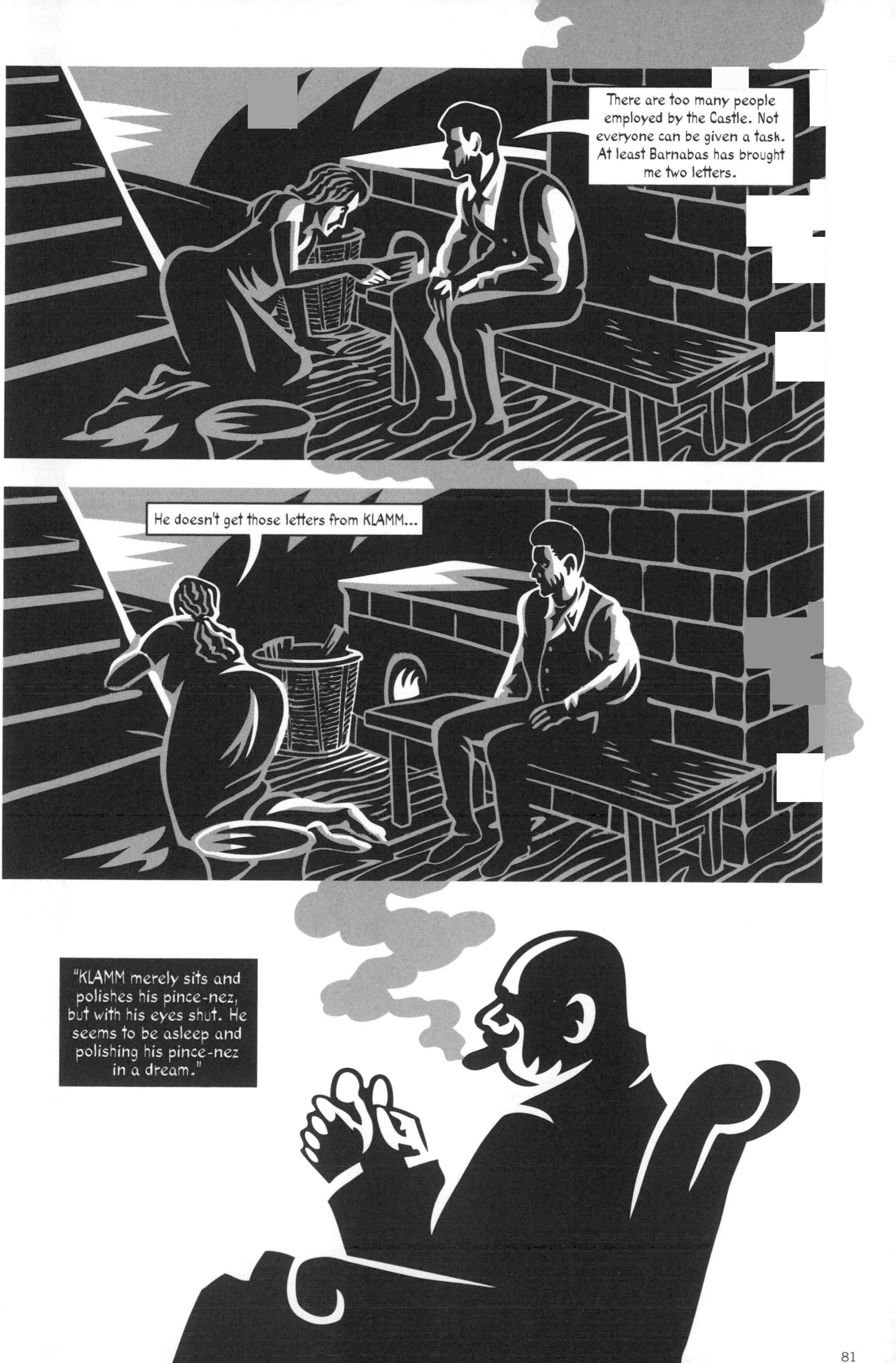
There are too many people employed by the Castle. Not everyone can be given a task. At least Barnabas has brought me two letters.
He doesn't get those letters from KLAMM...
"KLAMM merely sits and polishes his pince-nez, but with his eyes shut. He seems to be asleep and polishing his pince-nez in a dream."

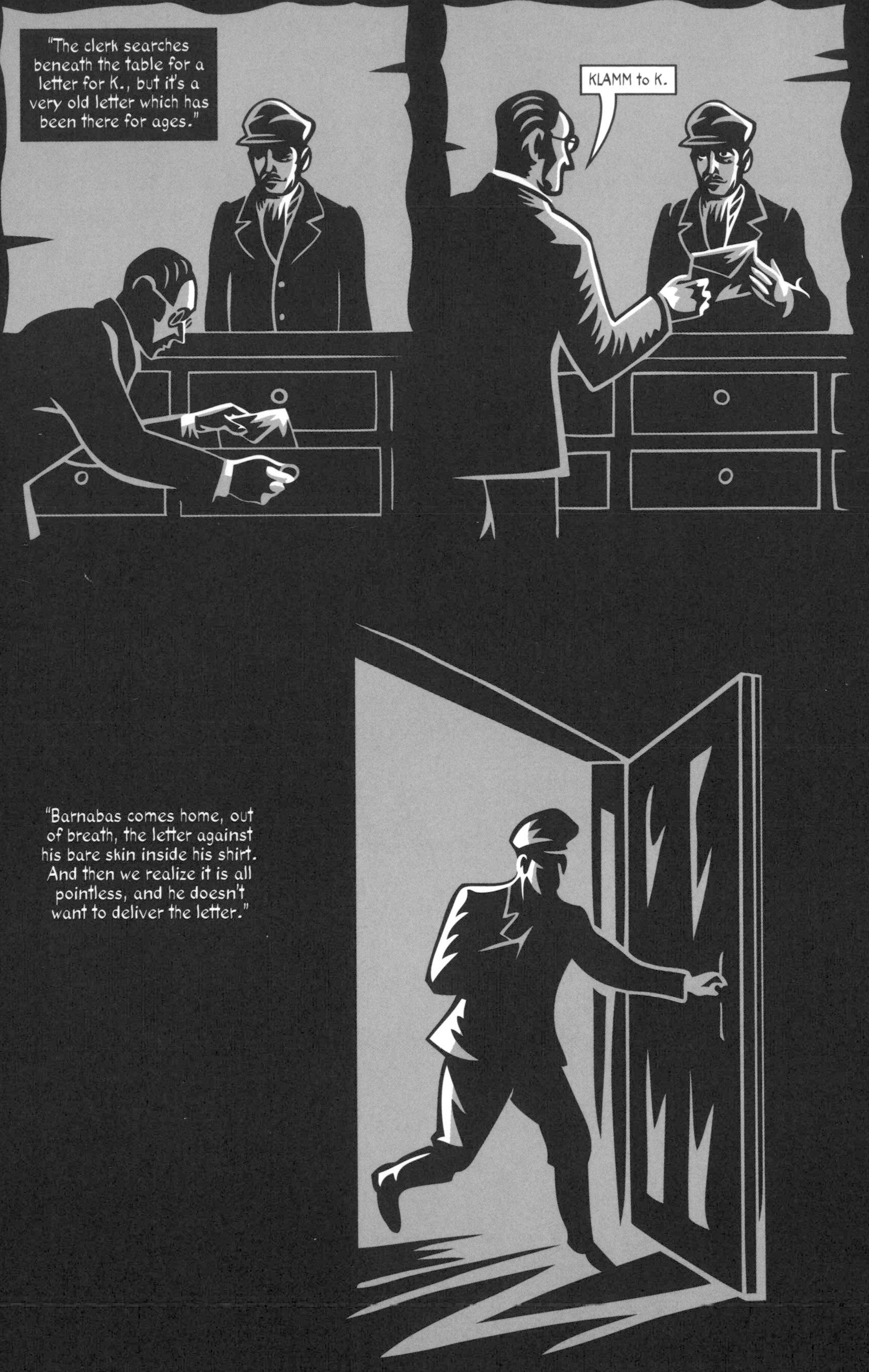
"The clerk searches beneath the table for a letter for K., but it's a very old letter which has been there for ages."
KLAMM to K.
"Barnabas comes home, out of breath, the letter against his bare skin inside his shirt. And then we realize it is all pointless, and he doesn't want to deliver the letter."

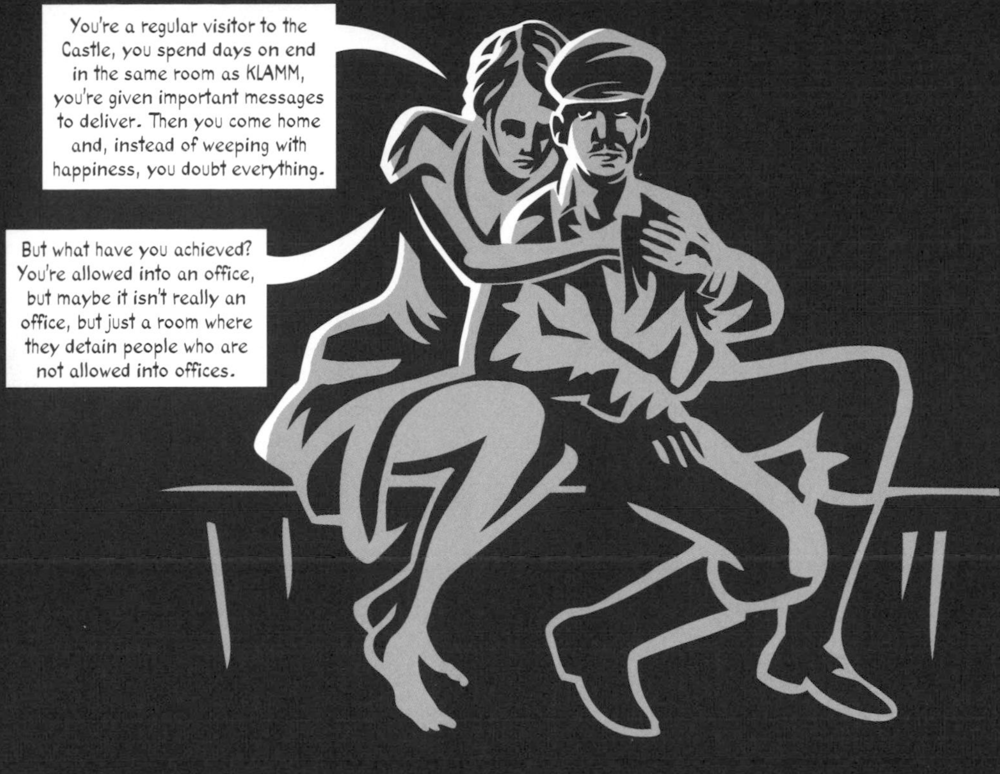
You're a regular visitor to the Castle, you spend days on end in the same room as KLAMM, you're given important messages to deliver. Then you come home and, instead of weeping with happiness, you doubt everything.
But what have you achieved? You're allowed into an office, but maybe it isn't really an office, but just a room where they detain people who are not allowed into offices.

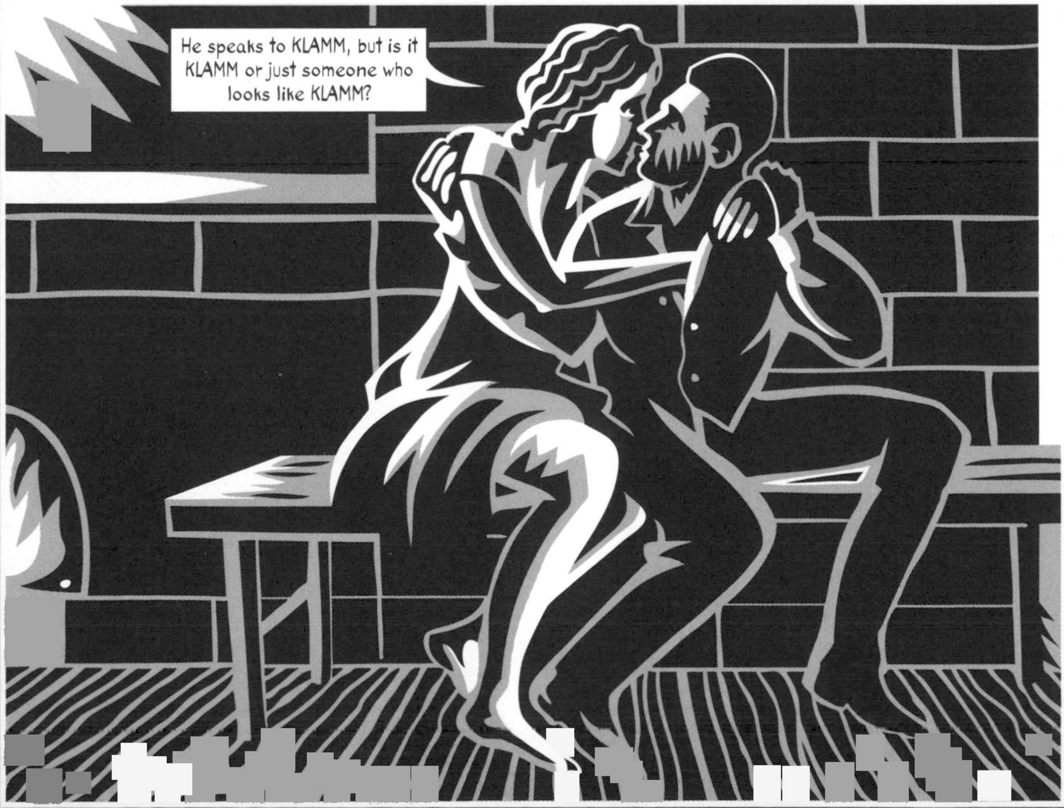
He speaks to KLAMM, but is it KLAMM or just someone who looks like KLAMM?

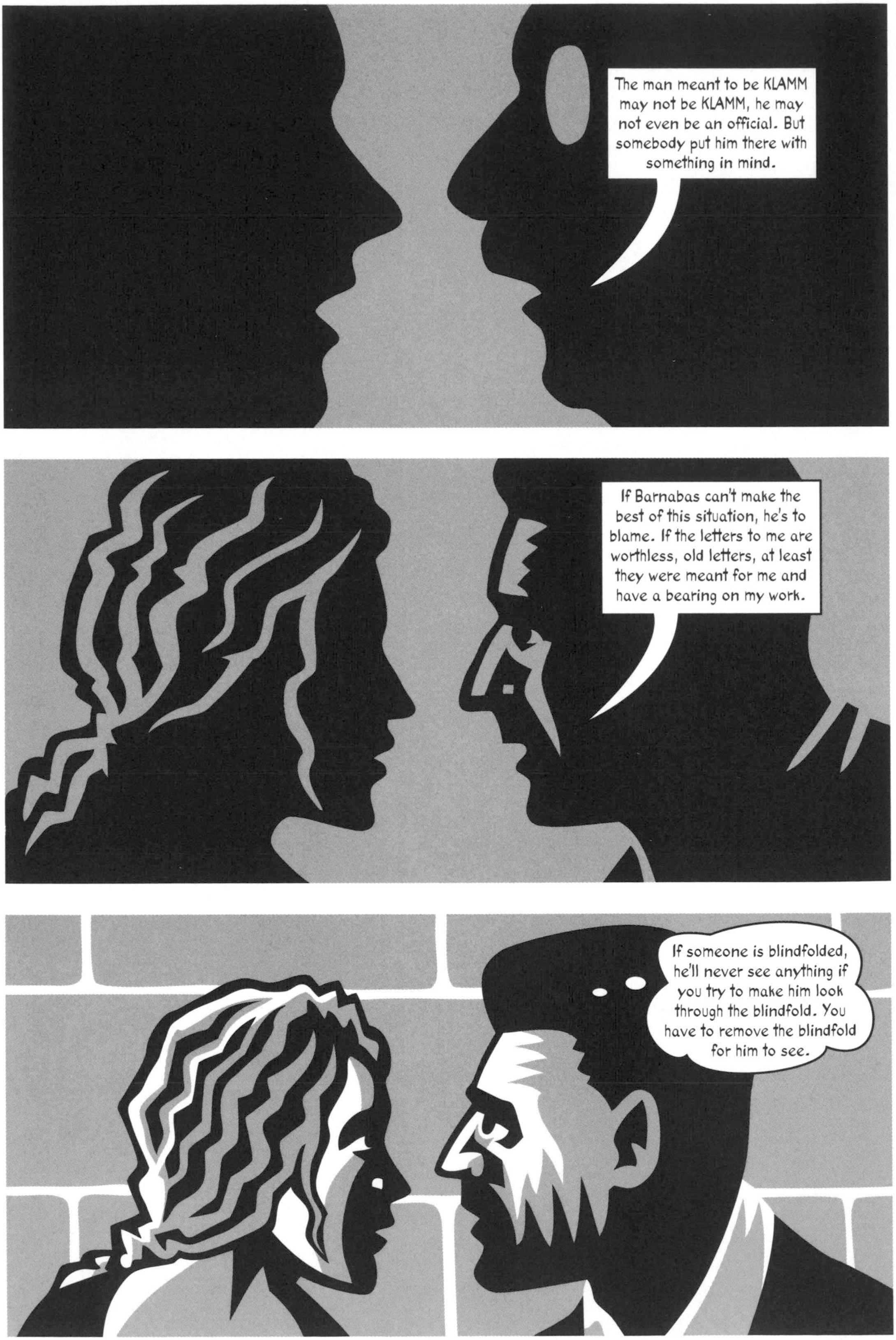
The man meant to be KLAMM may not be KLAMM, he may not even be an official. But somebody put him there with something in mind.
If Barnabas can't make the best of this situation, he's to blame. If the letters to me are worthless, old letters, at least they were meant for me and have a bearing on my work.
If someone is blindfolded, he'll never see anything if you try to make him look through the blindfold. You have to remove the blindfold for him to see.

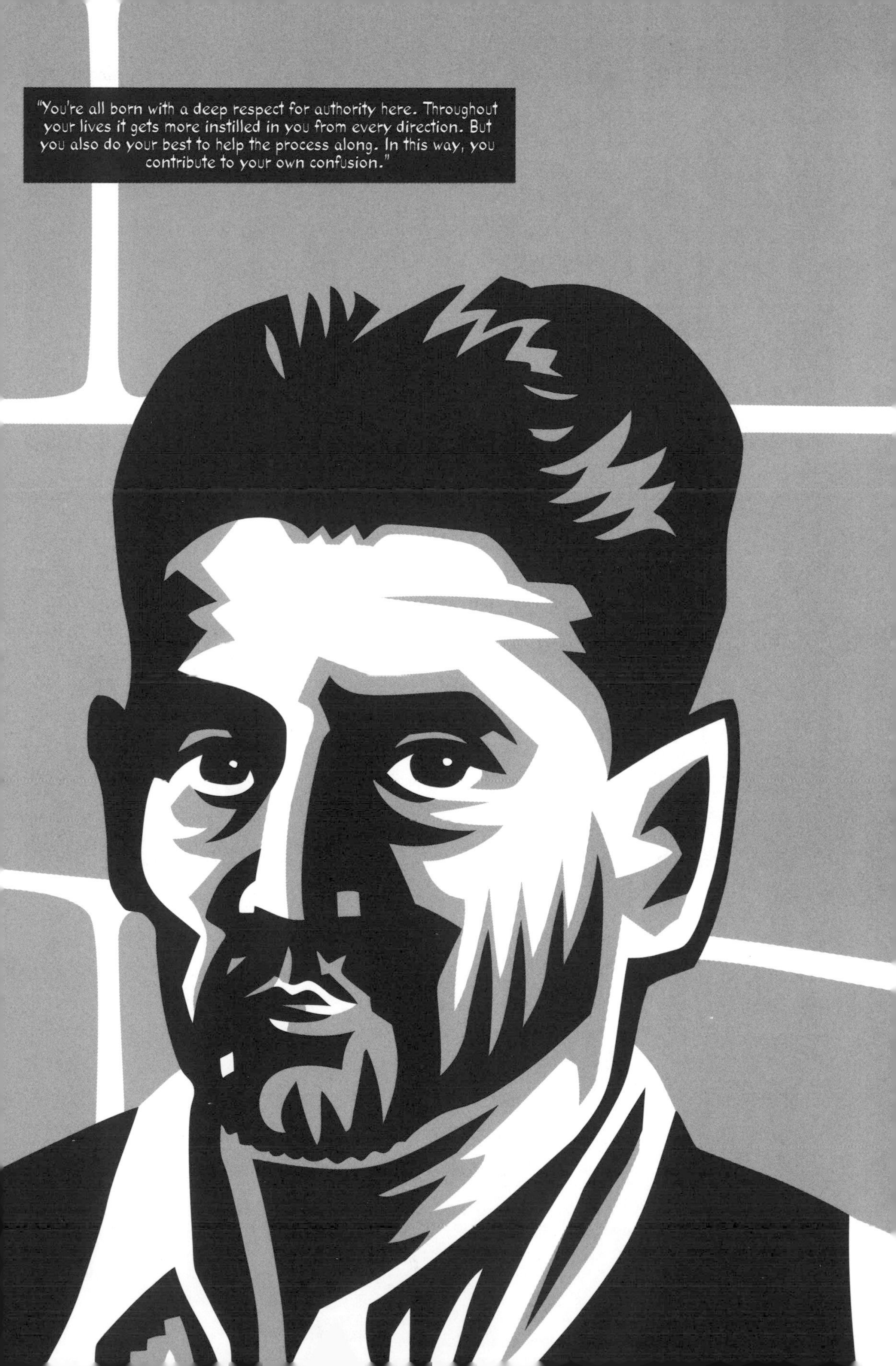
"You're all born with a deep respect for authority here. Throughout your lives it gets more instilled in you from every direction. But you also do your best to help the process along. In this way, you contribute to your own confusion."

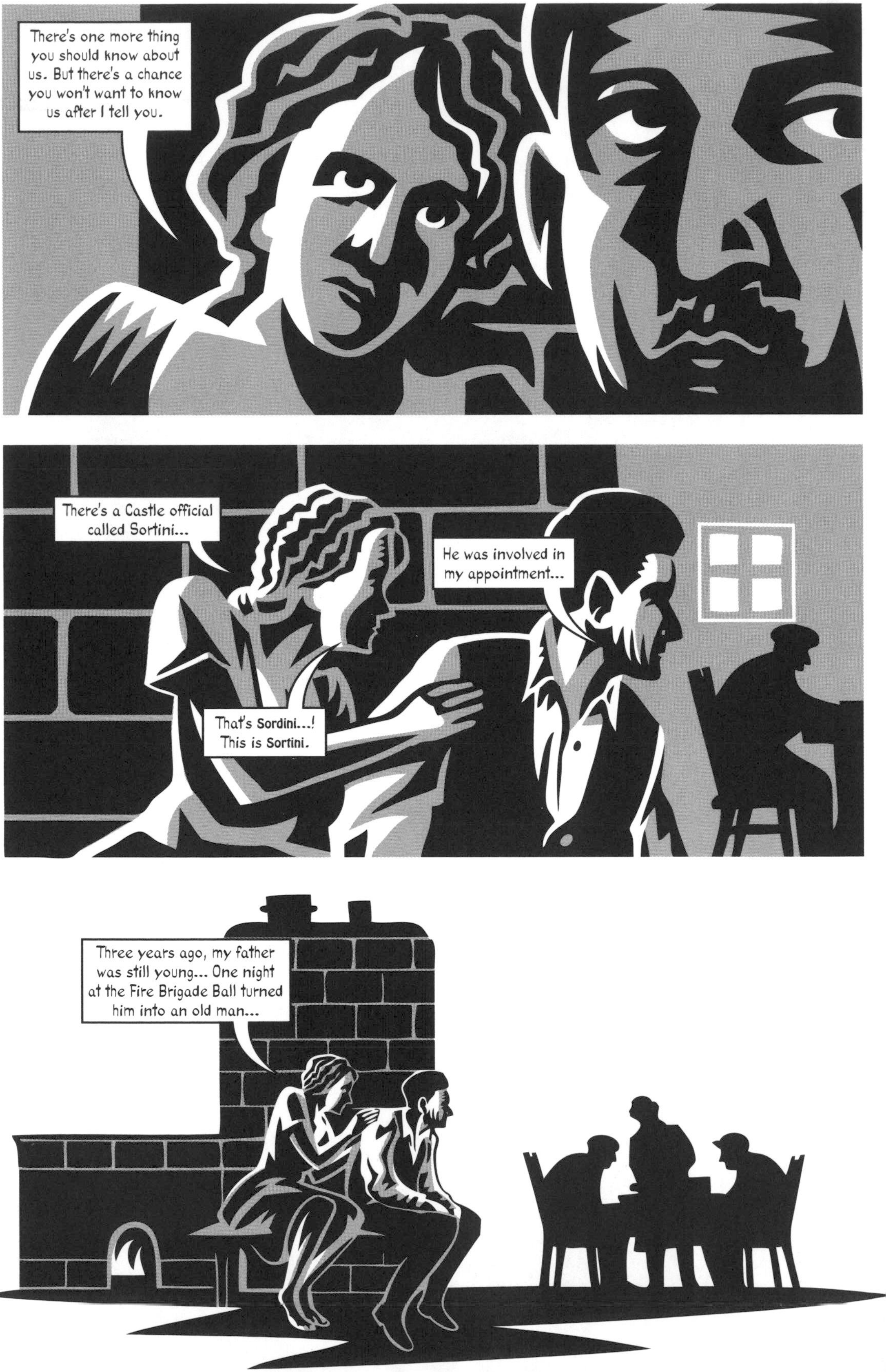
There's one more thing you should know about us. But there's a chance you won't want to know us after I tell you.
There's a Castle official called Sortini...
He was involved in my appointment...
That's Sordini...! This is Sortini.
Three years ago, my father was still young... One night at the Fire Brigade Ball turned him into an old man...

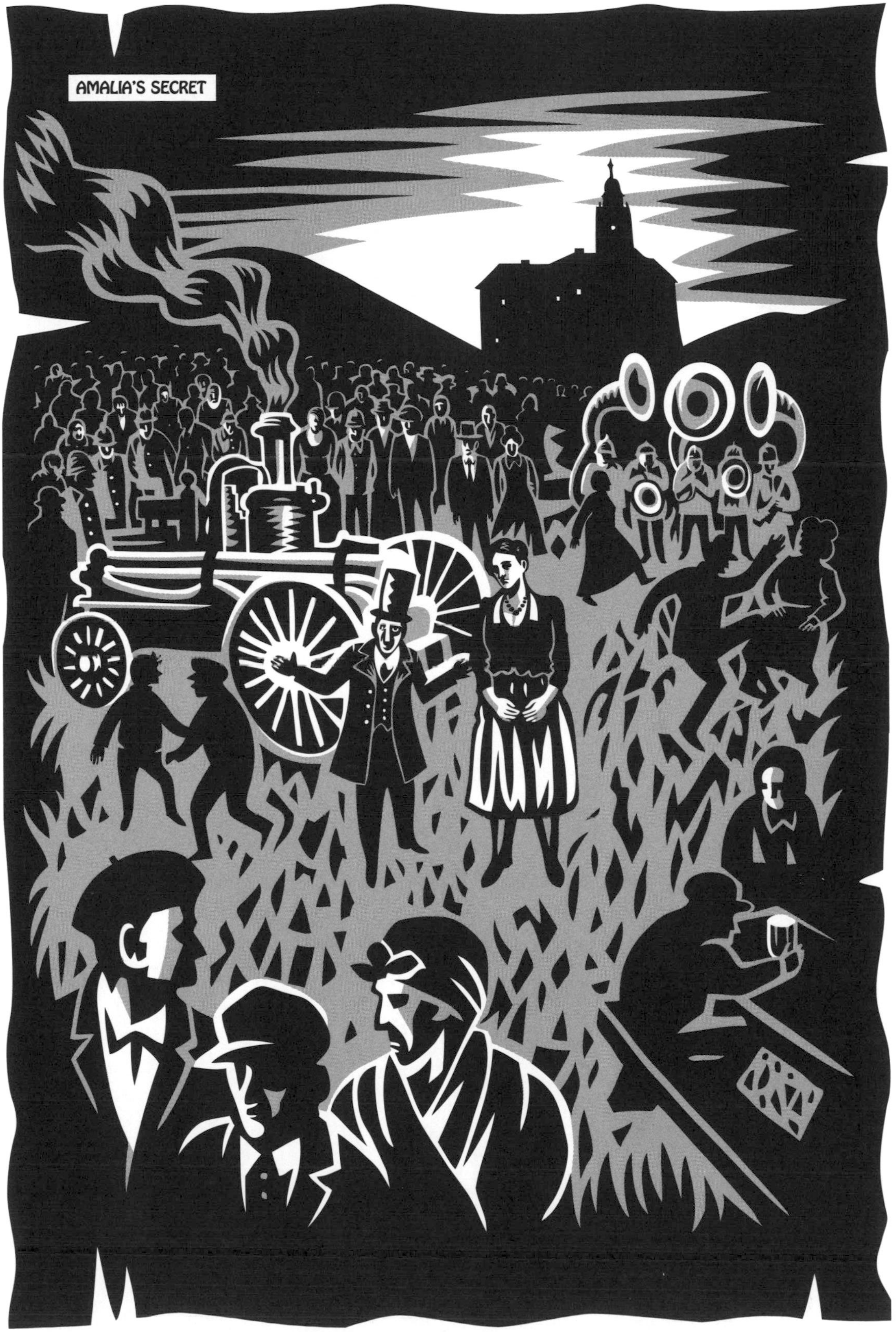
AMALIA'S SECRET

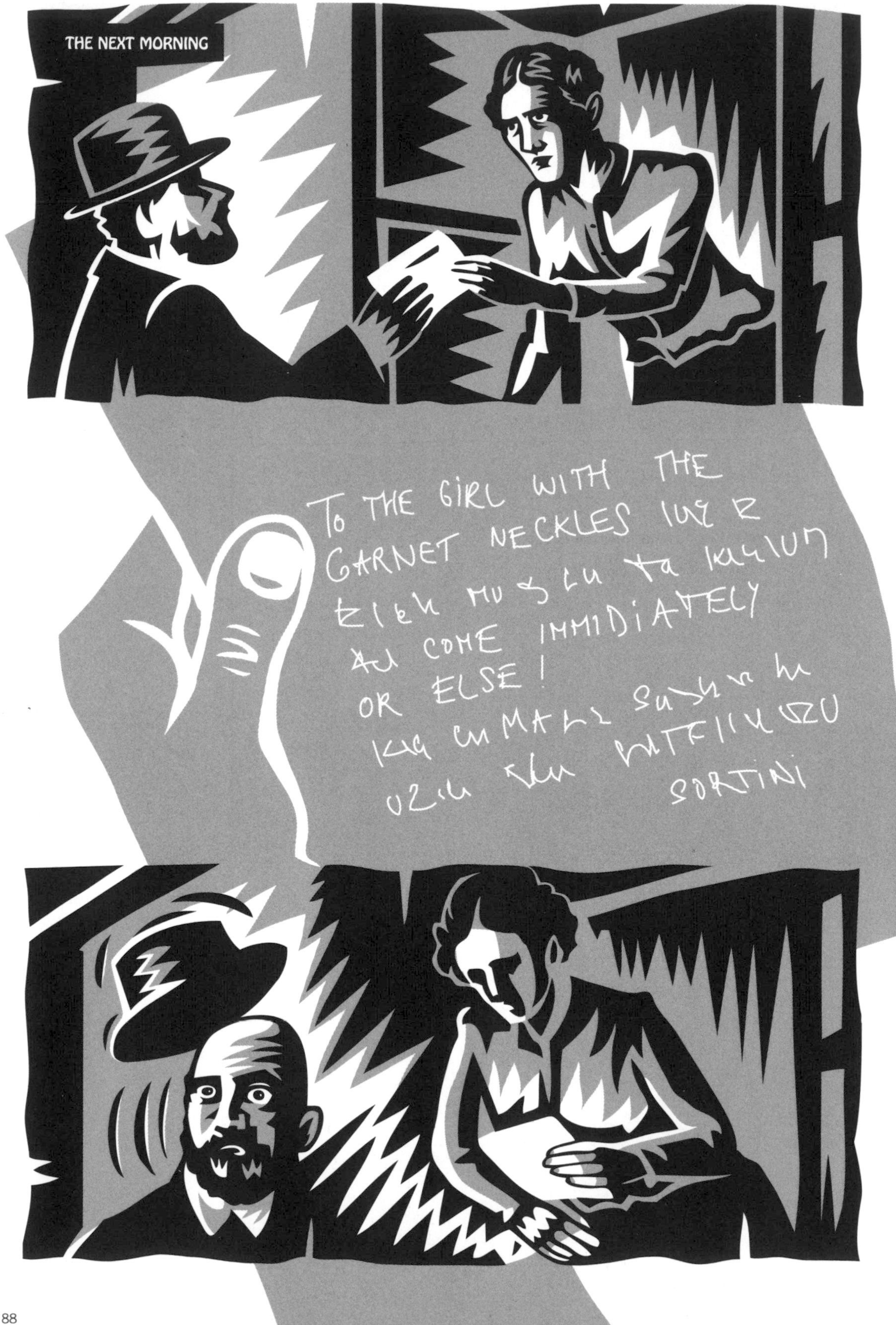
THE NEXT MORNING
TO THE GIRL WITH THE
GARNET NECKLES
COME IMMIDIATELY
OR ELSE!
SORTINI

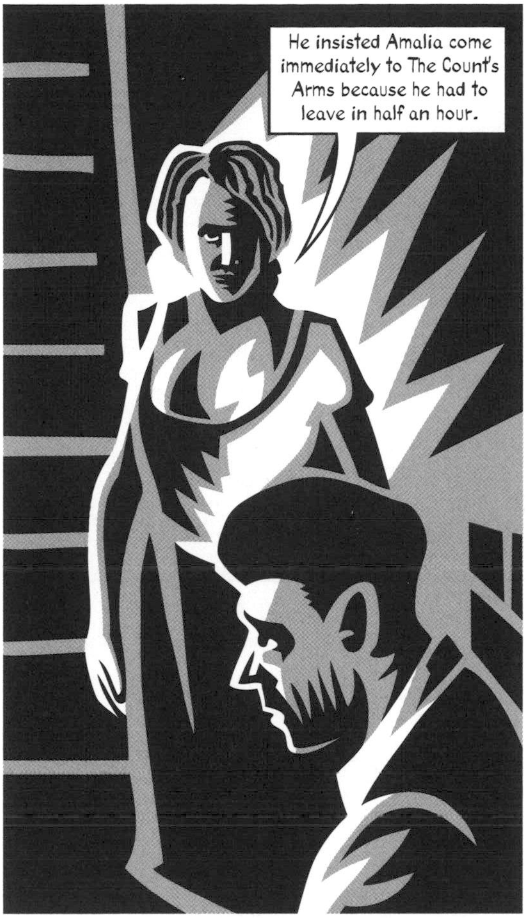
He insisted Amalia come immediately to The Count's Arms because he had to leave in half an hour.

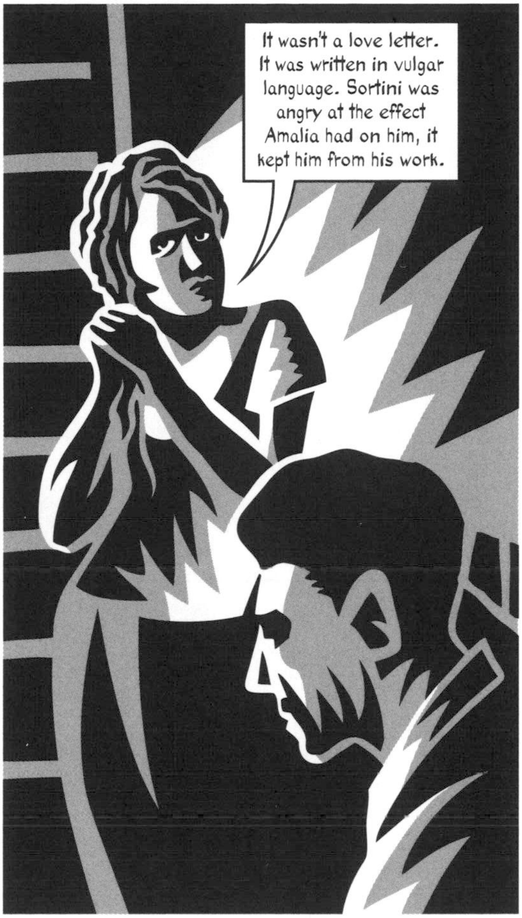
It wasn't a love letter. It was written in vulgar language. Sortini was angry at the effect Amalia had on him, it kept him from his work.

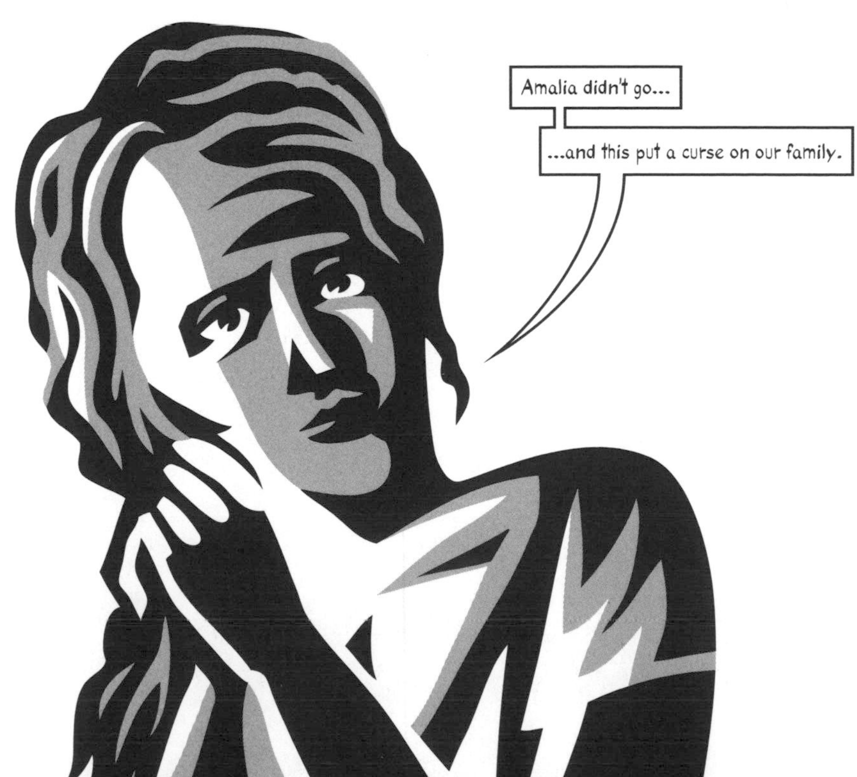
Amalia didn't go...
...and this put a curse on our family.

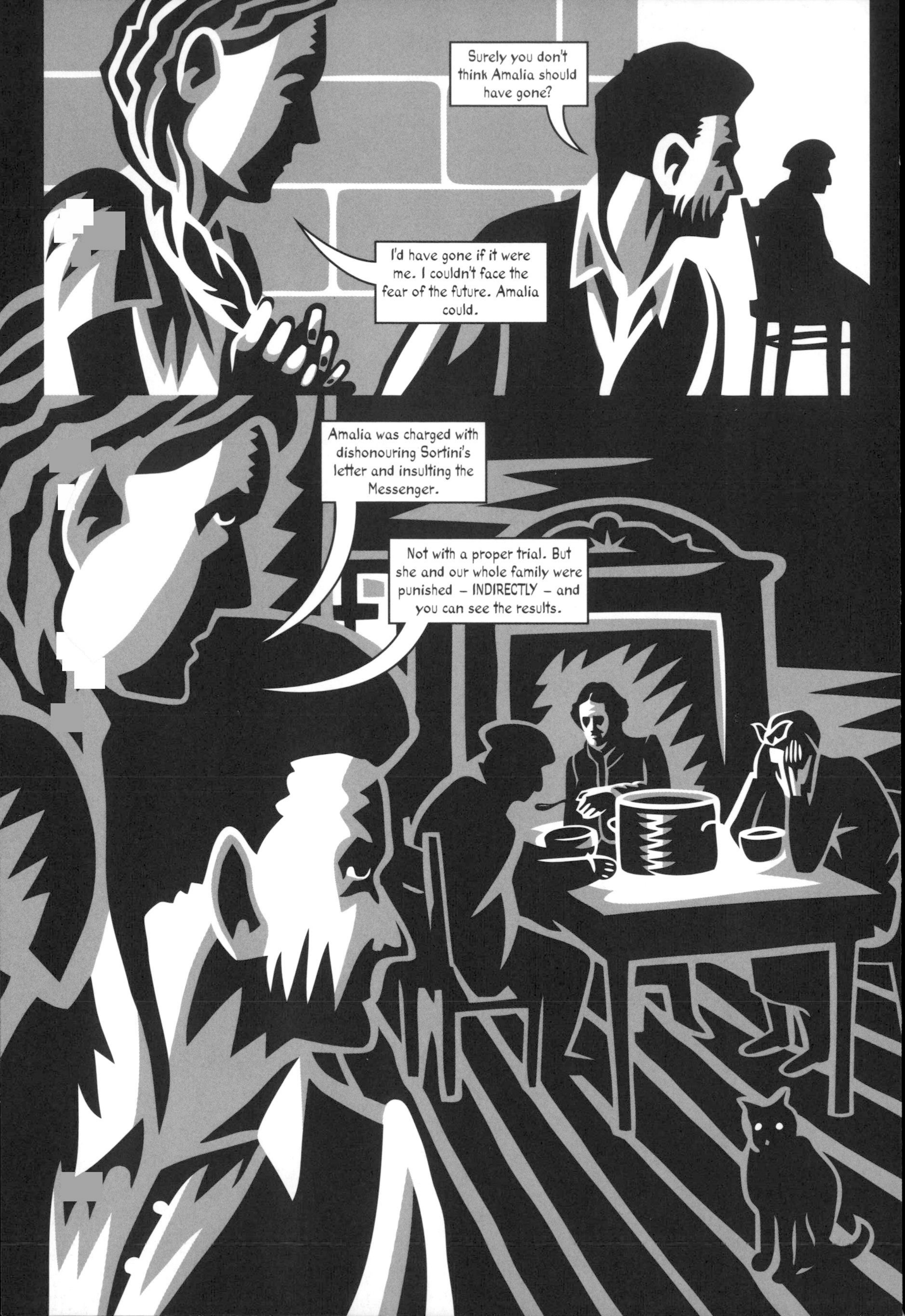
Surely you don't think Amalia should have gone?
I'd have gone if it were me. I couldn't face the fear of the future. Amalia could.
Amalia was charged with dishonouring Sortini's letter and insulting the Messenger.
Not with a proper trial. But she and our whole family were punished – INDIRECTLY – and you can see the results.

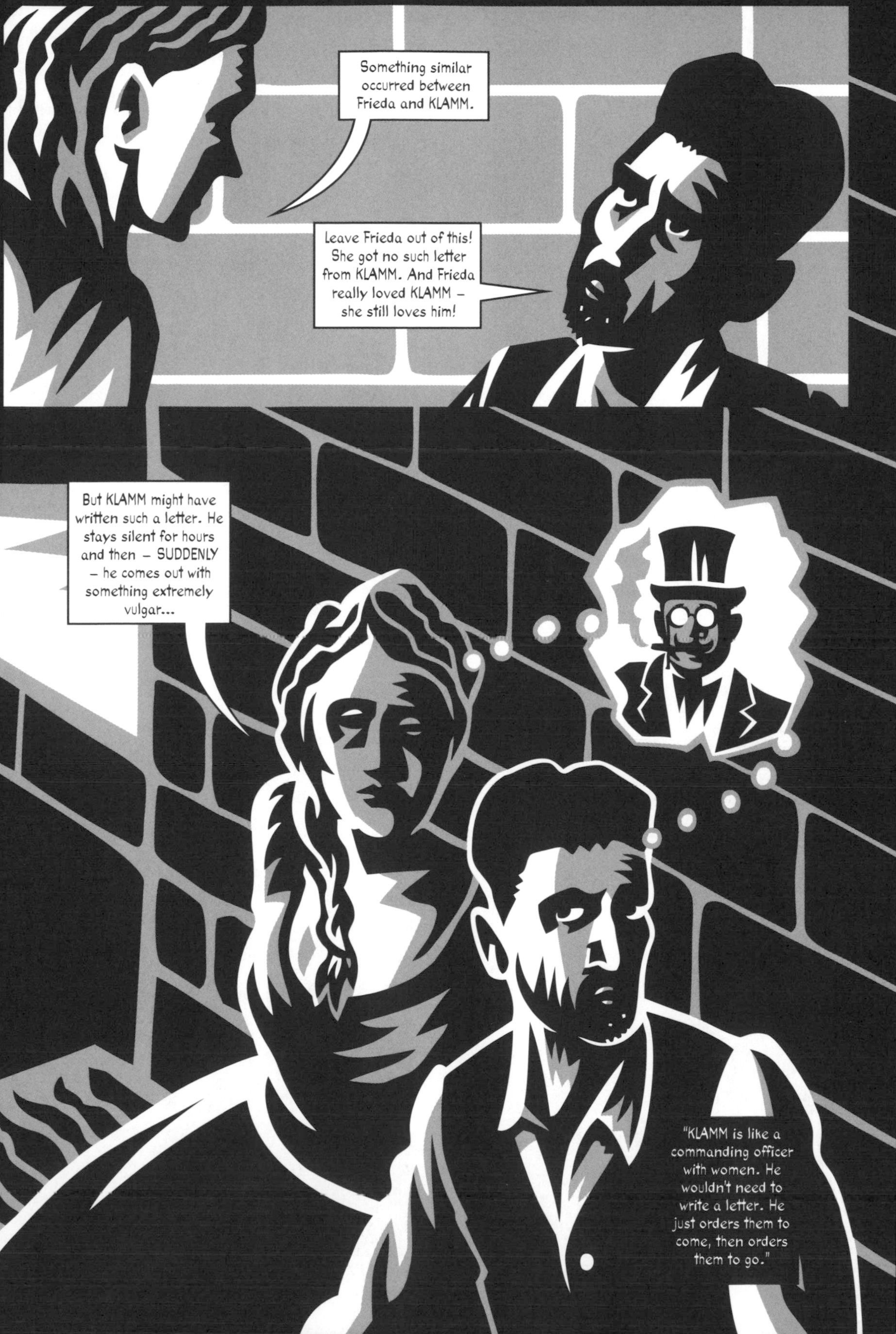
Something similar occurred between Frieda and KLAMM.
Leave Frieda out of this! She got no such letter from KLAMM. And Frieda really loved KLAMM – she still loves him!
But KLAMM might have written such a letter. He stays silent for hours and then – SUDDENLY – he comes out with something extremely vulgar...
"KLAMM is like a commanding officer with women. He wouldn't need to write a letter. He just orders them to come, then orders them to go."

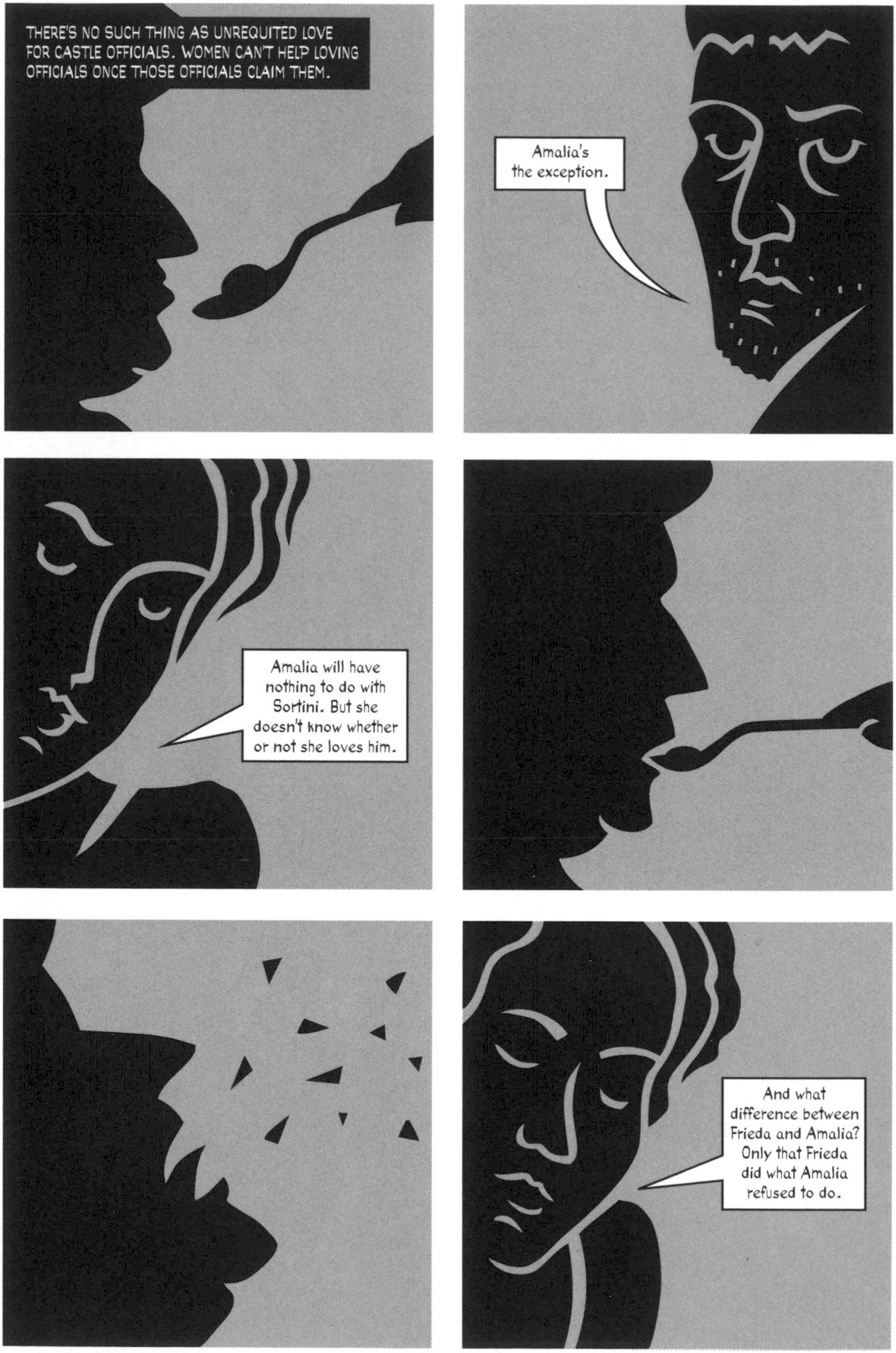
THERE'S NO SUCH THING AS UNREQUITED LOVE FOR CASTLE OFFICIALS. WOMEN CAN'T HELP LOVING OFFICIALS ONCE THOSE OFFICIALS CLAIM THEM.
Amalia's the exception.
Amalia will have nothing to do with Sortini. But she doesn't know whether or not she loves him.
And what difference between Frieda and Amalia? Only that Frieda did what Amalia refused to do.

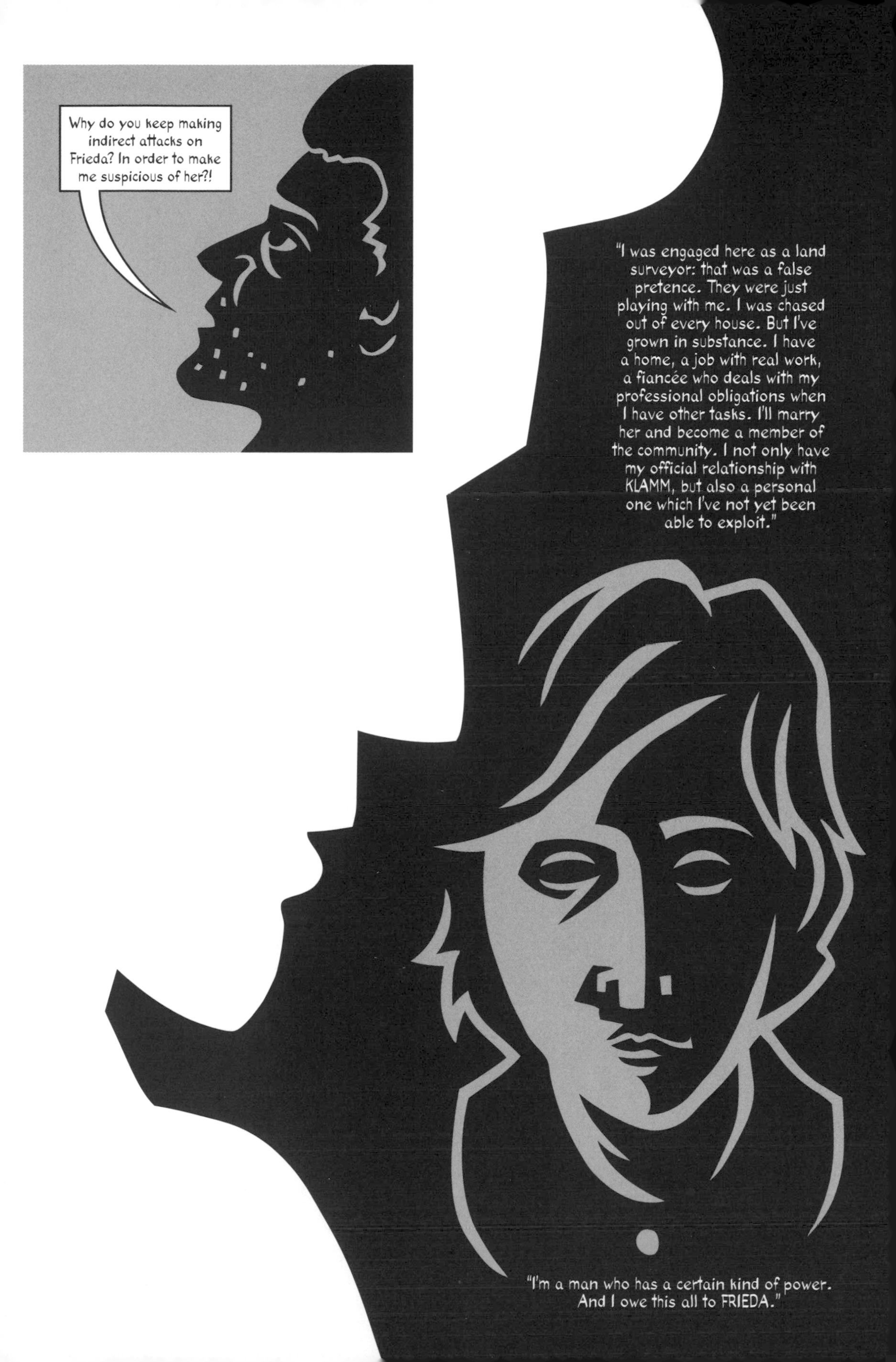
Why do you keep making indirect attacks on Frieda? In order to make me suspicious of her?!
"I was engaged here as a land surveyor: that was a false pretence. They were just playing with me. I was chased out of every house. But I've grown in substance. I have a home, a job with real work, a fiancée who deals with my professional obligations when I have other tasks. I'll marry her and become a member of the community. I not only have my official relationship with KLAMM, but also a personal one which I've not yet been able to exploit."
"I'm a man who has a certain kind of power. And I owe this all to FRIEDA."

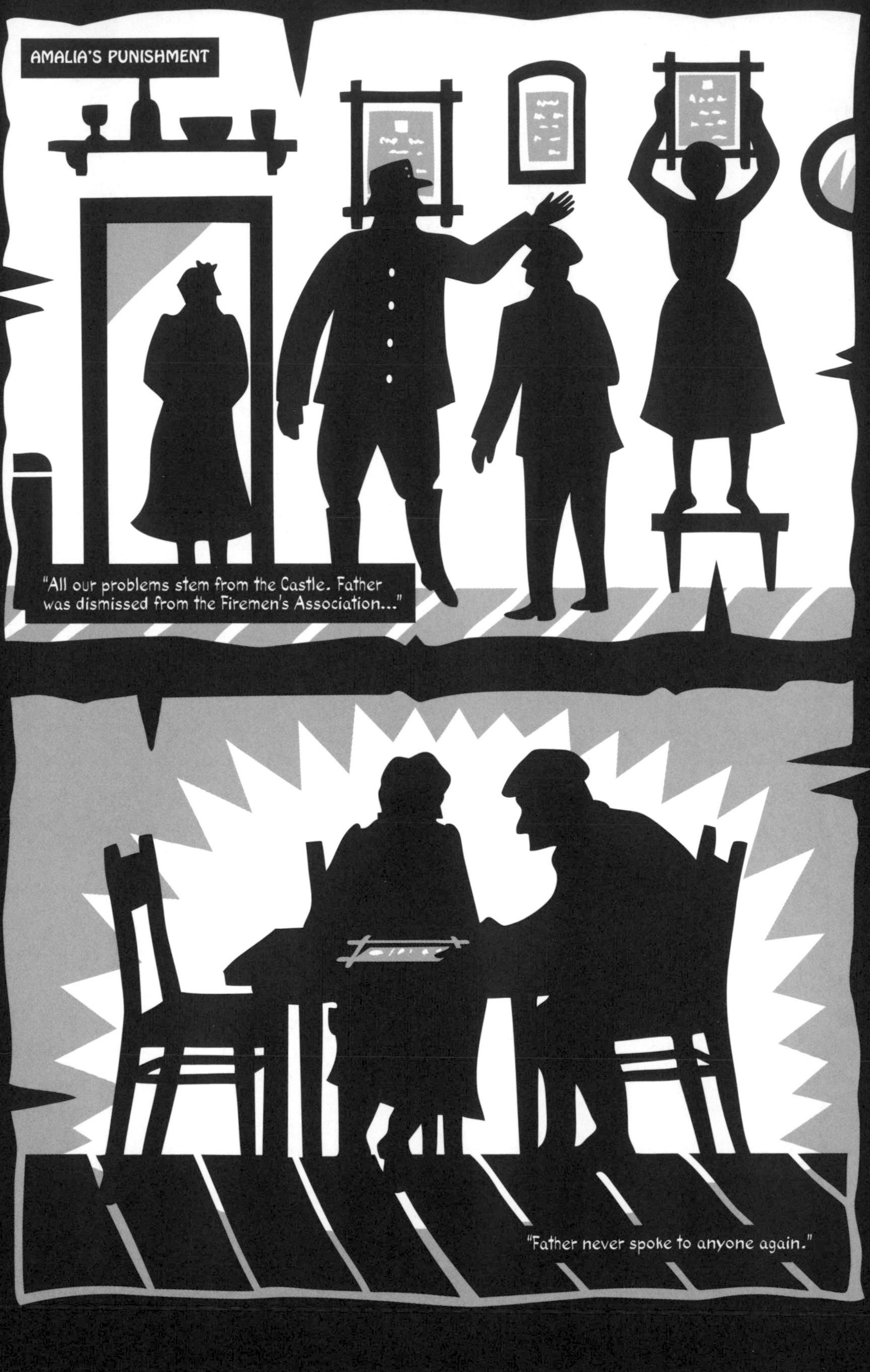
AMALIA'S PUNISHMENT
"All our problems stem from the Castle. Father was dismissed from the Firemen's Association..."
"Father never spoke to anyone again."

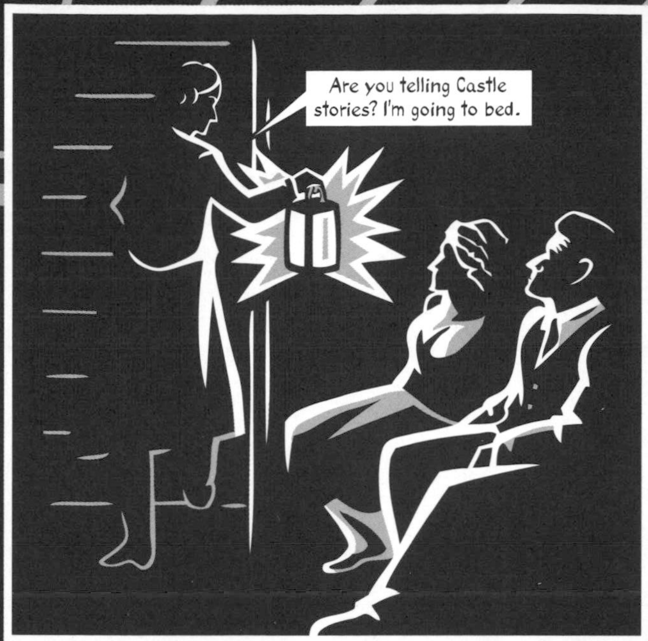
Are you telling Castle stories? I'm going to bed.

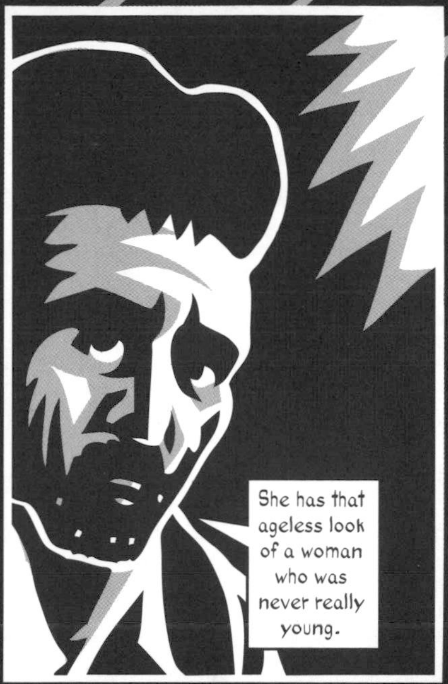
She has that ageless look of a woman who was never really young.

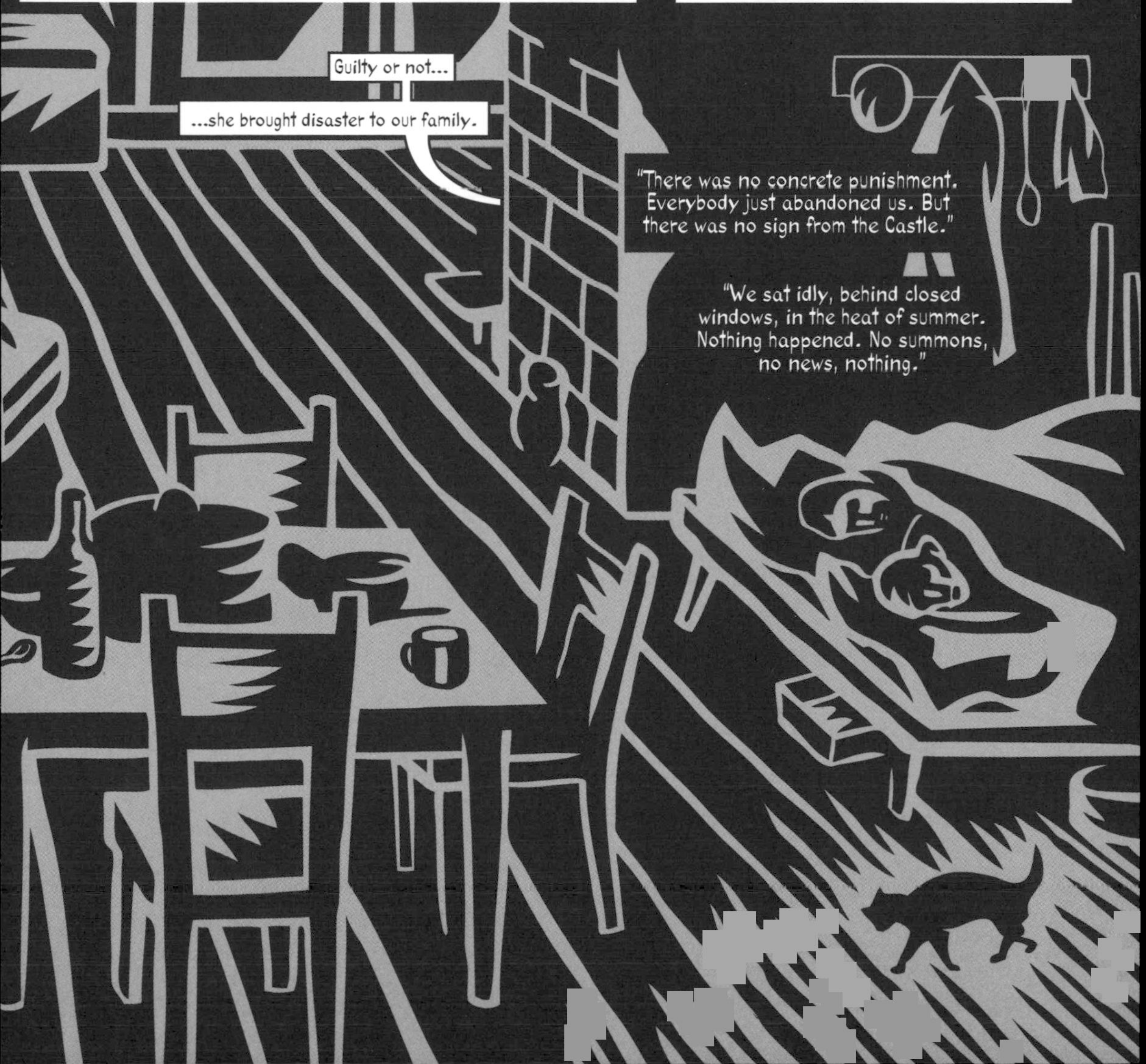
Guilty or not...
...she brought disaster to our family.
"There was no concrete punishment. Everybody just abandoned us. But there was no sign from the Castle."
"We sat idly, behind closed windows, in the heat of summer. Nothing happened. No summons, no news, nothing."

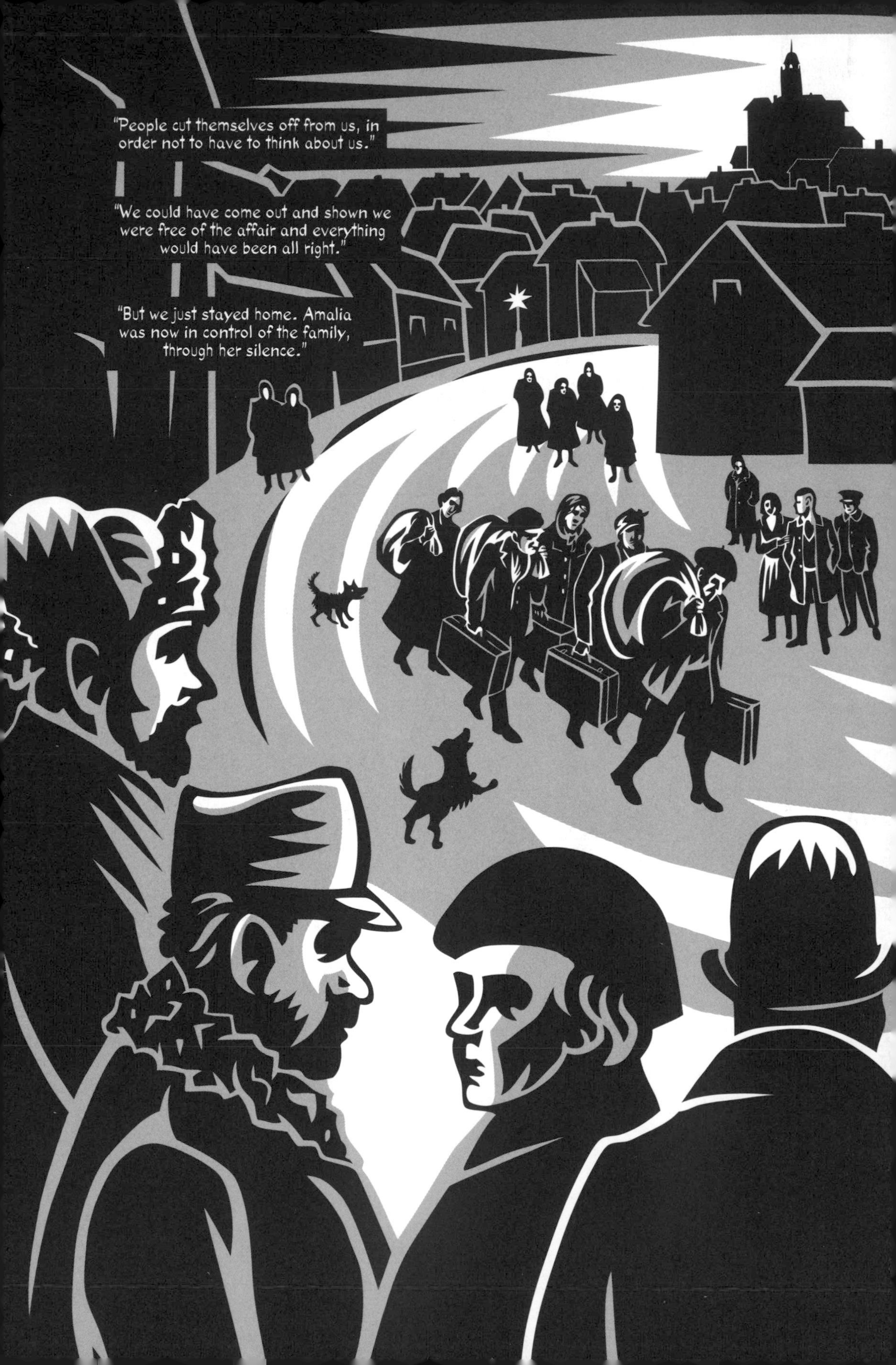
"People cut themselves off from us, in order not to have to think about us."
"We could have come out and shown we were free of the affair and everything would have been all right."
"But we just stayed home. Amalia was now in control of the family, through her silence."

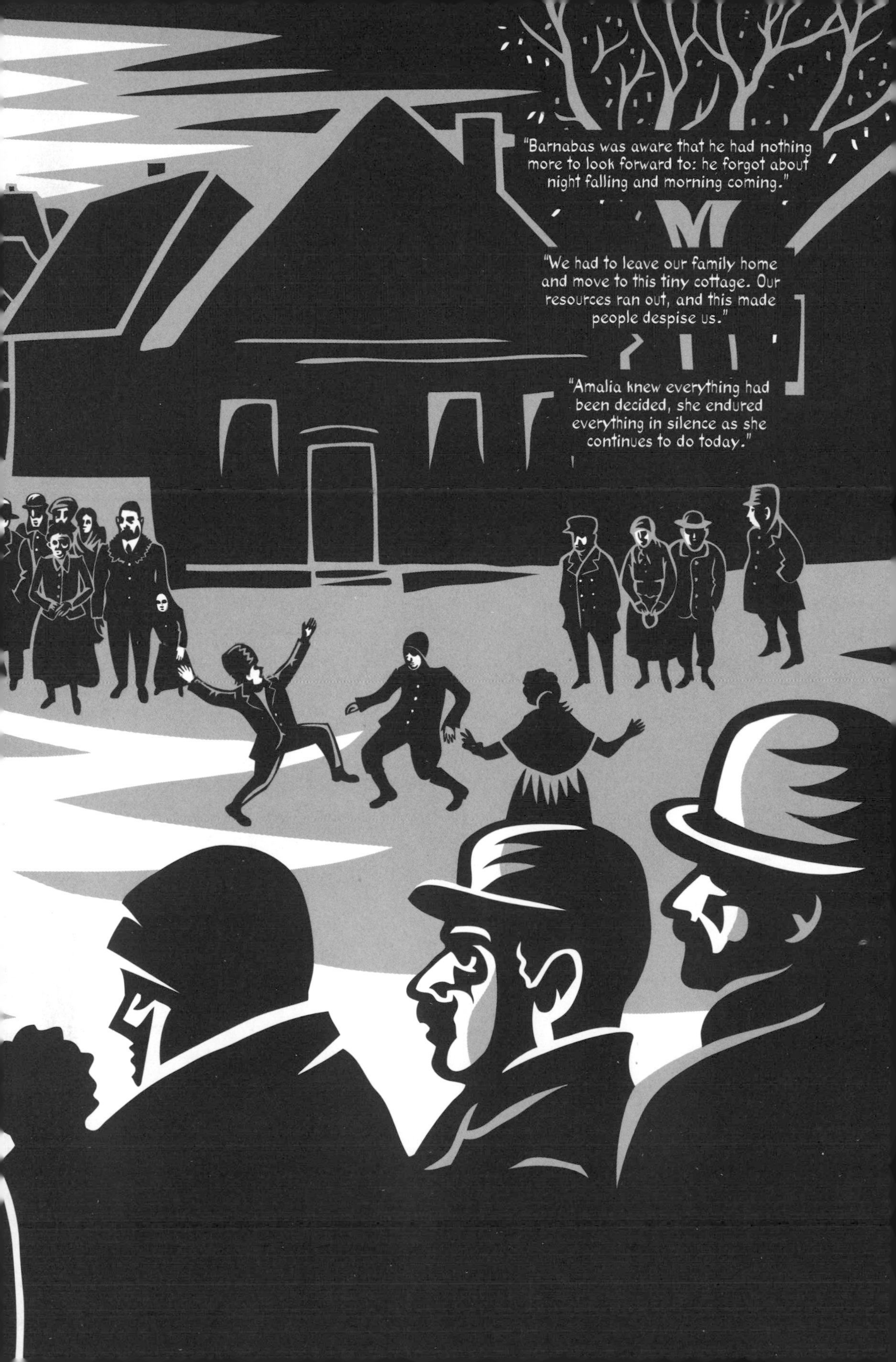
"Barnabas was aware that he had nothing more to look forward to: he forgot about night falling and morning coming."
"We had to leave our family home and move to this tiny cottage. Our resources ran out, and this made people despise us."
"Amalia knew everything had been decided, she endured everything in silence as she continues to do today."

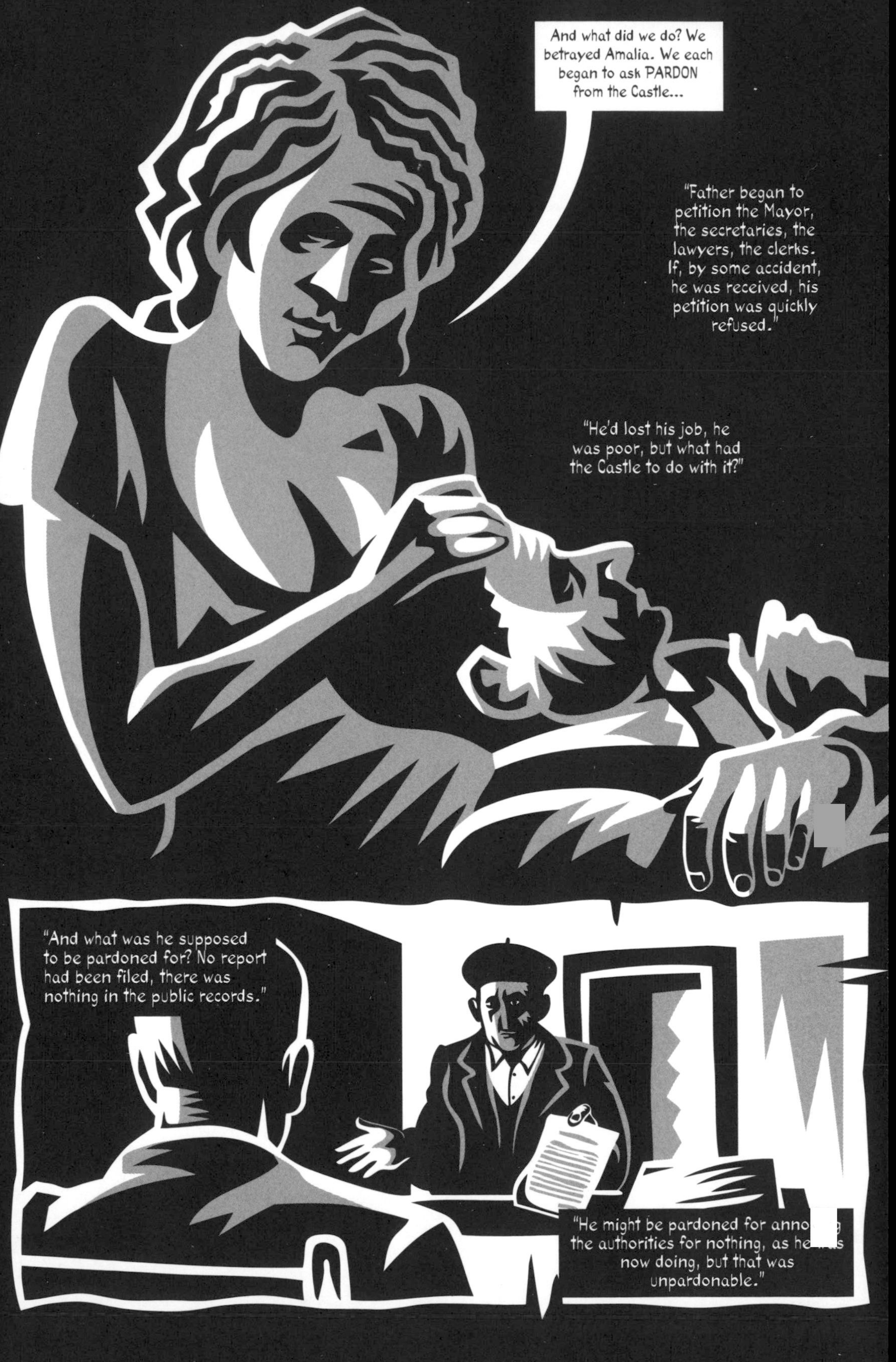
And what did we do? We betrayed Amalia. We each began to ask PARDON from the Castle...
"Father began to petition the Mayor, the secretaries, the lawyers, the clerks. If, by some accident, he was received, his petition was quickly refused."
"He'd lost his job, he was poor, but what had the Castle to do with it?"
"And what was he supposed to be pardoned for? No report had been filed, there was nothing in the public records."
"He might be pardoned for anno g the authorities for nothing, as he s now doing, but that was unpardonable."

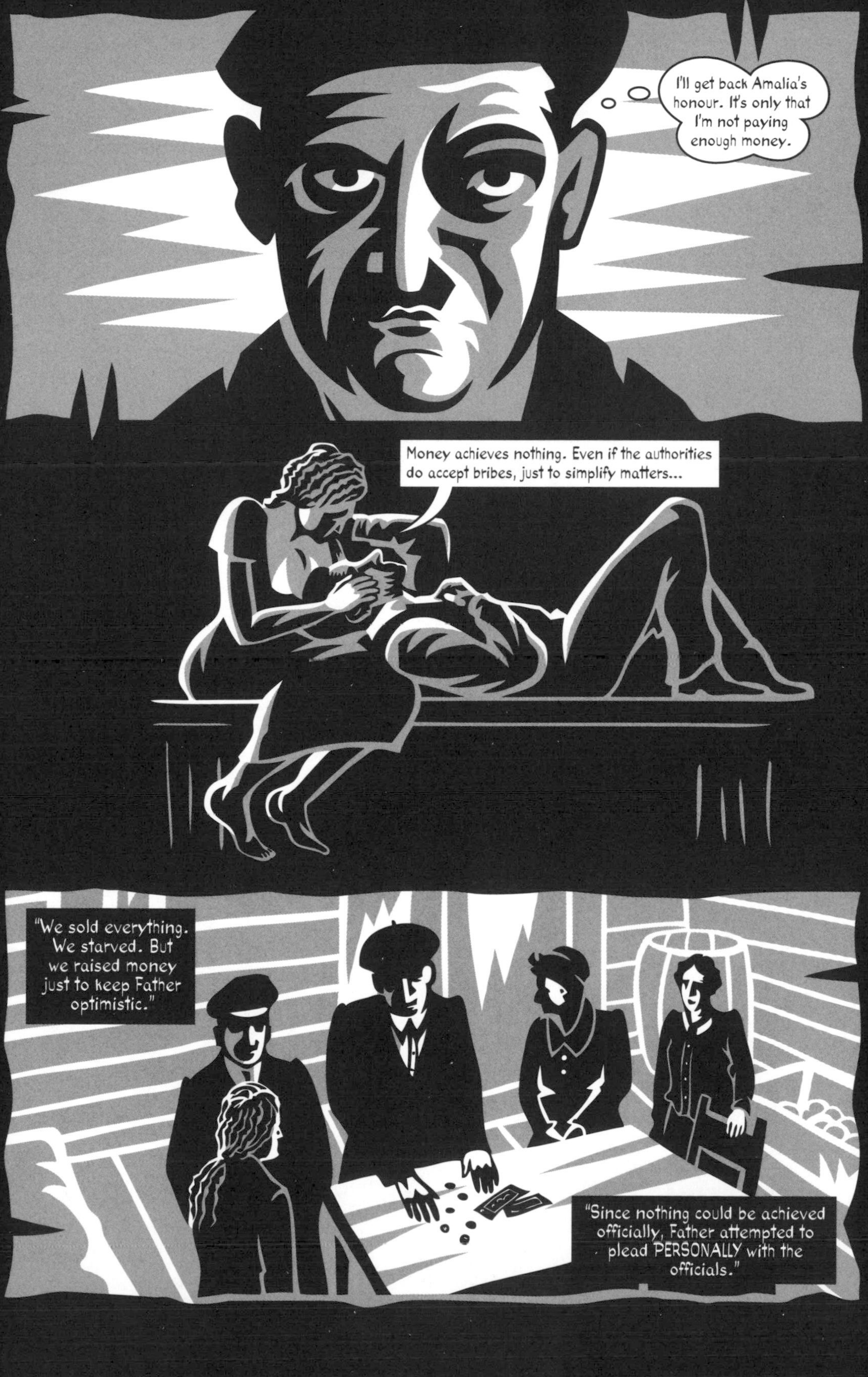
I'll get back Amalia's honour. It's only that I'm not paying enough money.
Money achieves nothing. Even if the authorities do accept bribes, just to simplify matters...
"We sold everything. We starved. But we raised money just to keep Father optimistic."
"Since nothing could be achieved officially, Father attempted to plead PERSONALLY with the officials."

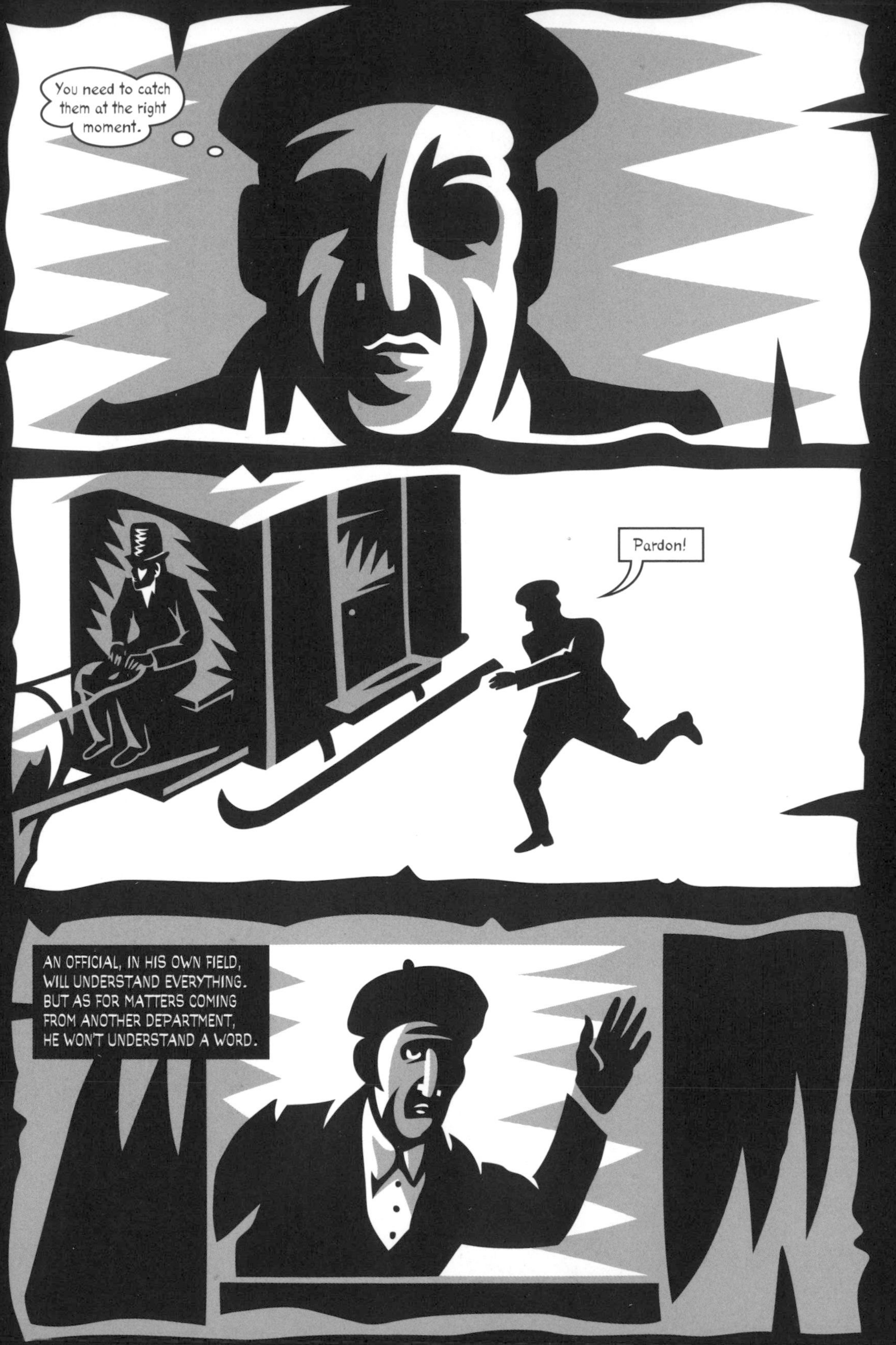
You need to catch them at the right moment.
Pardon!
AN OFFICIAL, IN HIS OWN FIELD, WILL UNDERSTAND EVERYTHING. BUT AS FOR MATTERS COMING FROM ANOTHER DEPARTMENT, HE WON'T UNDERSTAND A WORD.

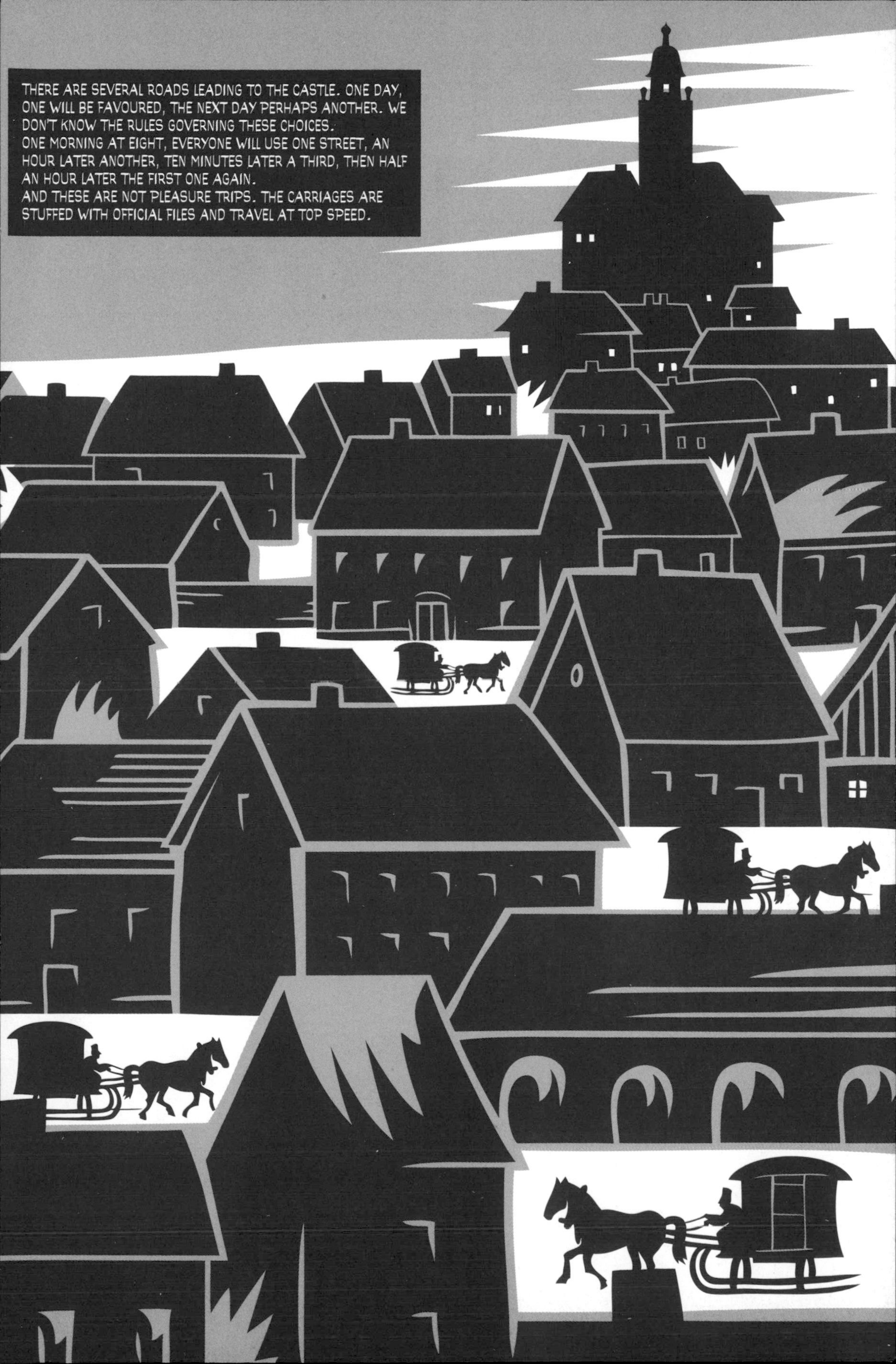
THERE ARE SEVERAL ROADS LEADING TO THE CASTLE. ONE DAY, ONE WILL BE FAVOURED, THE NEXT DAY PERHAPS ANOTHER. WE DON'T KNOW THE RULES GOVERNING THESE CHOICES.
ONE MORNING AT EIGHT, EVERYONE WILL USE ONE STREET, AN HOUR LATER ANOTHER, TEN MINUTES LATER A THIRD, THEN HALF AN HOUR LATER THE FIRST ONE AGAIN.
AND THESE ARE NOT PLEASURE TRIPS. THE CARRIAGES ARE STUFFED WITH OFFICIAL FILES AND TRAVEL AT TOP SPEED.

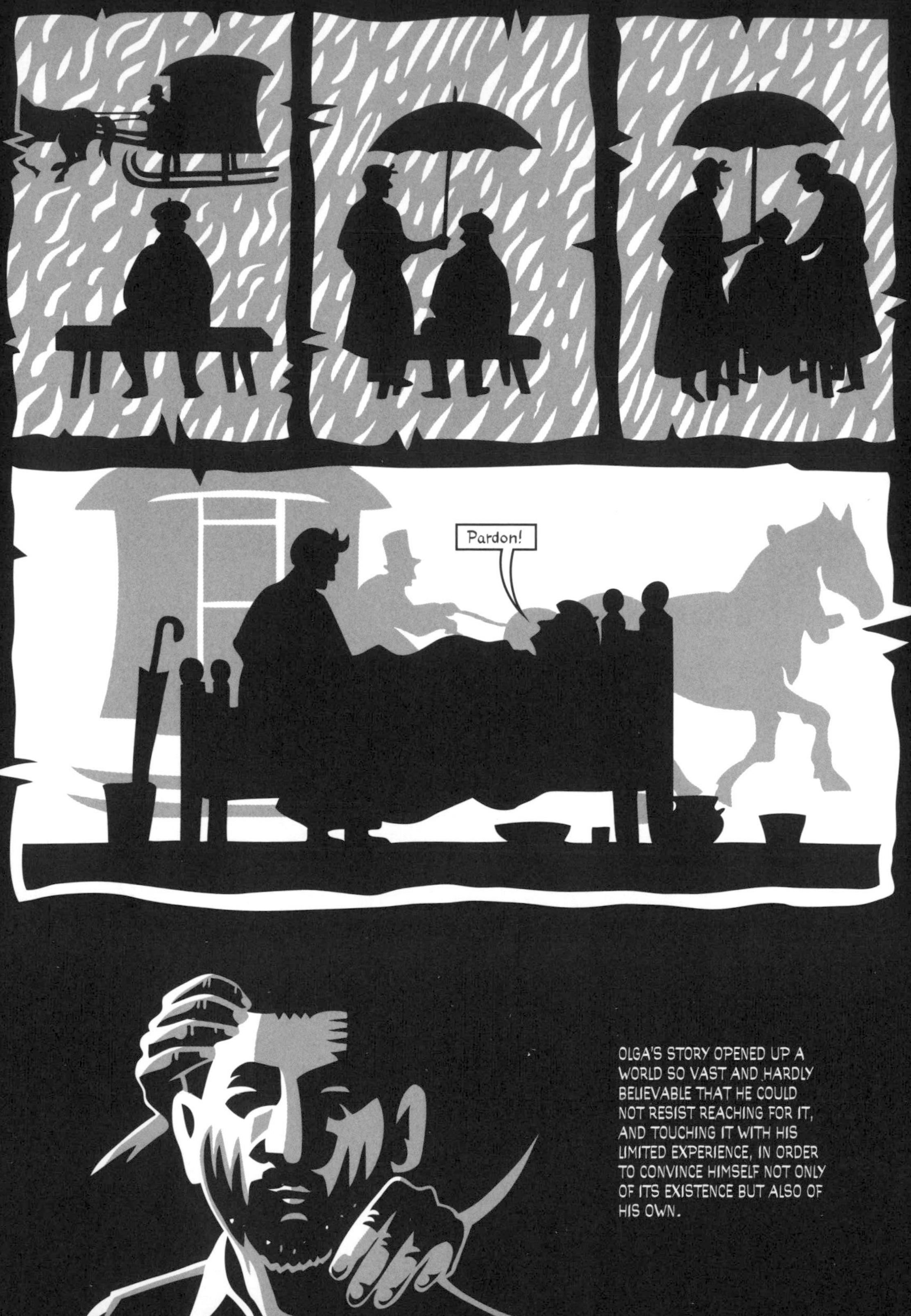
Pardon!
OLGA'S STORY OPENED UP A WORLD SO VAST AND HARDLY BELIEVABLE THAT HE COULD NOT RESIST REACHING FOR IT, AND TOUCHING IT WITH HIS LIMITED EXPERIENCE, IN ORDER TO CONVINCE HIMSELF NOT ONLY OF ITS EXISTENCE BUT ALSO OF HIS OWN.

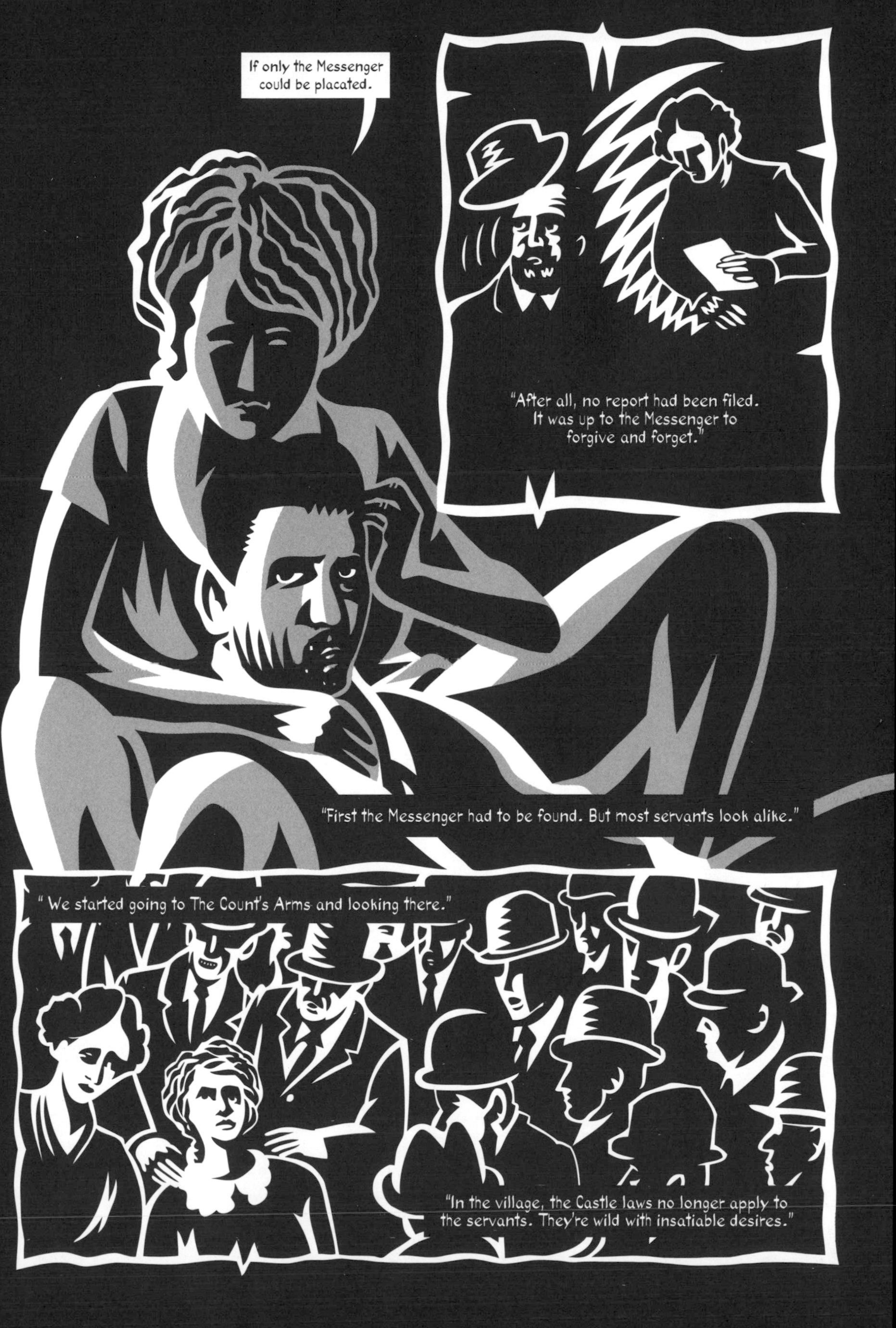

If only the Messenger could be placated.
"After all, no report had been filed. It was up to the Messenger to forgive and forget."
"First the Messenger had to be found. But most servants look alike."
" We started going to The Count's Arms and looking there."
"In the village, the Castle laws no longer apply to the servants. They're wild with insatiable desires."

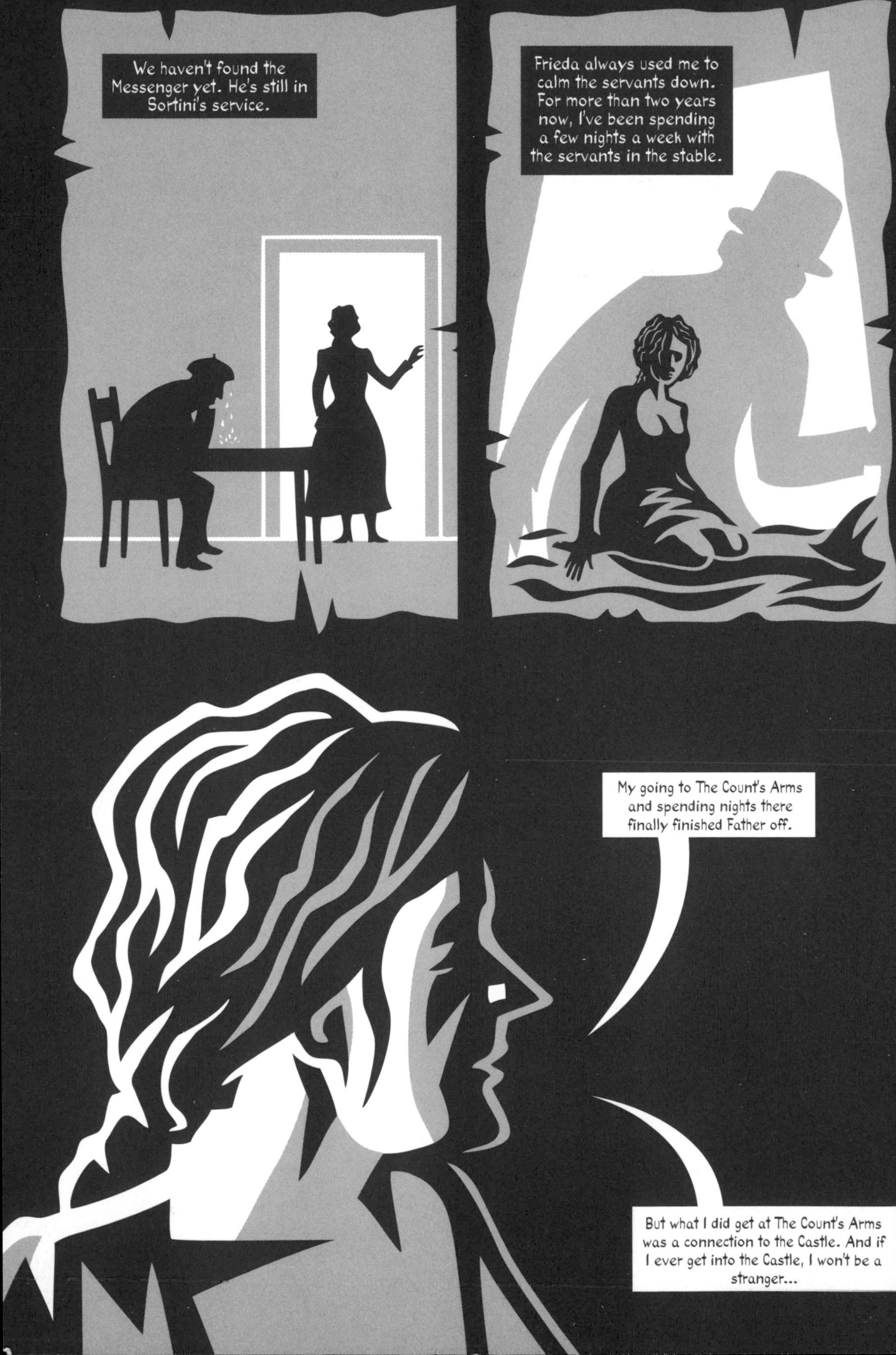

We haven't found the Messenger yet. He's still in Sortini's service.
Frieda always used me to calm the servants down. For more than two years now, I've been spending a few nights a week with the servants in the stable.
My going to The Count's Arms and spending nights there finally finished Father off.
But what I did get at The Count's Arms was a connection to the Castle. And if I ever get into the Castle, I won't be a stranger...

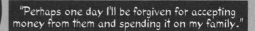
"The servants in the stable swore a hundred times that they looked forward to meeting me again in the Castle."

"Perhaps one day I'll be forgiven for accepting money from them and spending it on my family."

"The servants always changed the subject when the Castle was brought up."

"Instead they talked a lot of nonsense while they took turns with me in the dark stable."

"And so I conceived of a new plan, based on Barnabas."

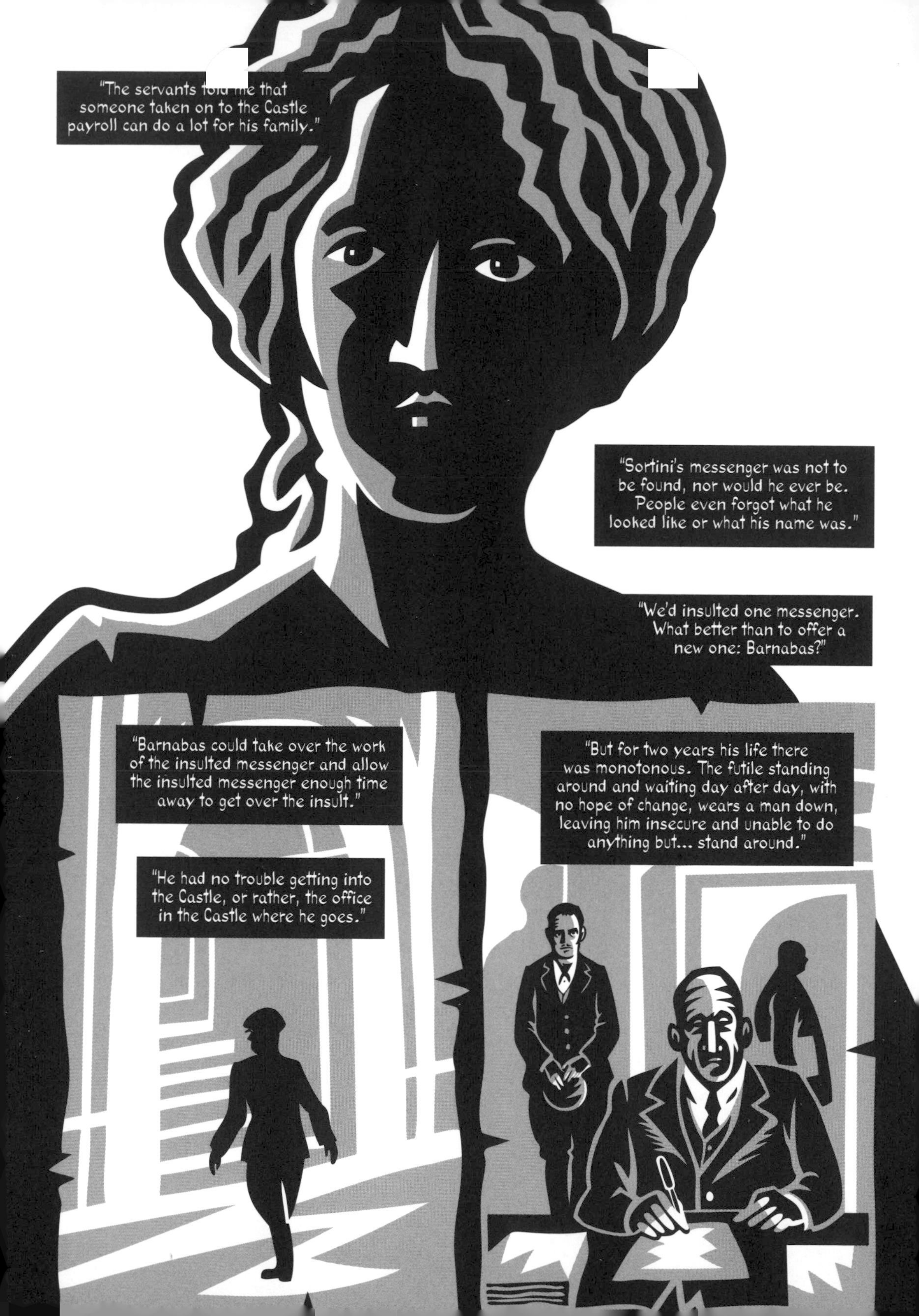
"The servants told me that someone taken on to the Castle payroll can do a lot for his family."
"Sortini's messenger was not to be found, nor would he ever be. People even forgot what he looked like or what his name was."
"We'd insulted one messenger. What better than to offer a new one: Barnabas?"
"Barnabas could take over the work of the insulted messenger and allow the insulted messenger enough time away to get over the insult."
"He had no trouble getting into the Castle, or rather, the office in the Castle where he goes."
"But for two years his life there was monotonous. The futile standing around and waiting day after day, with no hope of change, wears a man down, leaving him insecure and unable to do anything but... stand around."

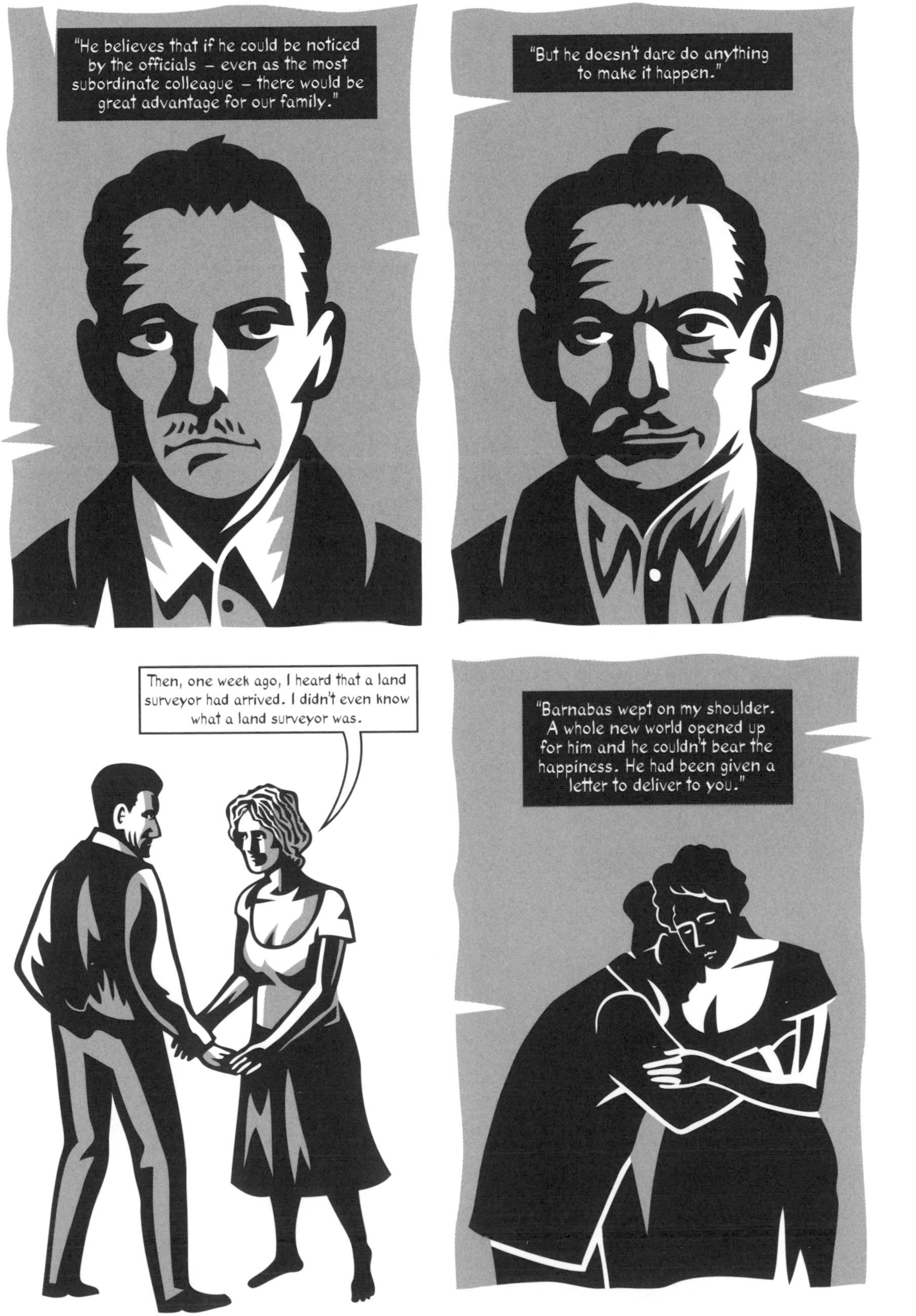
"He believes that if he could be noticed by the officials – even as the most subordinate colleague – there would be great advantage for our family."
"But he doesn't dare do anything to make it happen."
Then, one week ago, I heard that a land surveyor had arrived. I didn't even know what a land surveyor was.
"Barnabas wept on my shoulder. A whole new world opened up for him and he couldn't bear the happiness. He had been given a letter to deliver to you."

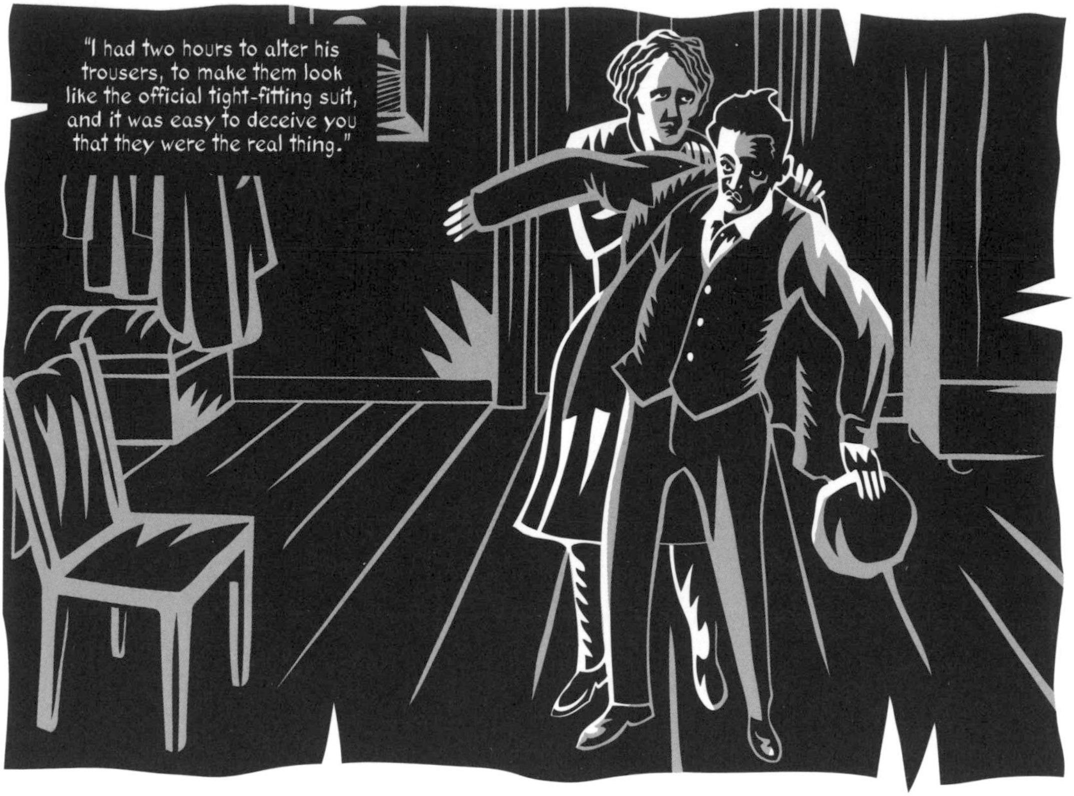
"I had two hours to alter his trousers, to make them look like the official tight-fitting suit, and it was easy to deceive you that they were the real thing."

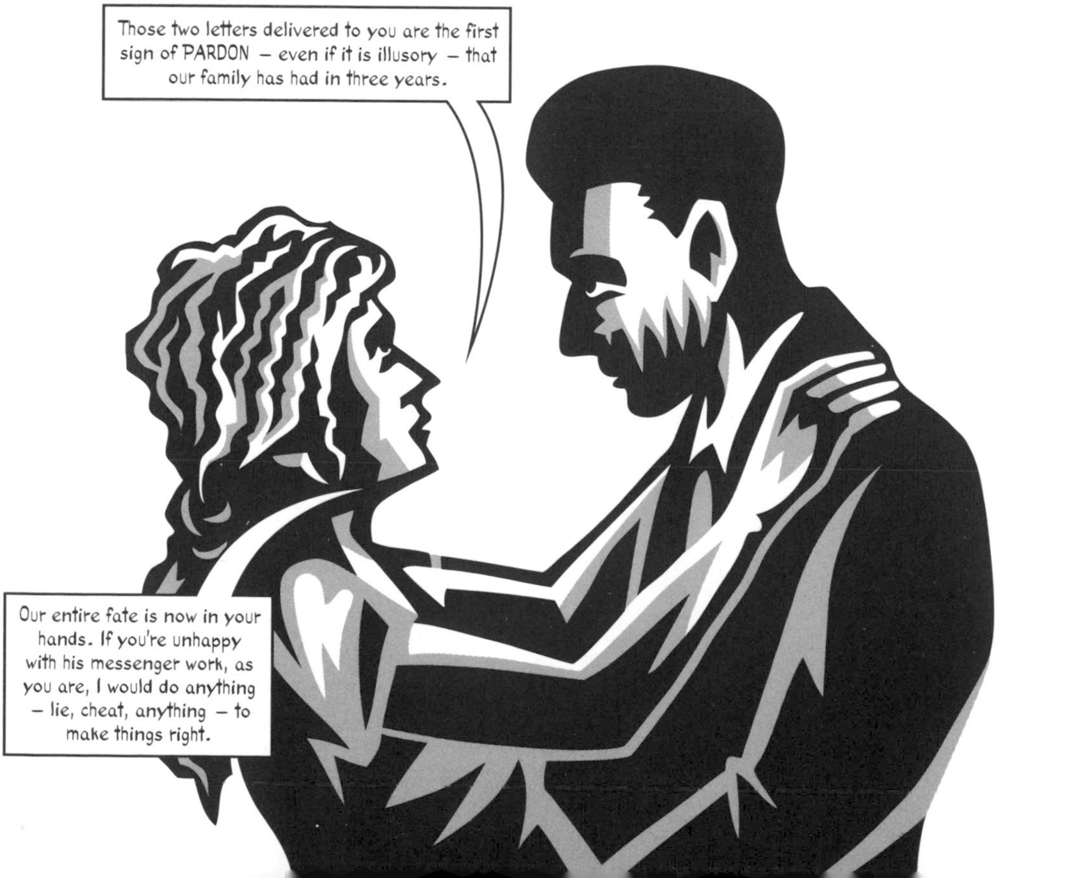
Those two letters delivered to you are the first sign of PARDON – even if it is illusory – that our family has had in three years.
Our entire fate is now in your hands. If you're unhappy with his messenger work, as you are, I would do anything – lie, cheat, anything – to make things right.

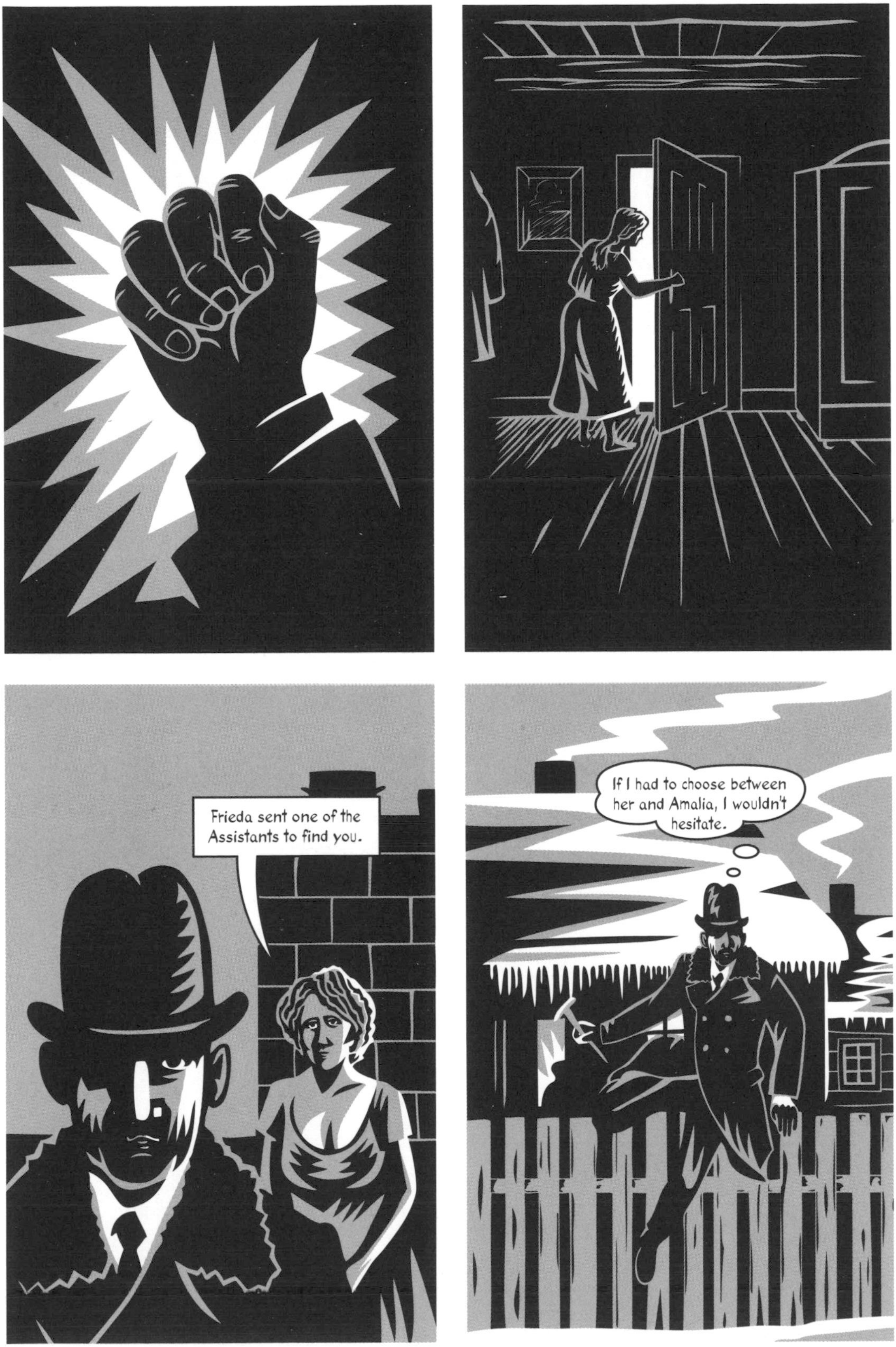
Frieda sent one of the Assistants to find you.
If I had to choose between her and Amalia, I wouldn't hesitate.

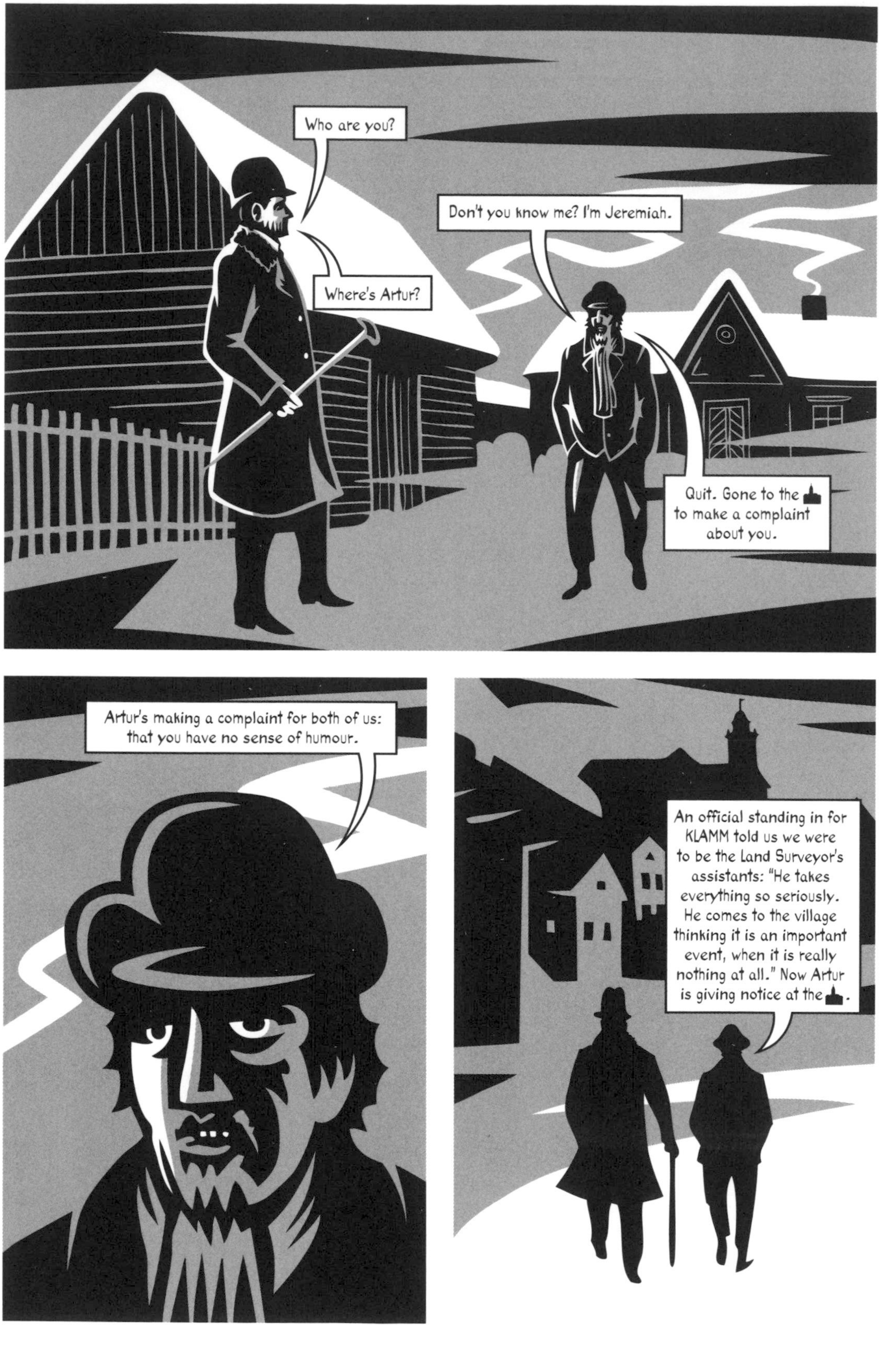
Who are you?
Where's Artur?
Don't you know me? I'm Jeremiah.
Quit. Gone to the to make a complaint about you.
Artur's making a complaint for both of us: that you have no sense of humour.
An official standing in for KLAMM told us we were to be the Land Surveyor's assistants: "He takes everything so seriously. He comes to the village thinking it is an important event, when it is really nothing at all." Now Artur is giving notice at the .

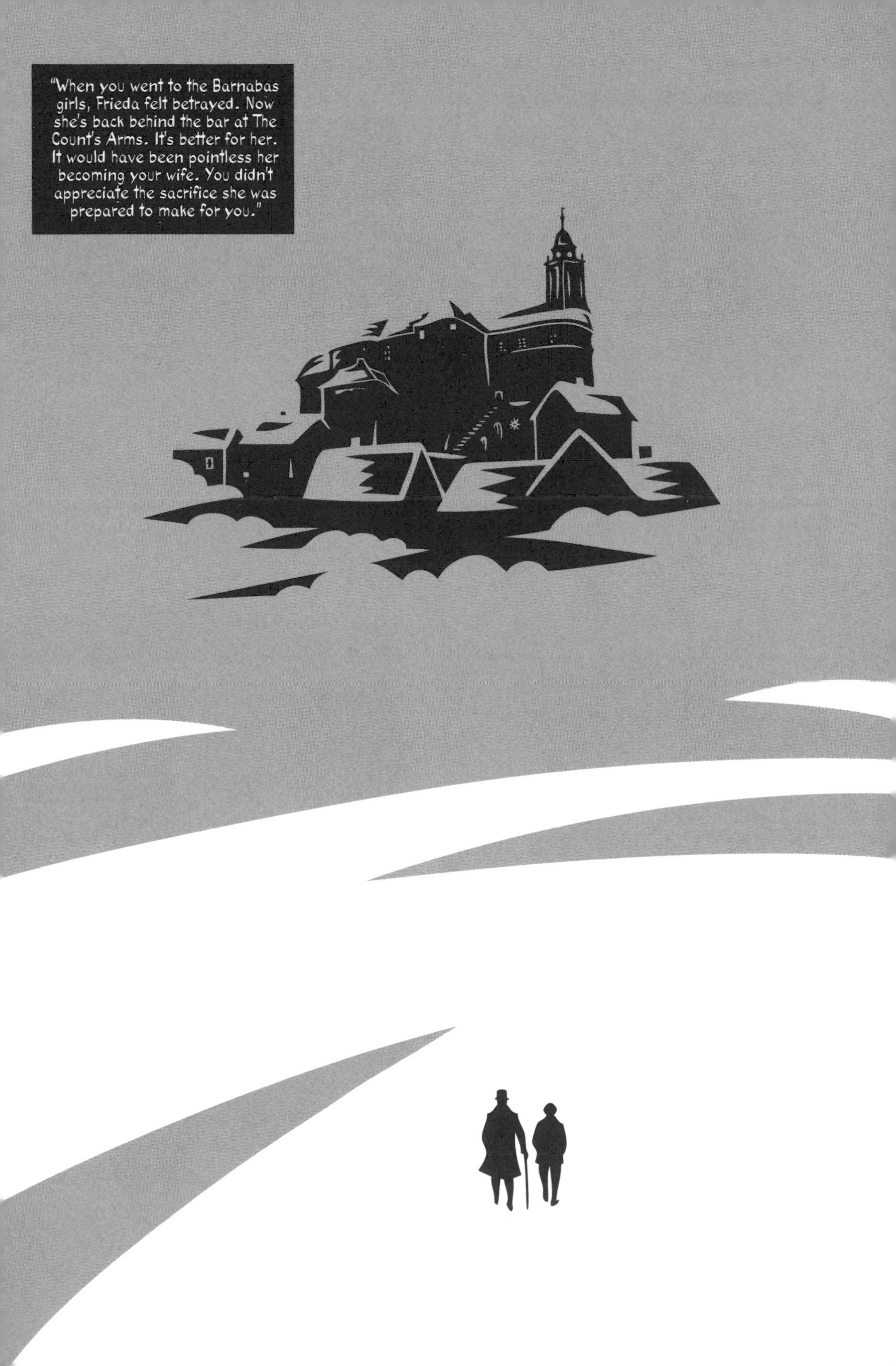
"When you went to the Barnabas girls, Frieda felt betrayed. Now she's back behind the bar at The Count's Arms. It's better for her. It would have been pointless her becoming your wife. You didn't appreciate the sacrifice she was prepared to make for you."

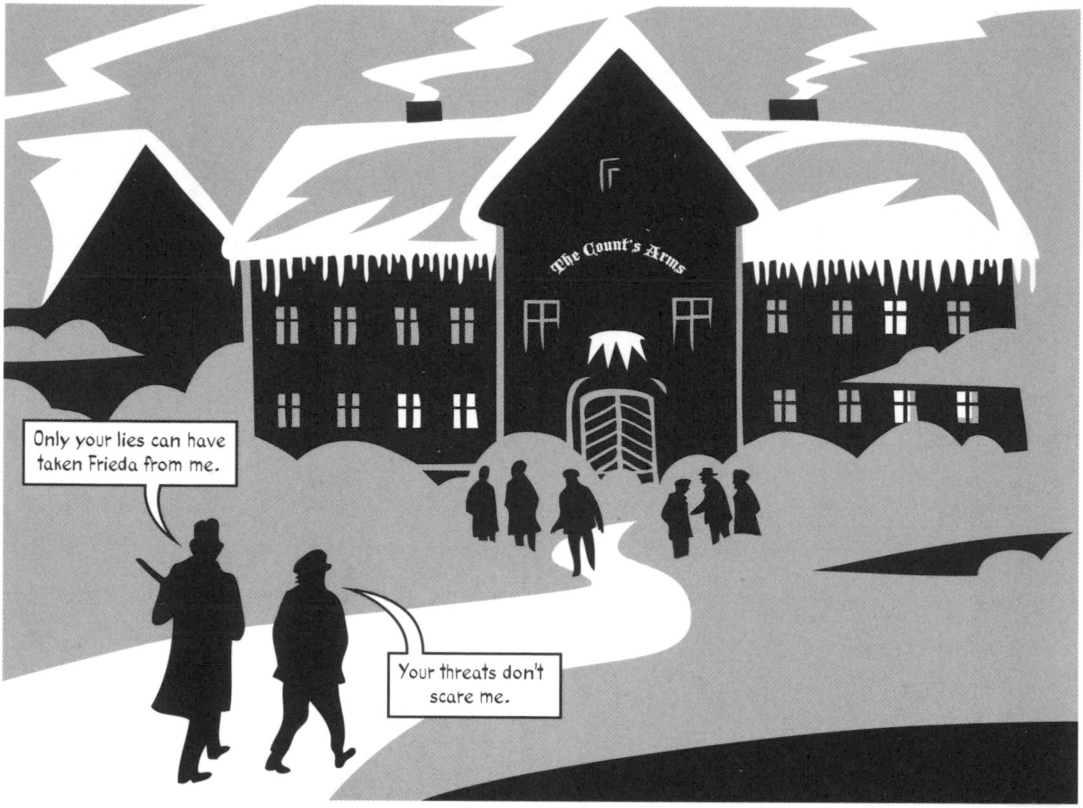
The Count's Arms
Only your lies can have taken Frieda from me.
Your threats don't scare me.

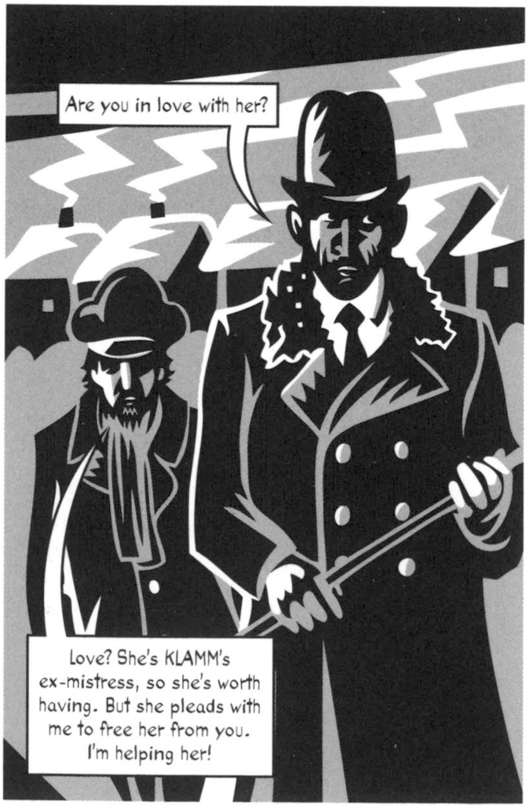
Are you in love with her?
Love? She's KLAMM's ex-mistress, so she's worth having. But she pleads with me to free her from you. I'm helping her!

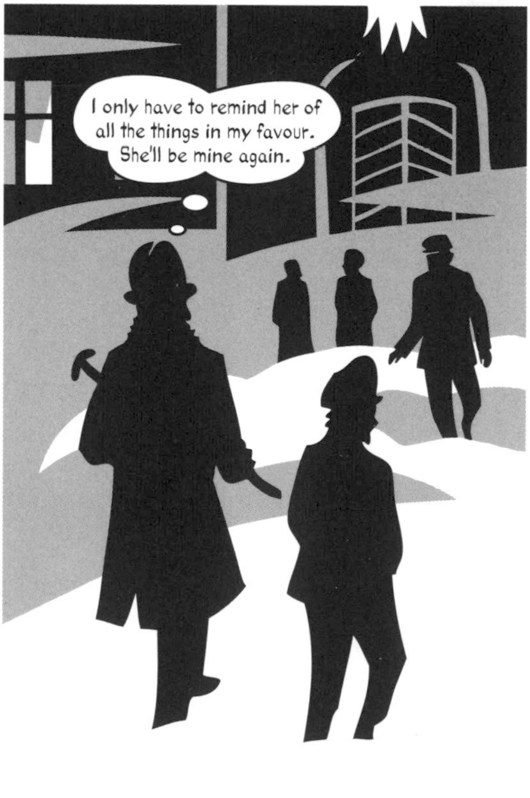
I only have to remind her of all the things in my favour. She'll be mine again.

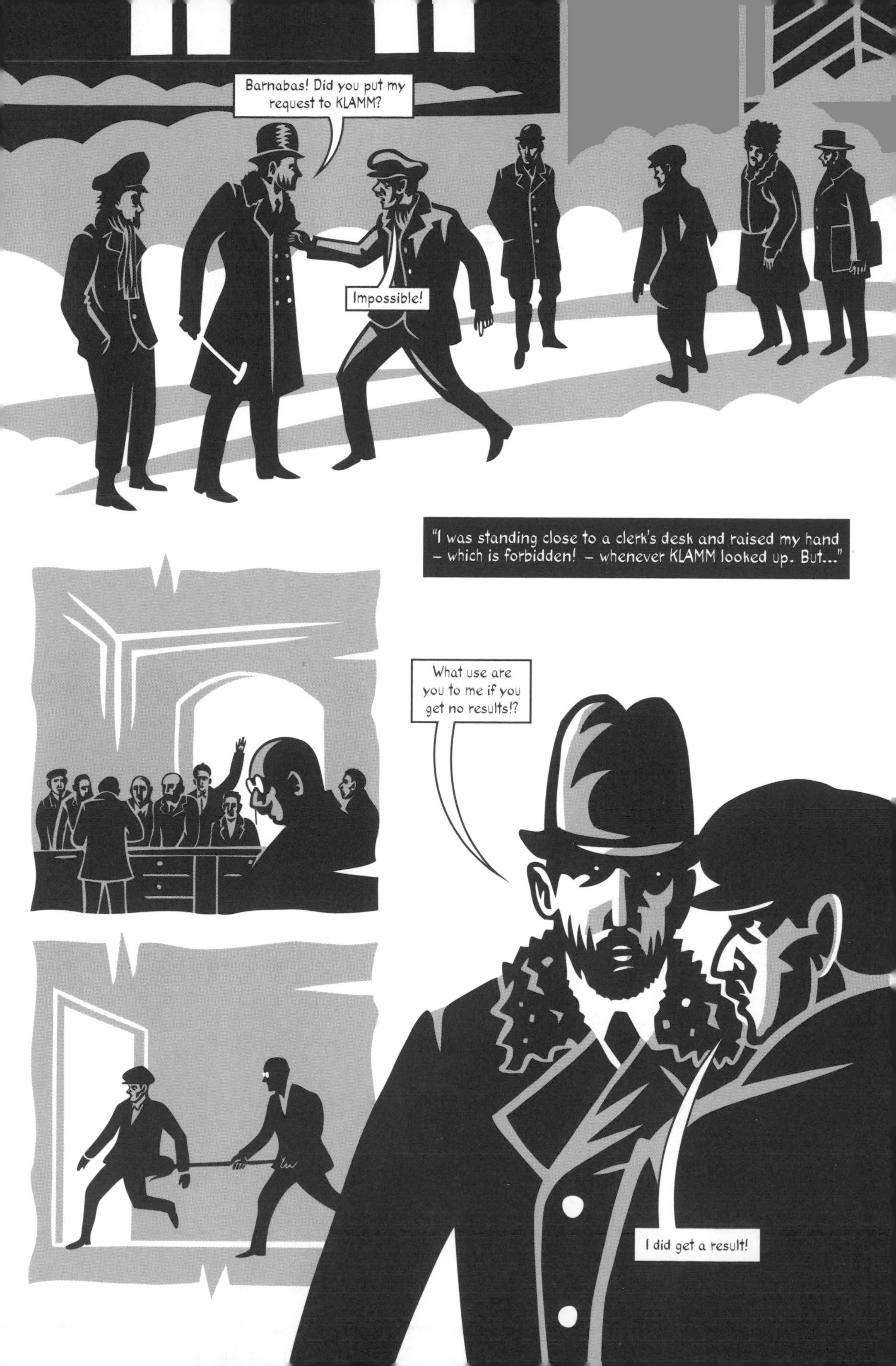
Barnabas! Did you put my request to KLAMM?
Impossible!
"I was standing close to a clerk's desk and raised my hand – which is forbidden! – whenever KLAMM looked up. But..."
What use are you to me if you get no results!?
I did get a result!

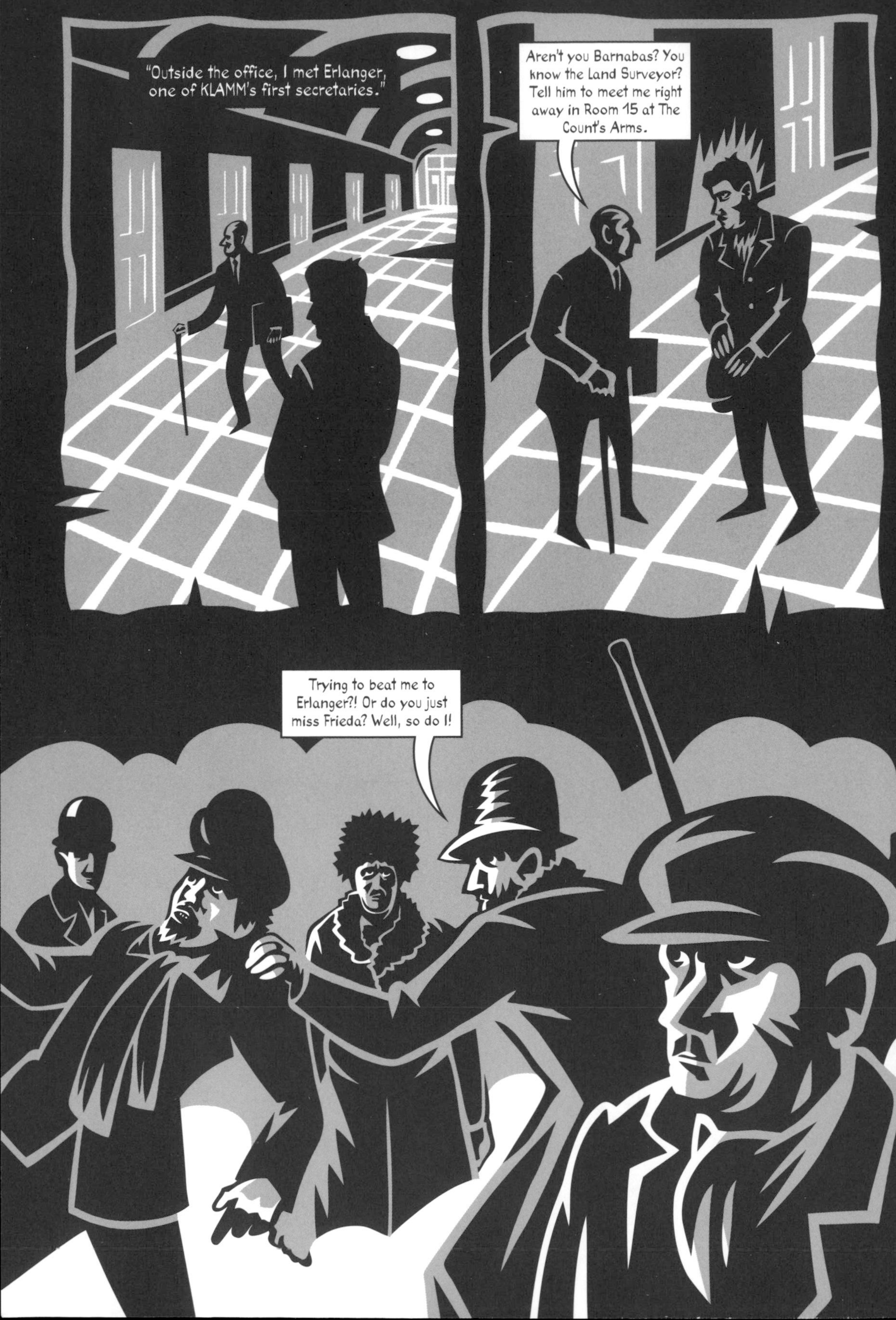
"Outside the office, I met Erlanger, one of KLAMM's first secretaries."
Aren't you Barnabas? You know the Land Surveyor? Tell him to meet me right away in Room 15 at The Count's Arms.
Trying to beat me to Erlanger?! Or do you just miss Frieda? Well, so do I!

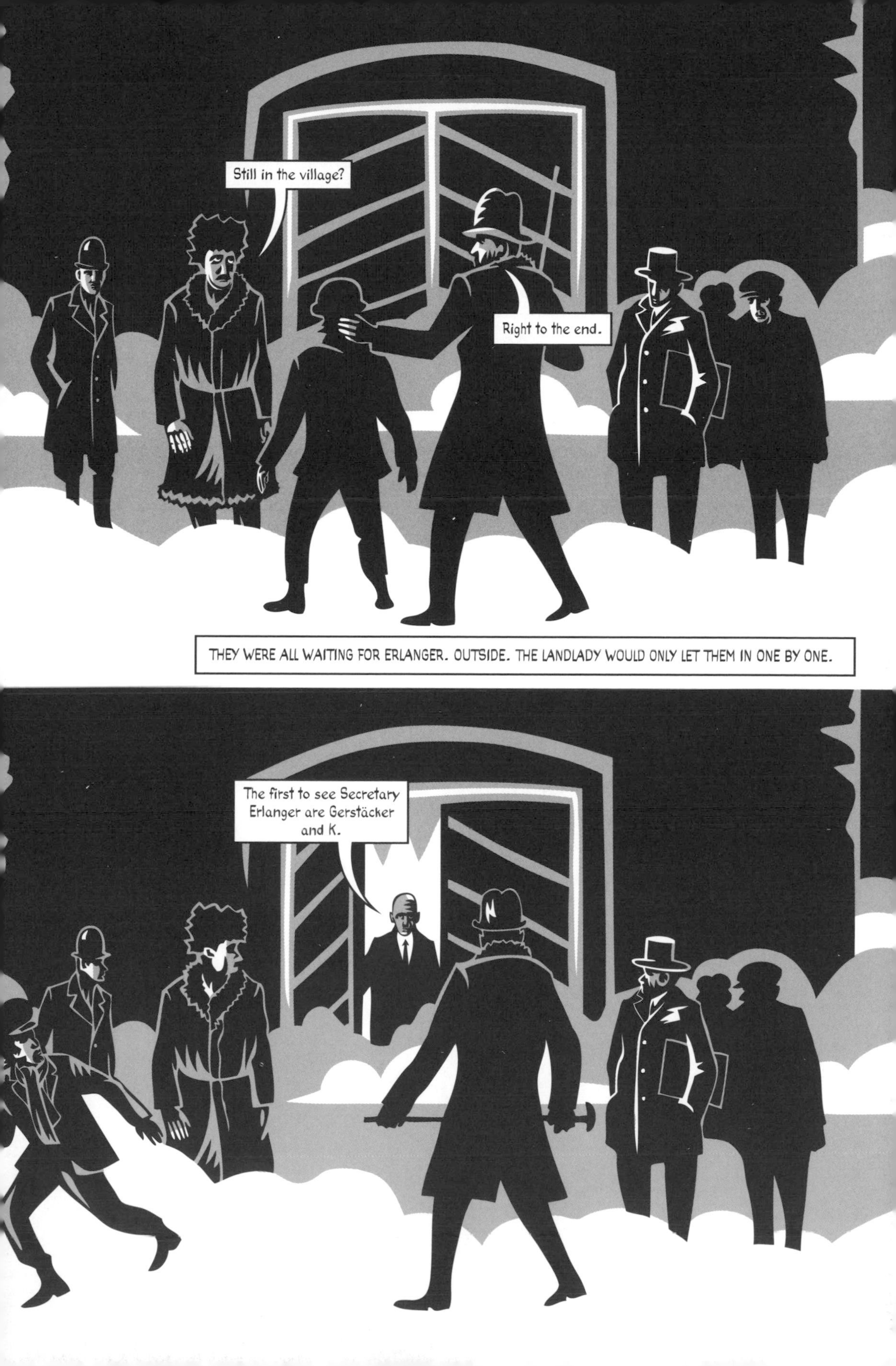
Still in the village?
Right to the end.
THEY WERE ALL WAITING FOR ERLANGER. OUTSIDE. THE LANDLADY WOULD ONLY LET THEM IN ONE BY ONE.
The first to see Secretary Erlanger are Gerstäcker and K.

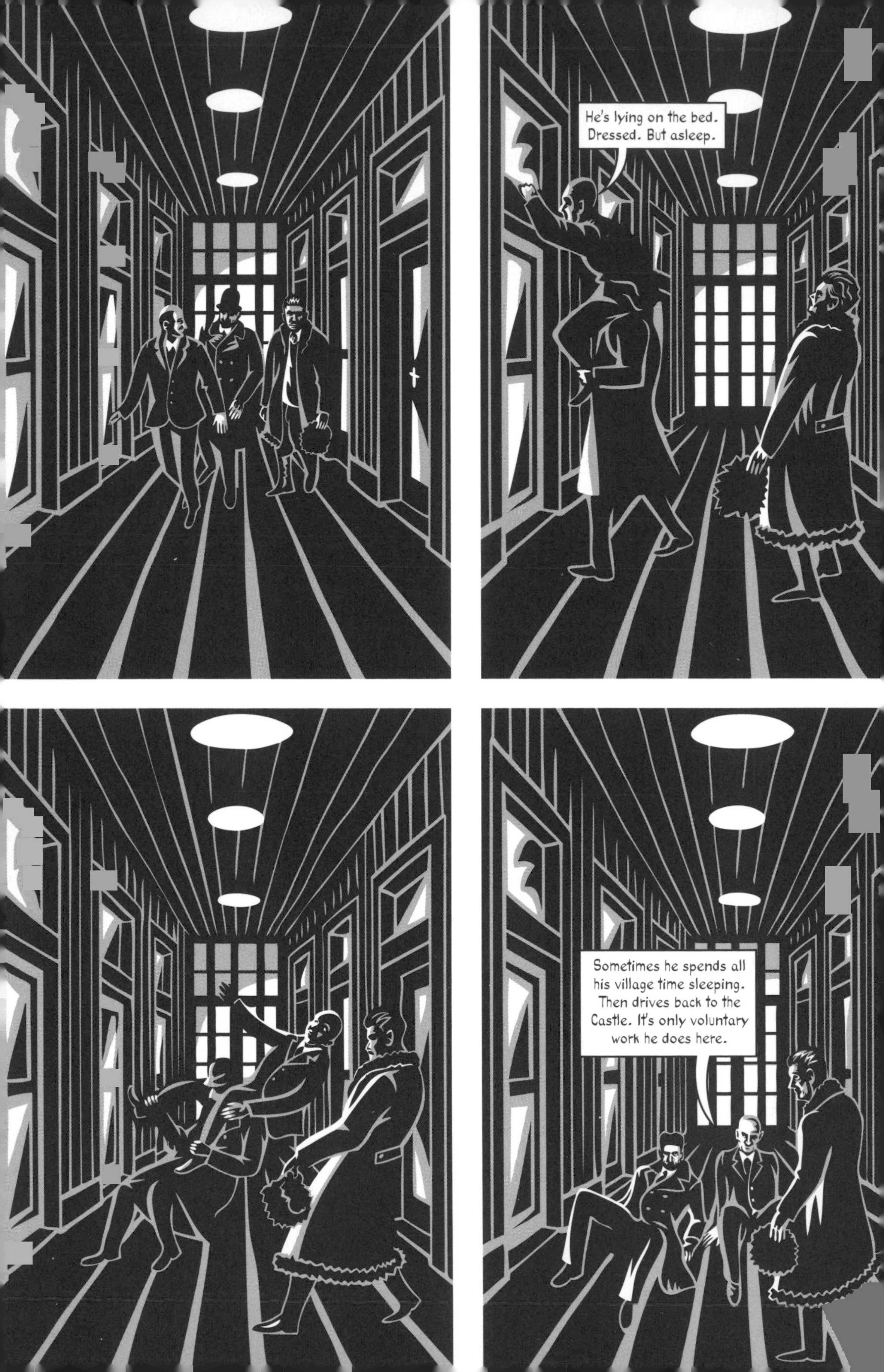
He's lying on the bed. Dressed. But asleep.
Sometimes he spends all his village time sleeping. Then drives back to the Castle. It's only voluntary work he does here.

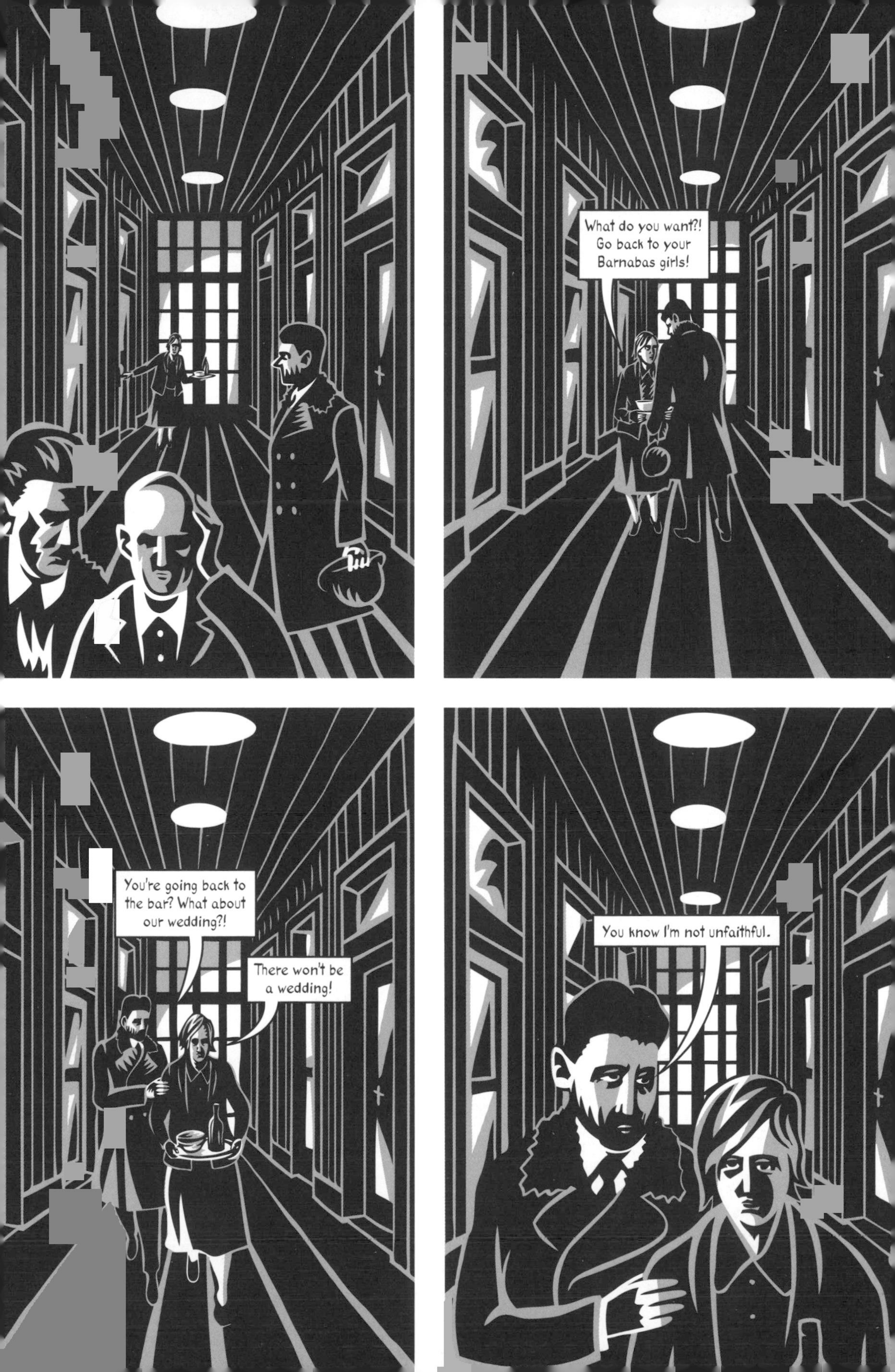
What do you want?! Go back to your Barnabas girls!
You're going back to the bar? What about our wedding?!
There won't be a wedding!
You know I'm not unfaithful.

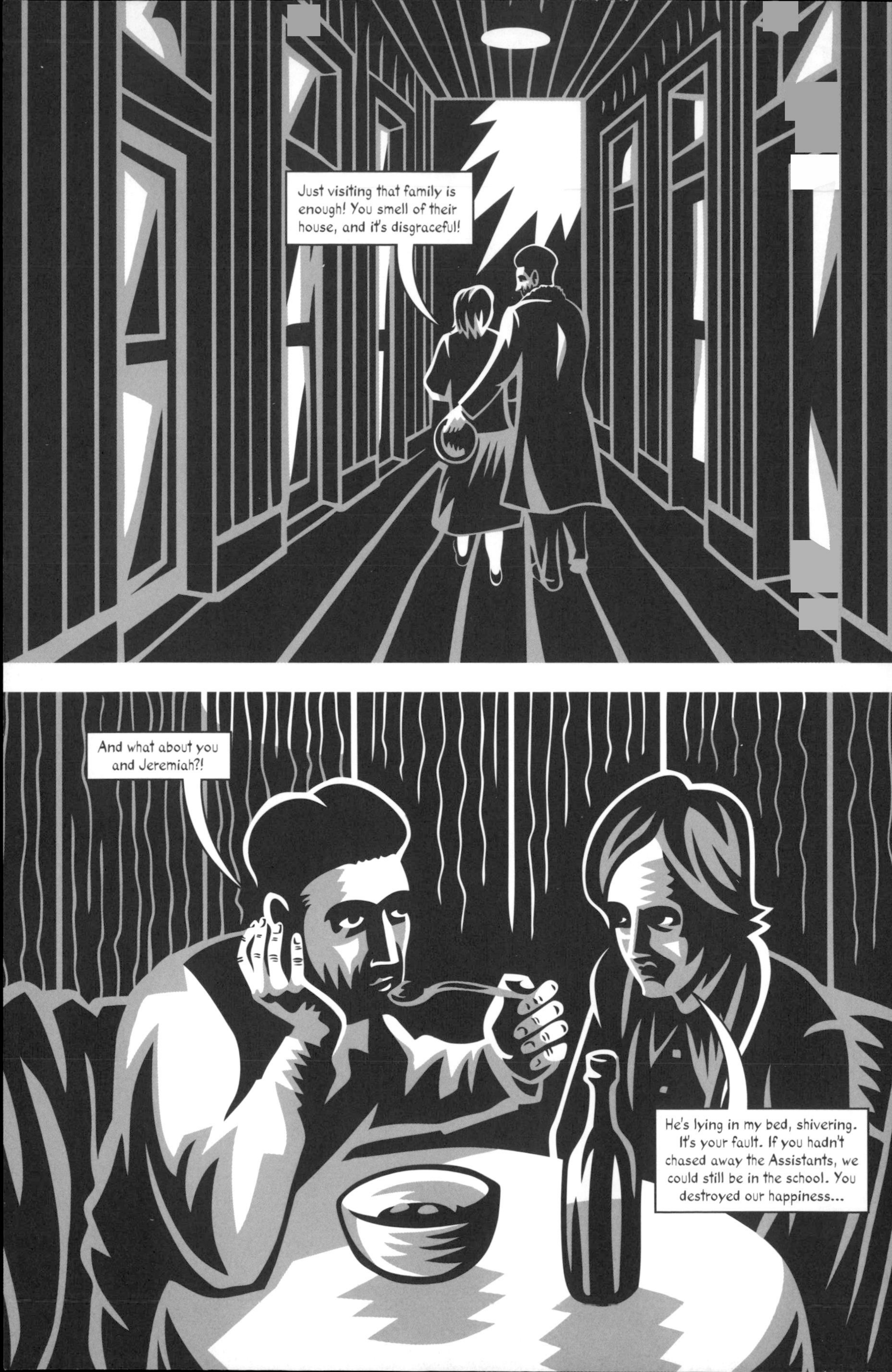
Just visiting that family is enough! You smell of their house, and it's disgraceful!
And what about you and Jeremiah?!
He's lying in my bed, shivering. It's your fault. If you hadn't chased away the Assistants, we could still be in the school. You destroyed our happiness...

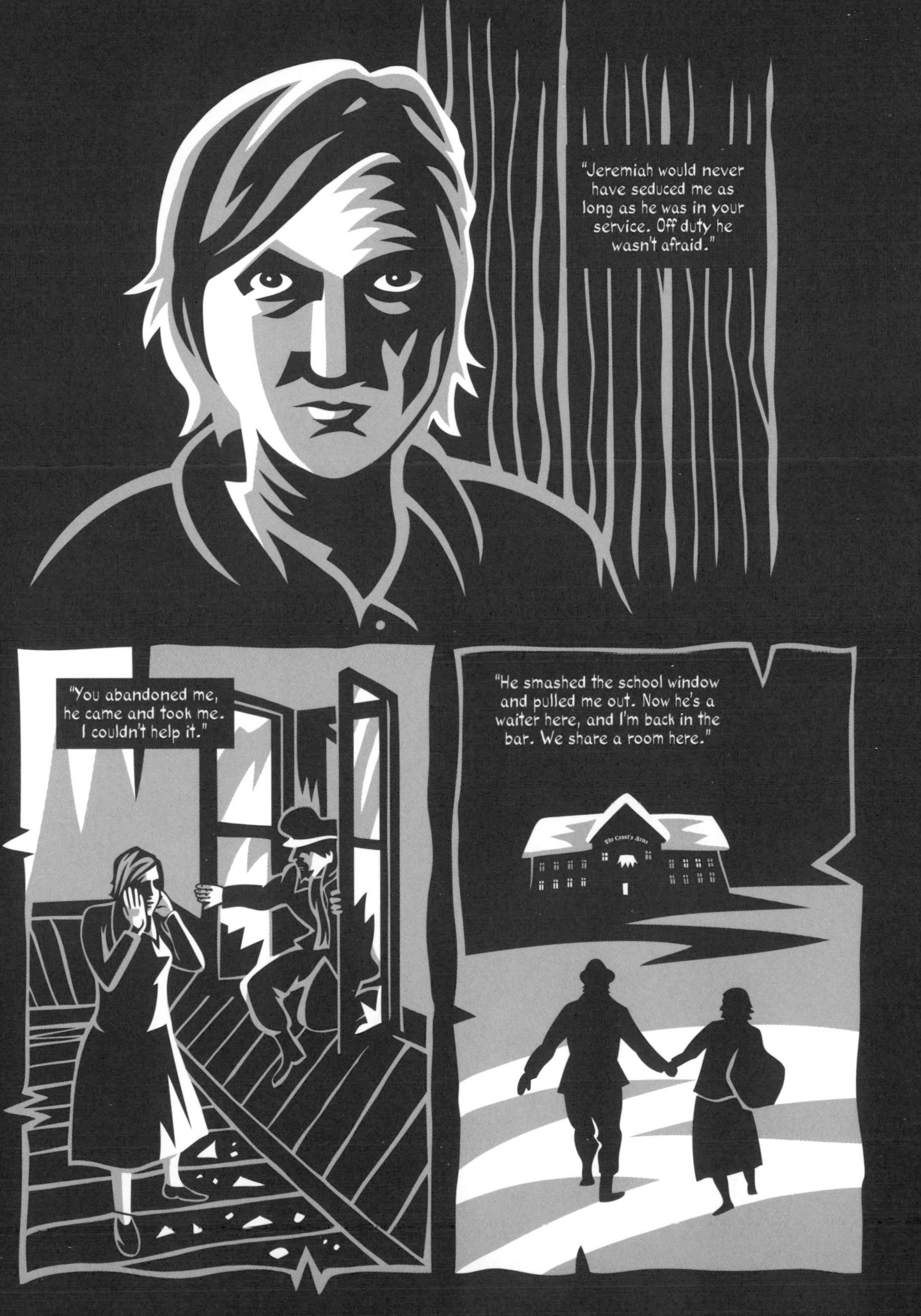
"Jeremiah would never have seduced me as long as he was in your service. Off duty he wasn't afraid."
"You abandoned me, he came and took me. I couldn't help it."
"He smashed the school window and pulled me out. Now he's a waiter here, and I'm back in the bar. We share a room here."
The Count's Arms

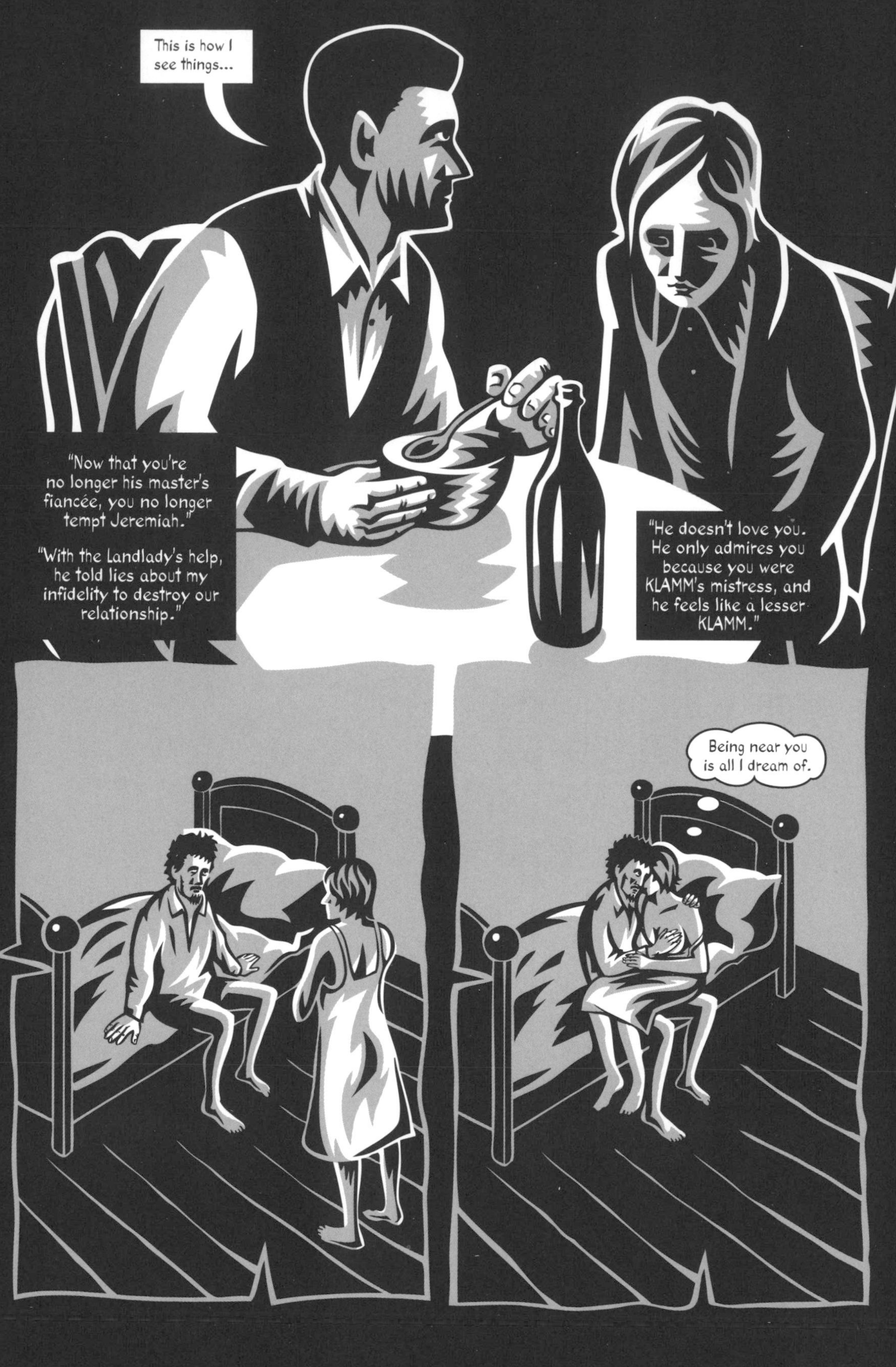
This is how I see things...
"Now that you're no longer his master's fiancée, you no longer tempt Jeremiah."
"With the Landlady's help, he told lies about my infidelity to destroy our relationship."
"He doesn't love you. He only admires you because you were KLAMM's mistress, and he feels like a lesser KLAMM."
Being near you is all I dream of.

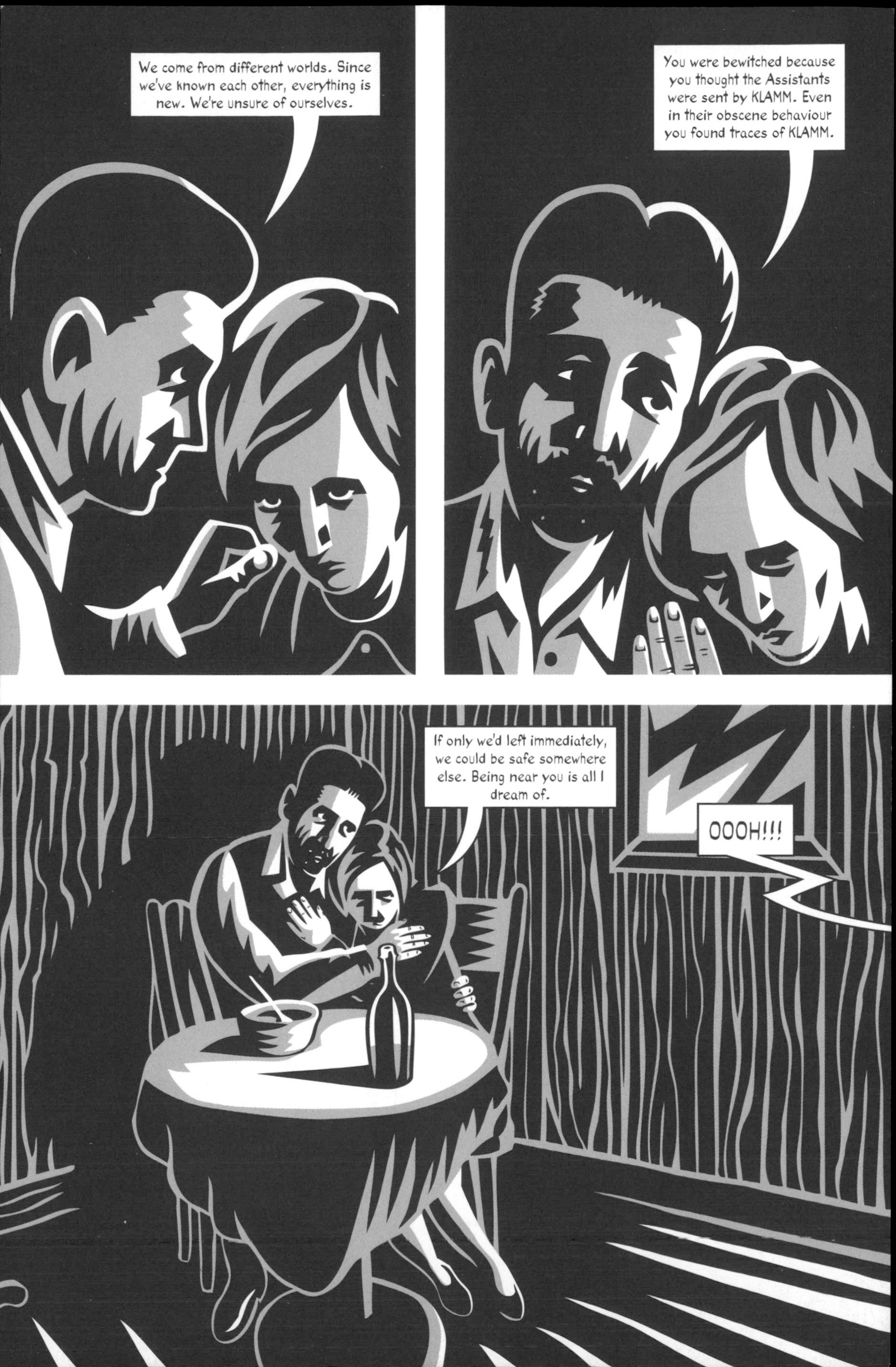
We come from different worlds. Since we've known each other, everything is new. We're unsure of ourselves.
You were bewitched because you thought the Assistants were sent by KLAMM. Even in their obscene behaviour you found traces of KLAMM.
If only we'd left immediately, we could be safe somewhere else. Being near you is all I dream of.
OOOH!!!

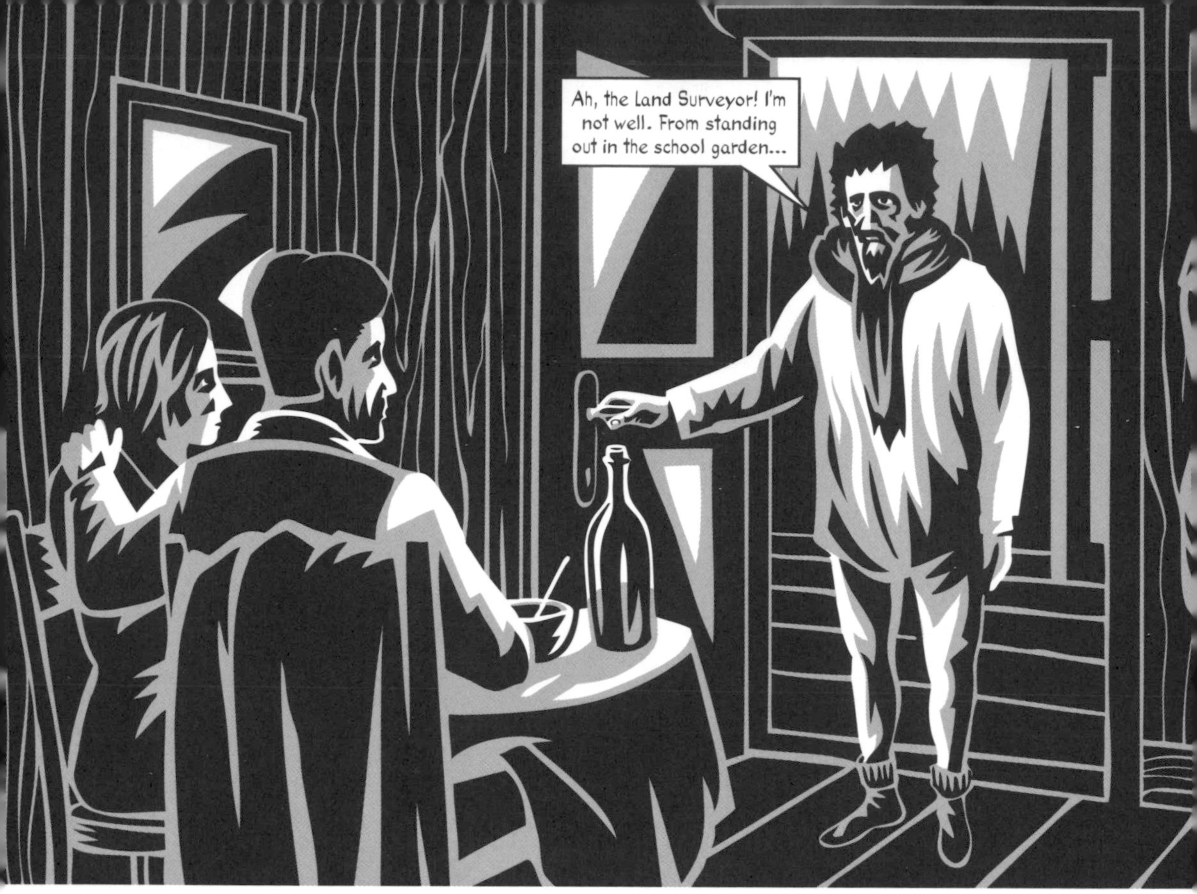
Ah, the Land Surveyor! I'm not well. From standing out in the school garden...

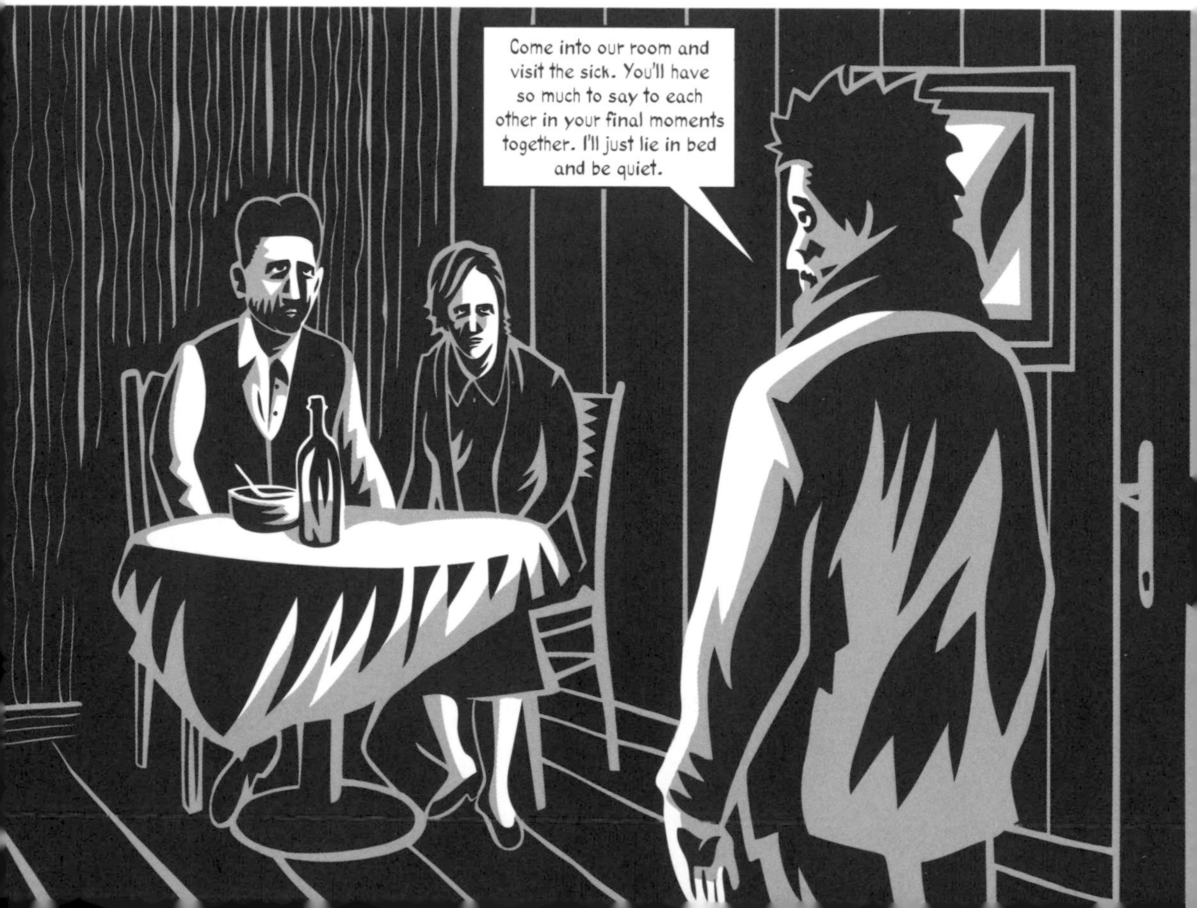
Come into our room and visit the sick. You'll have so much to say to each other in your final moments together. I'll just lie in bed and be quiet.

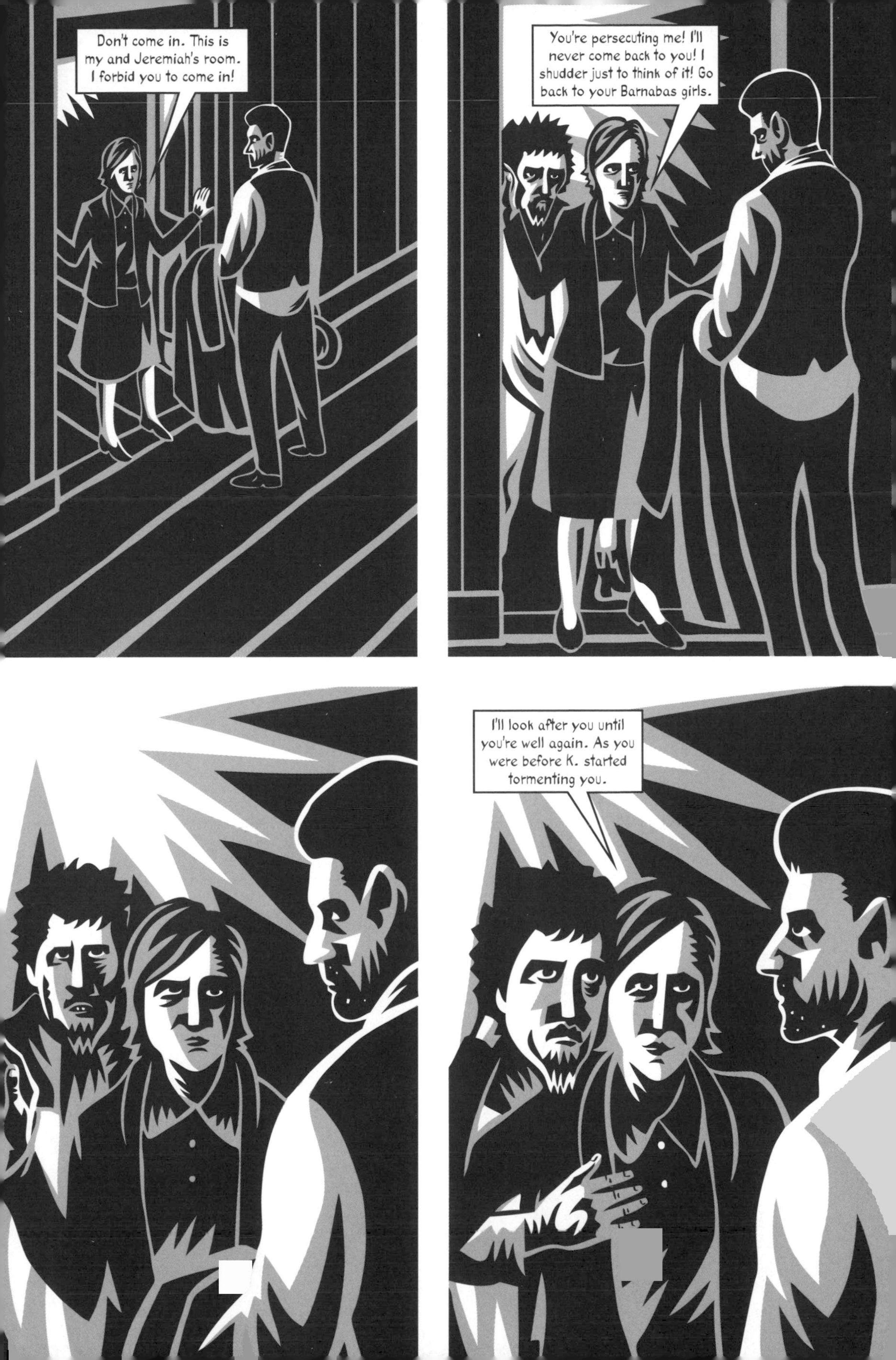
Don't come in. This is my and Jeremiah's room. I forbid you to come in!
You're persecuting me! I'll never come back to you! I shudder just to think of it! Go back to your Barnabas girls.
I'll look after you until you're well again. As you were before K. started tormenting you.

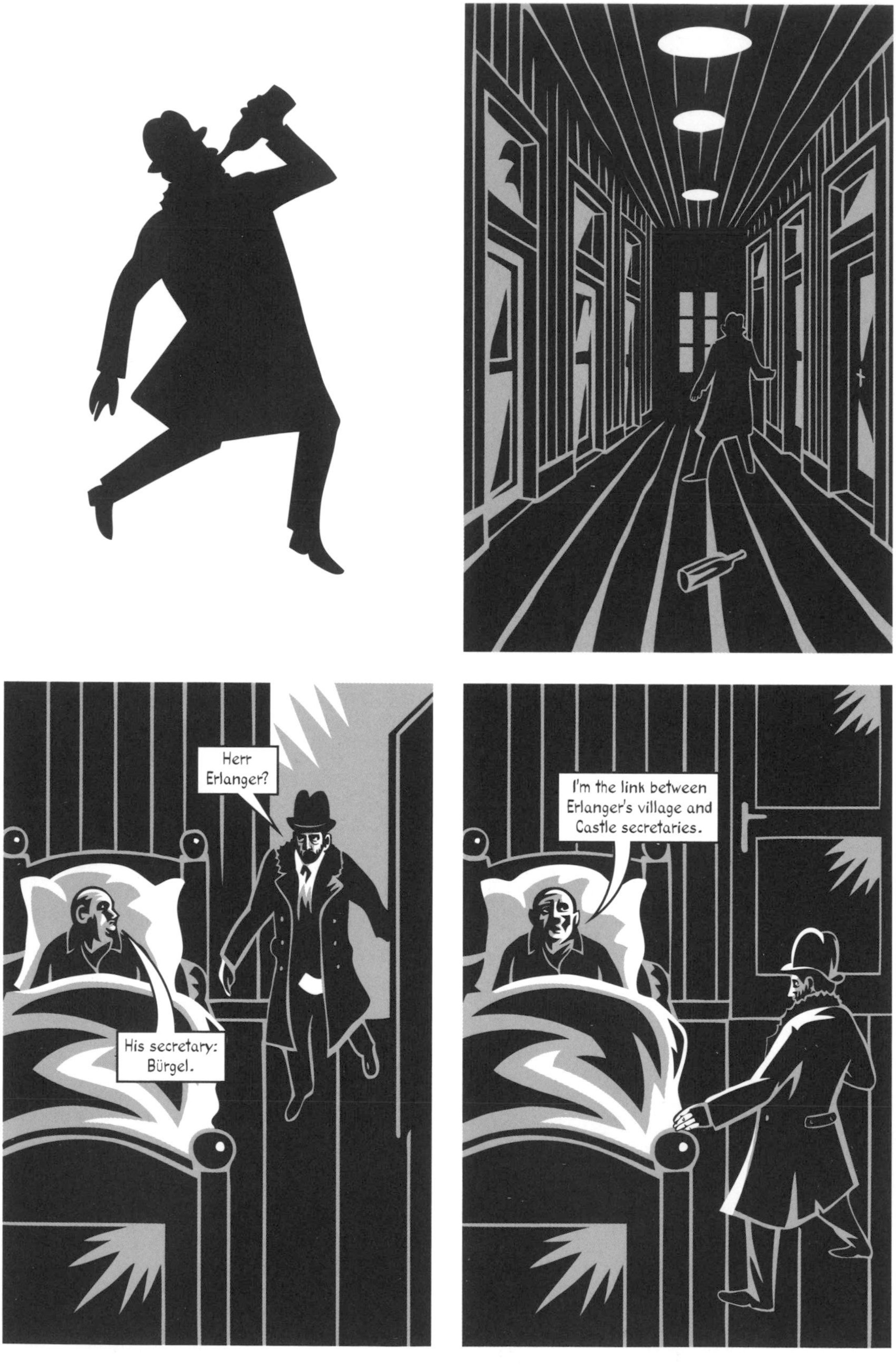
Herr
Erlanger?
His secretary:
Bürgel.
I'm the link between
Erlanger's village and
Castle secretaries.

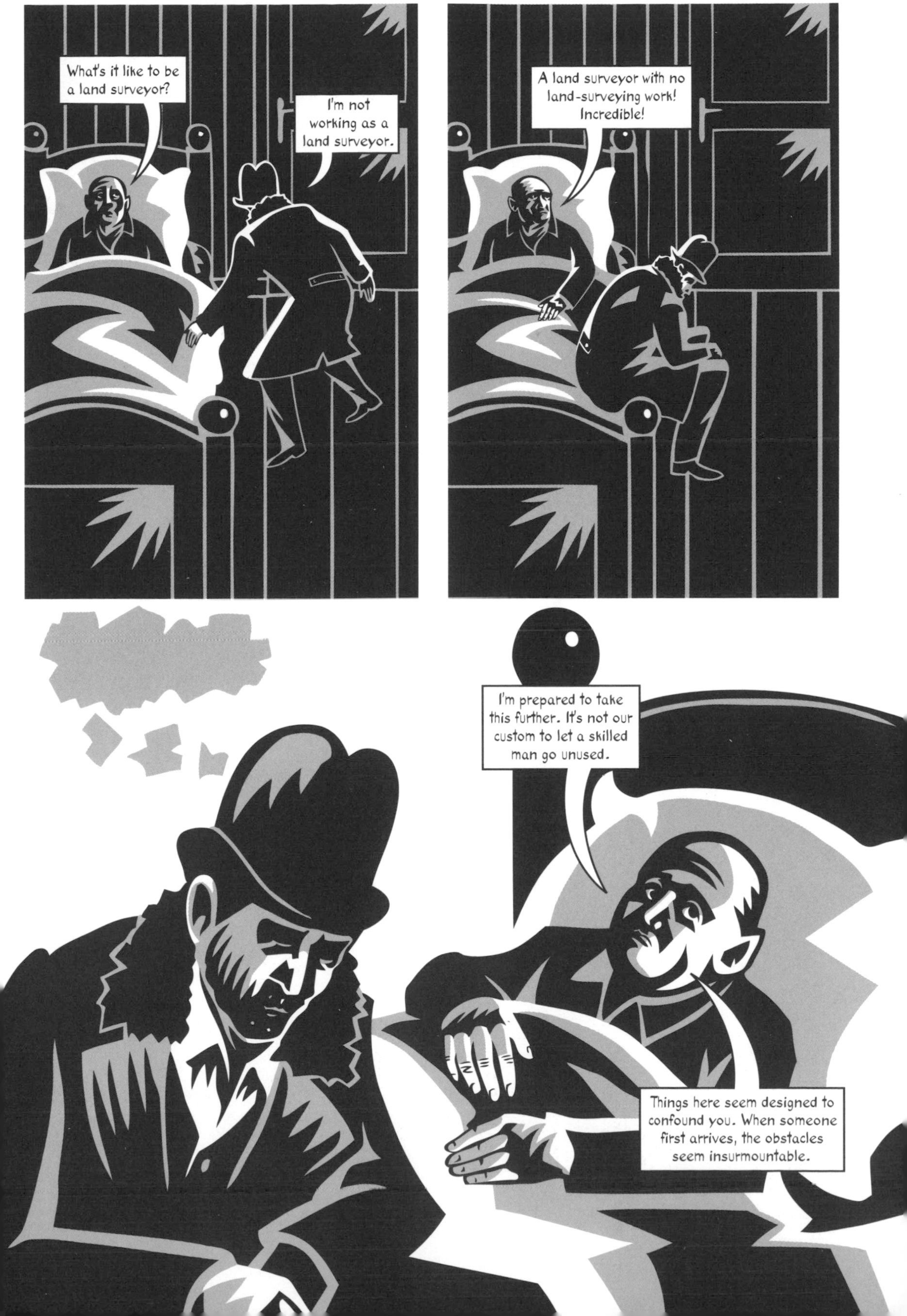
What's it like to be a land surveyor?
I'm not working as a land surveyor.
A land surveyor with no land-surveying work! Incredible!
I'm prepared to take this further. It's not our custom to let a skilled man go unused.
Things here seem designed to confound you. When someone first arrives, the obstacles seem insurmountable.

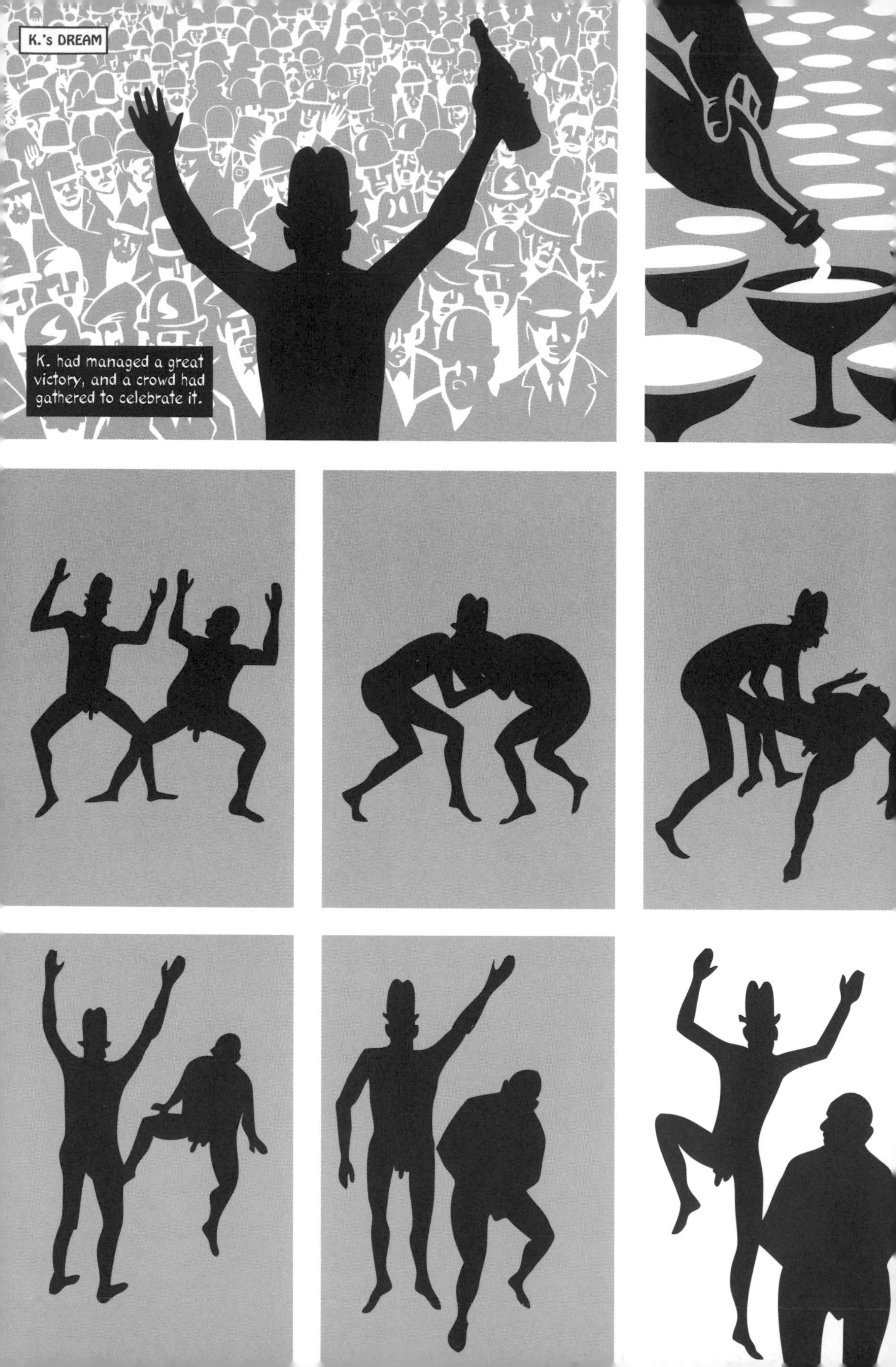
K.'s DREAM
K. had managed a great victory, and a crowd had gathered to celebrate it.

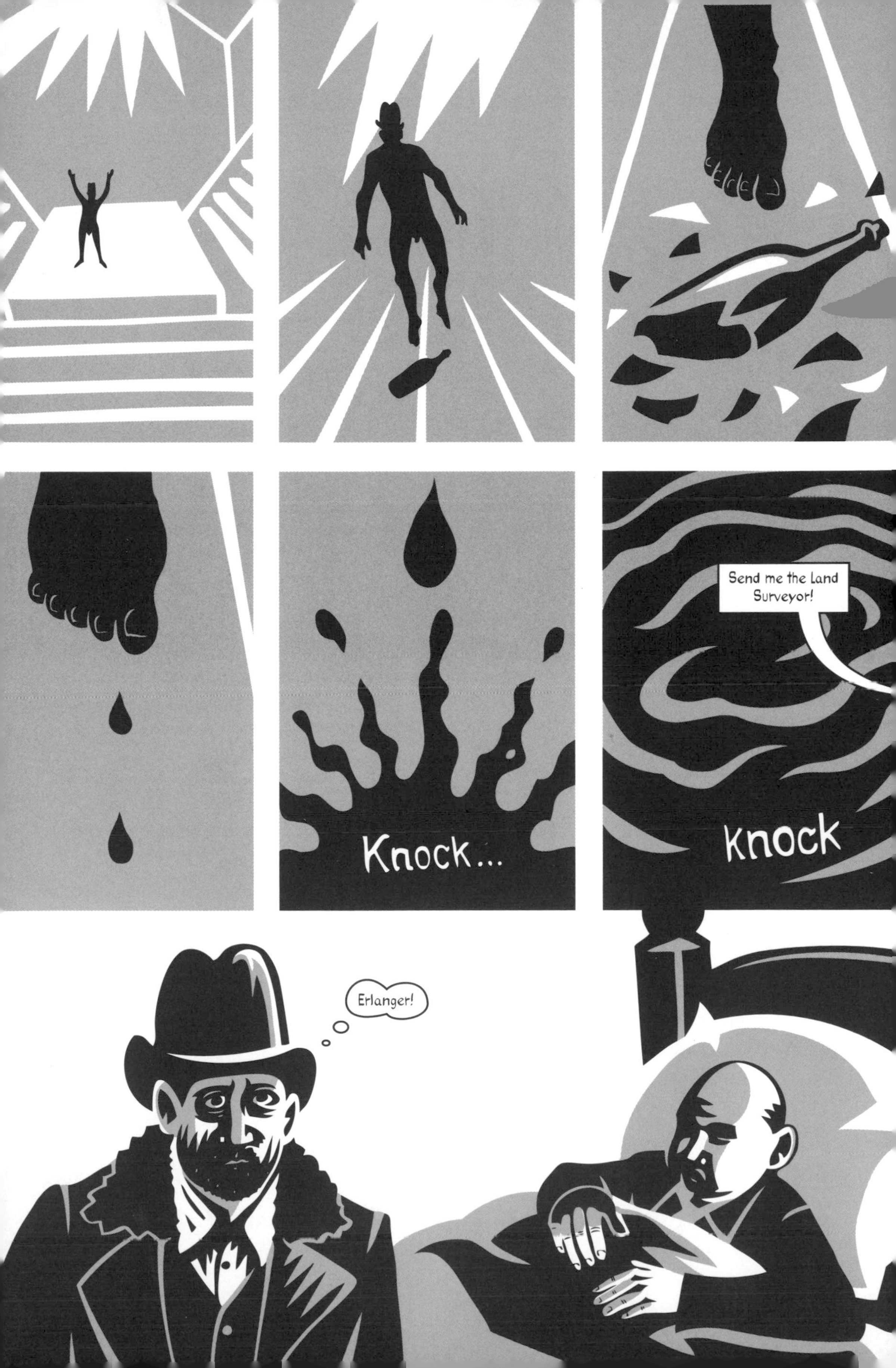
Knock...
Send me the Land Surveyor!
knock
Erlanger!

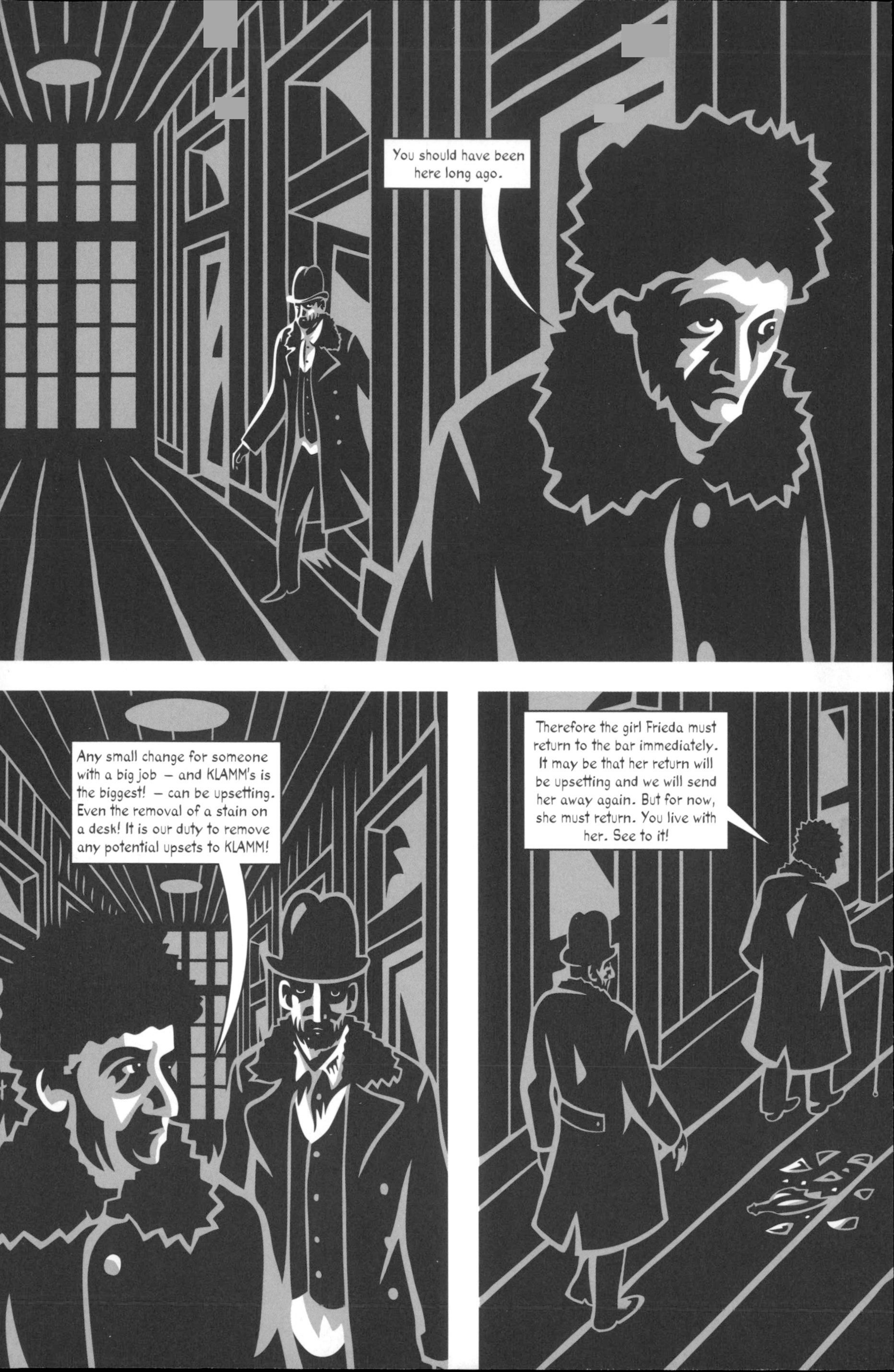

You should have been here long ago.
Any small change for someone with a big job – and KLAMM's is the biggest! – can be upsetting. Even the removal of a stain on a desk! It is our duty to remove any potential upsets to KLAMM!
Therefore the girl Frieda must return to the bar immediately. It may be that her return will be upsetting and we will send her away again. But for now, she must return. You live with her. See to it!

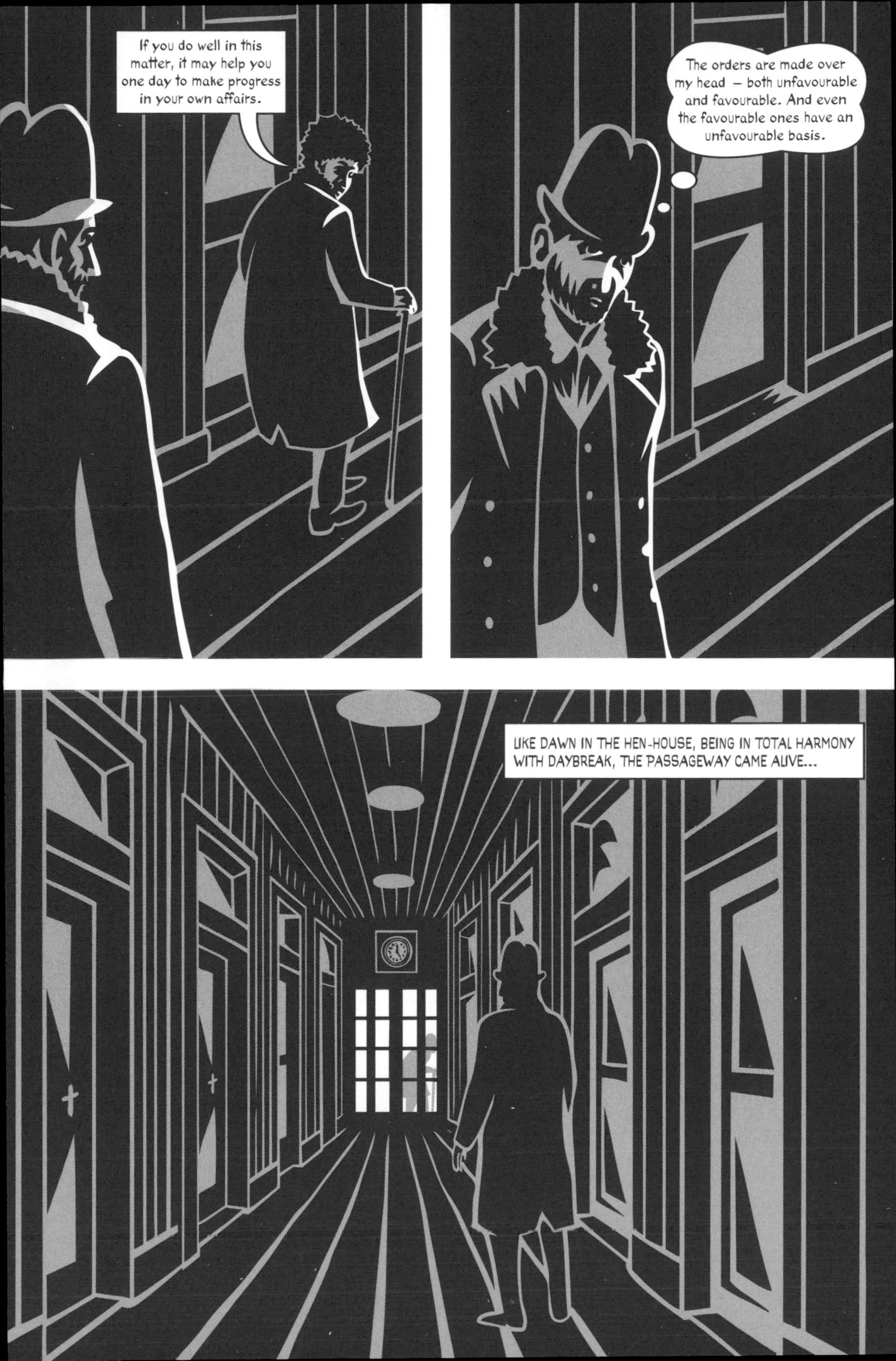
If you do well in this matter, it may help you one day to make progress in your own affairs.
The orders are made over my head – both unfavourable and favourable. And even the favourable ones have an unfavourable basis.
LIKE DAWN IN THE HEN-HOUSE, BEING IN TOTAL HARMONY WITH DAYBREAK, THE PASSAGEWAY CAME ALIVE...

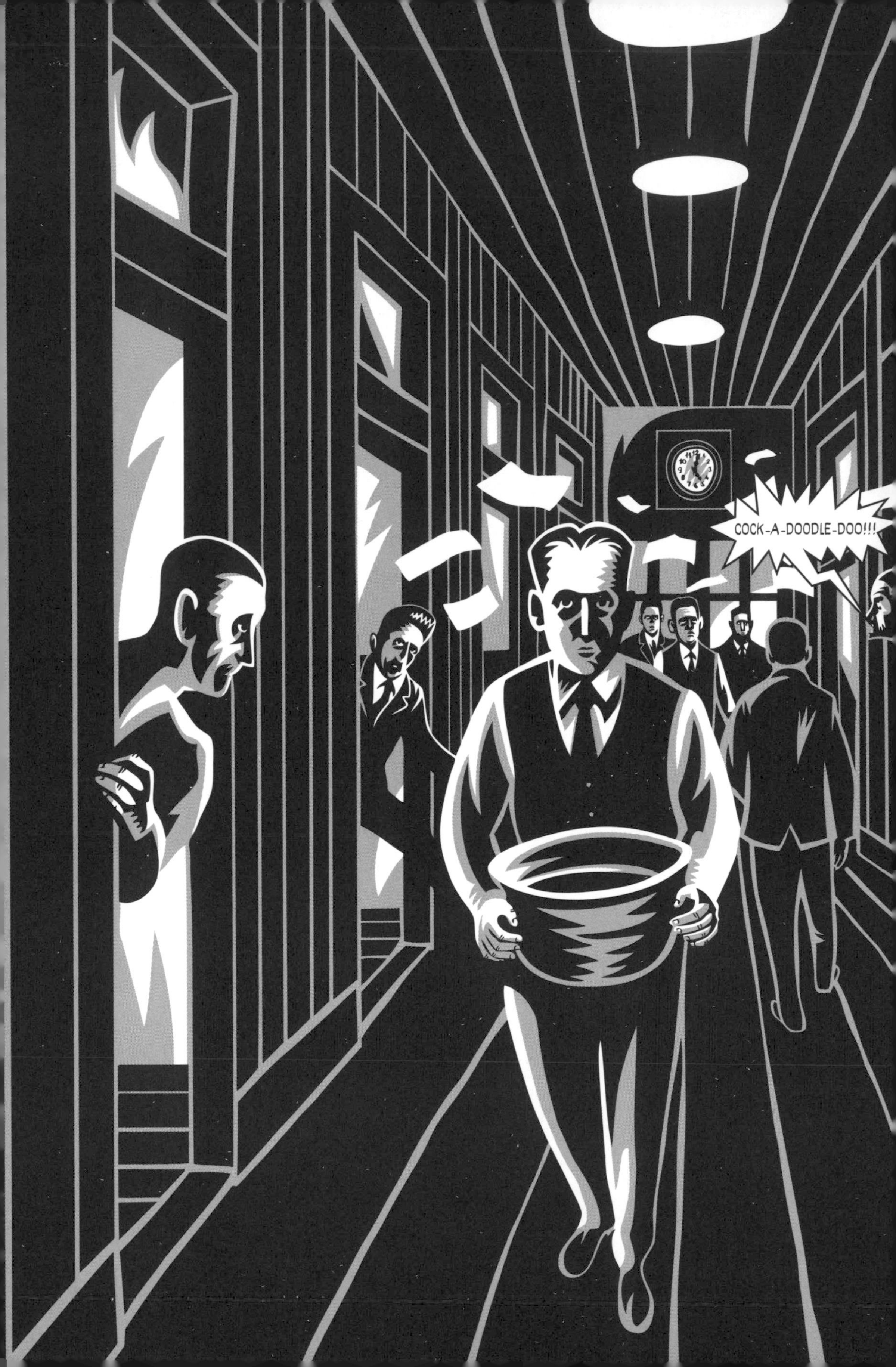
COCK-A-DOODLE-DOO!!!

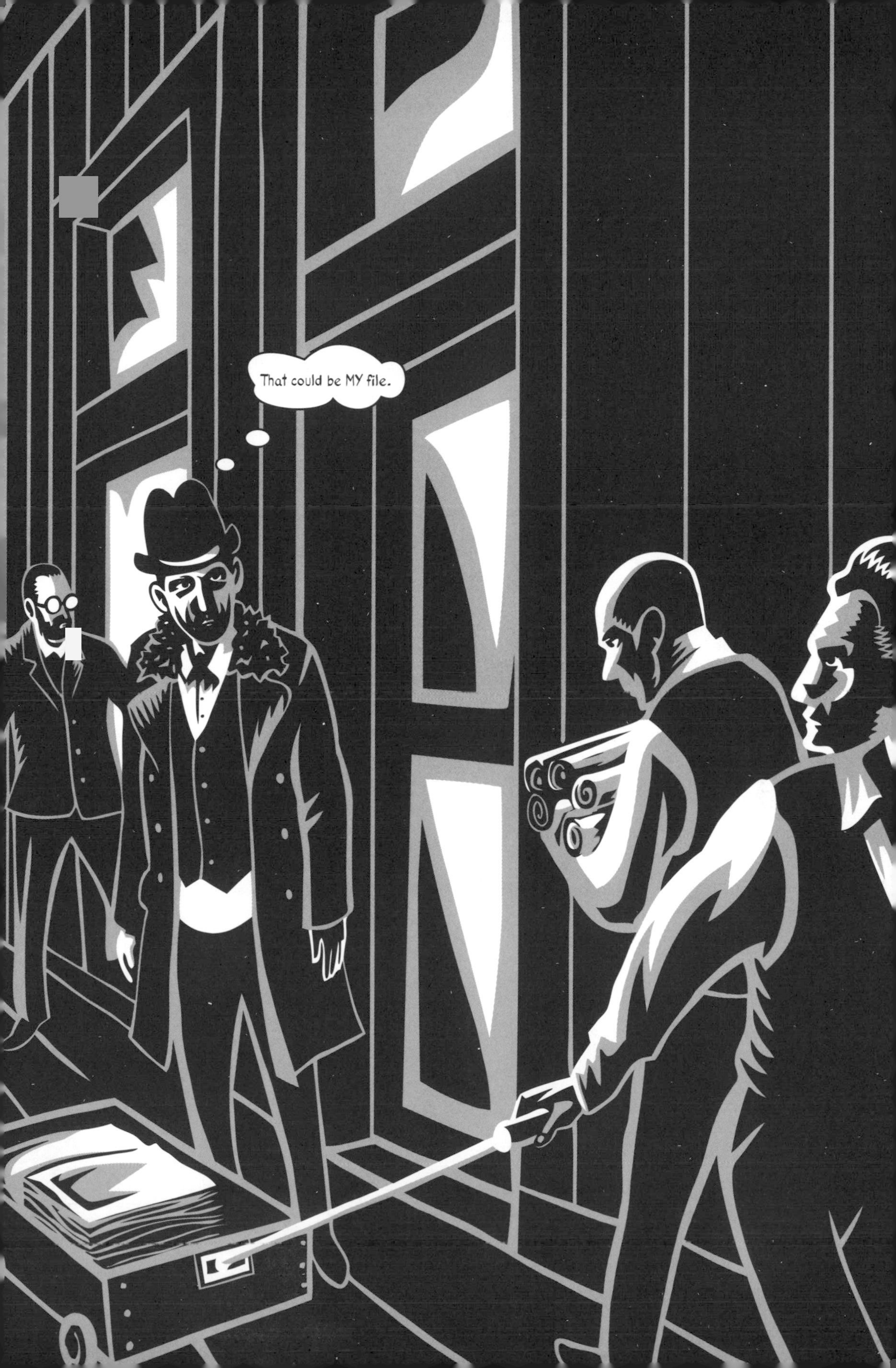
That could be MY file.

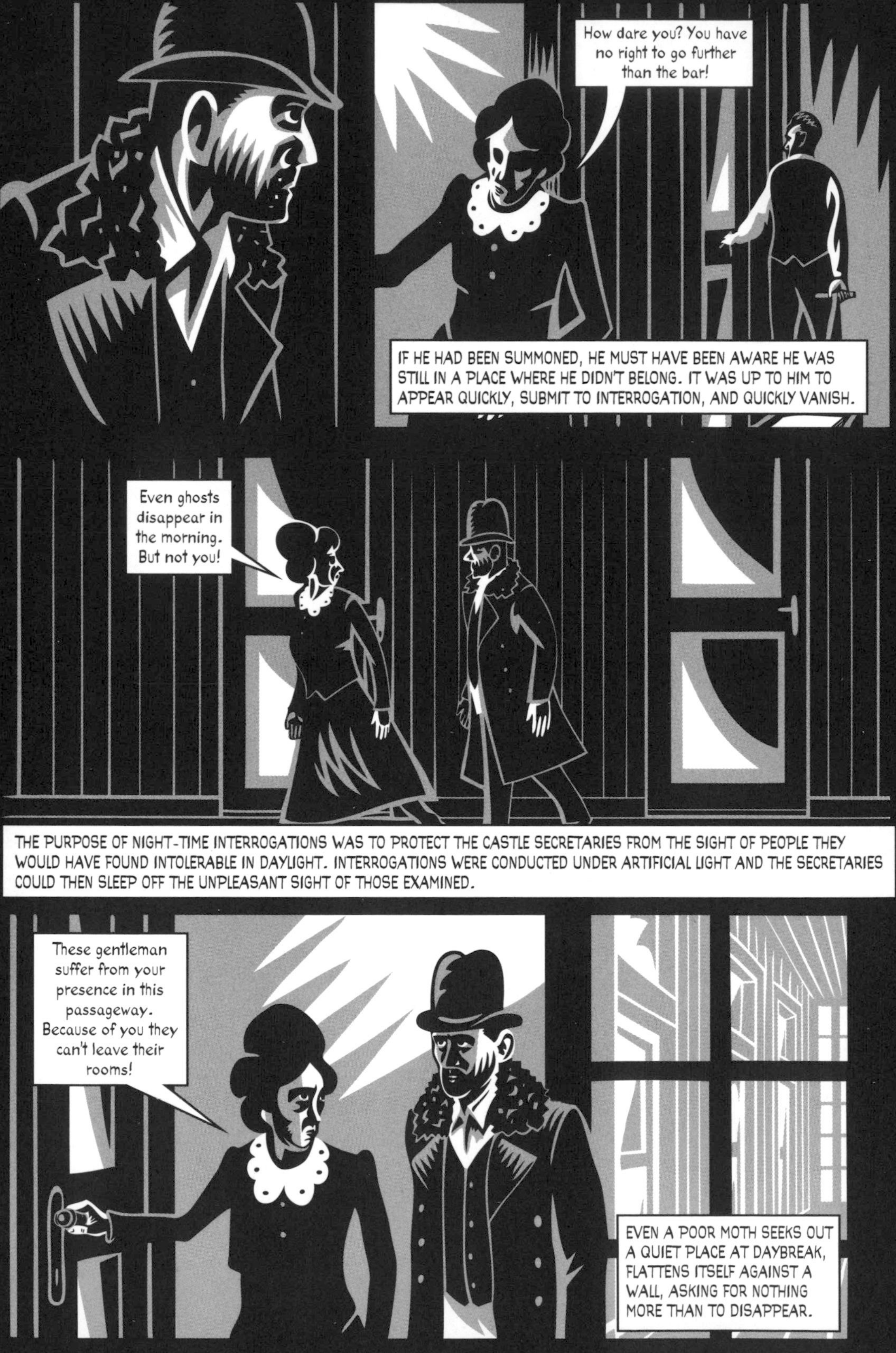
How dare you? You have no right to go further than the bar!
IF HE HAD BEEN SUMMONED, HE MUST HAVE BEEN AWARE HE WAS STILL IN A PLACE WHERE HE DIDN'T BELONG. IT WAS UP TO HIM TO APPEAR QUICKLY, SUBMIT TO INTERROGATION, AND QUICKLY VANISH.
Even ghosts disappear in the morning. But not you!
THE PURPOSE OF NIGHT-TIME INTERROGATIONS WAS TO PROTECT THE CASTLE SECRETARIES FROM THE SIGHT OF PEOPLE THEY WOULD HAVE FOUND INTOLERABLE IN DAYLIGHT. INTERROGATIONS WERE CONDUCTED UNDER ARTIFICIAL LIGHT AND THE SECRETARIES COULD THEN SLEEP OFF THE UNPLEASANT SIGHT OF THOSE EXAMINED.
These gentleman suffer from your presence in this passageway. Because of you they can't leave their rooms!
EVEN A POOR MOTH SEEKS OUT A QUIET PLACE AT DAYBREAK, FLATTENS ITSELF AGAINST A WALL, ASKING FOR NOTHING MORE THAN TO DISAPPEAR.

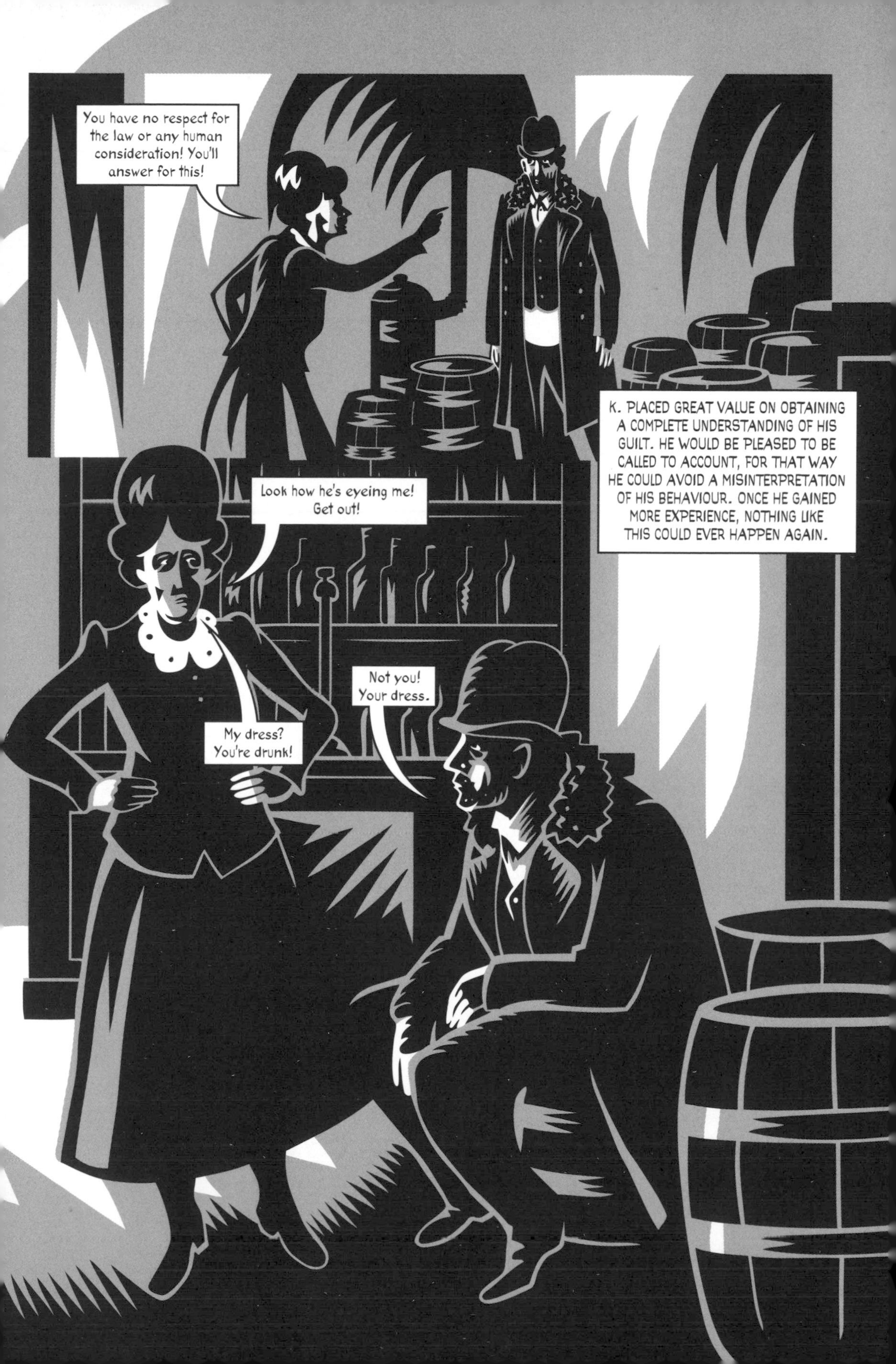
You have no respect for the law or any human consideration! You'll answer for this!
K. PLACED GREAT VALUE ON OBTAINING A COMPLETE UNDERSTANDING OF HIS GUILT. HE WOULD BE PLEASED TO BE CALLED TO ACCOUNT, FOR THAT WAY HE COULD AVOID A MISINTERPRETATION OF HIS BEHAVIOUR. ONCE HE GAINED MORE EXPERIENCE, NOTHING LIKE THIS COULD EVER HAPPEN AGAIN.
Look how he's eyeing me! Get out!
Not you! Your dress.
My dress? You're drunk!

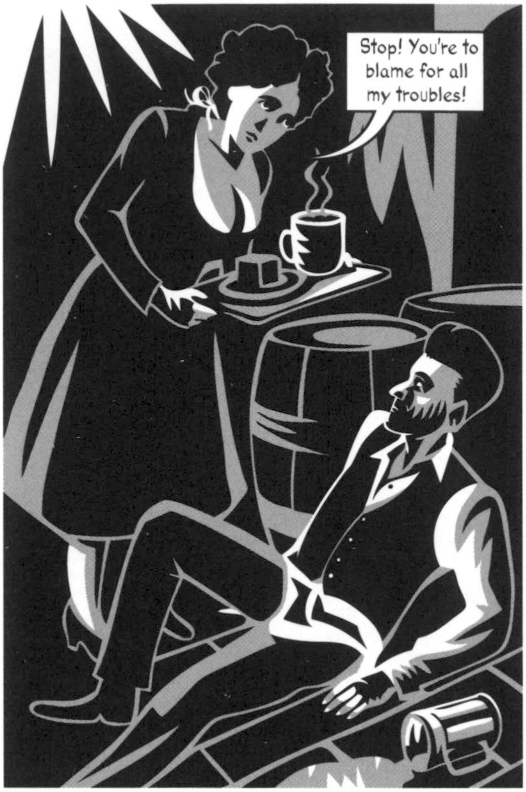
Stop! You're to blame for all my troubles!

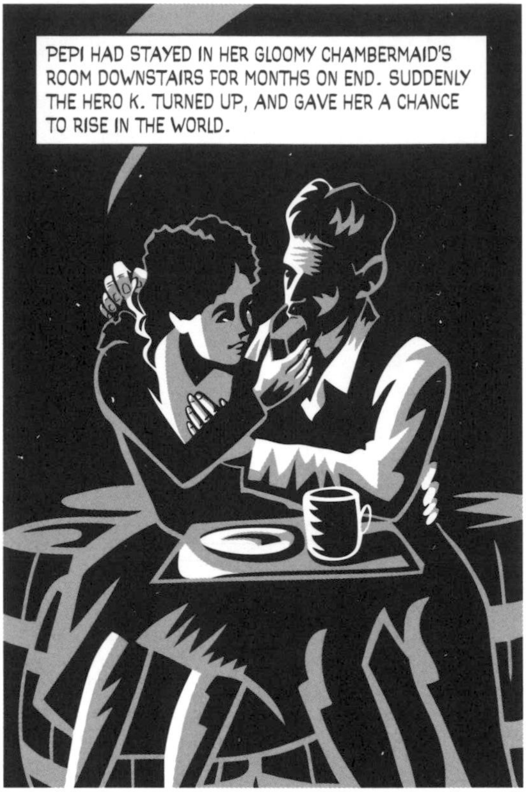
PEPI HAD STAYED IN HER GLOOMY CHAMBERMAID'S ROOM DOWNSTAIRS FOR MONTHS ON END. SUDDENLY THE HERO K. TURNED UP, AND GAVE HER A CHANCE TO RISE IN THE WORLD.

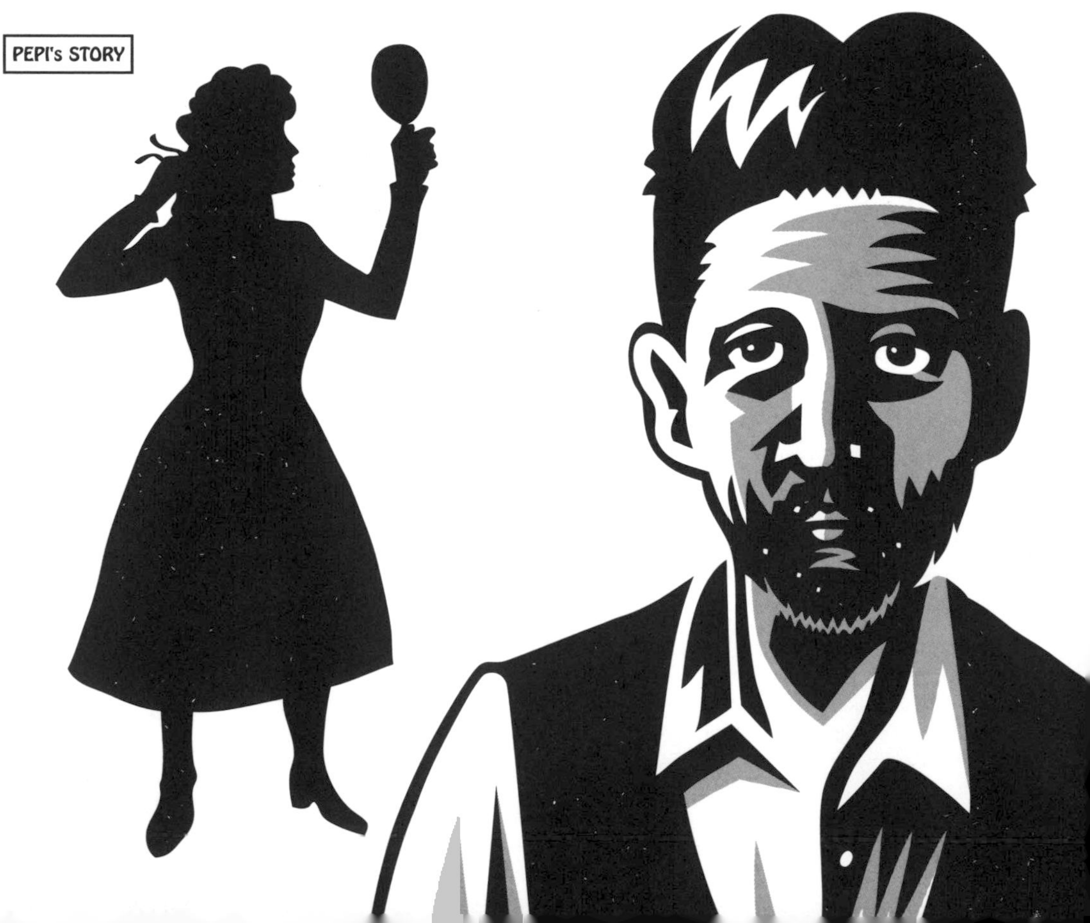
PEPI's STORY

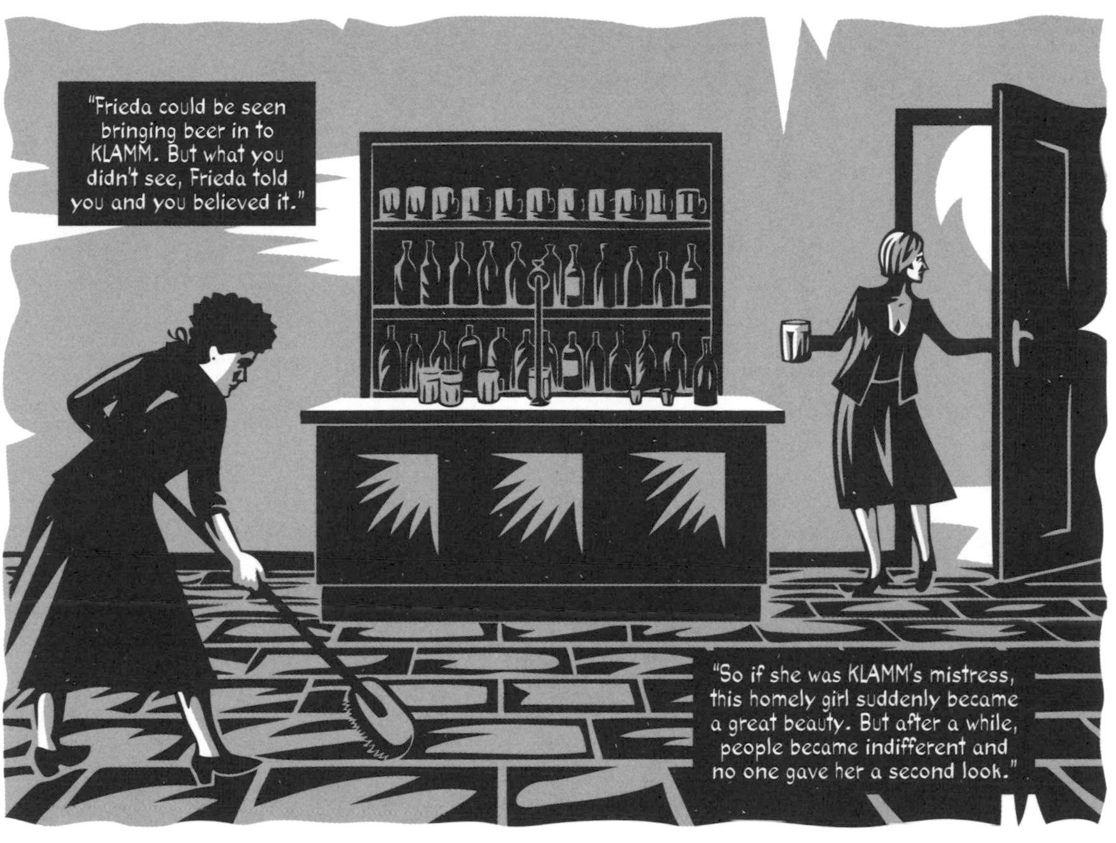
"Frieda could be seen bringing beer in to KLAMM. But what you didn't see, Frieda told you and you believed it."
"So if she was KLAMM's mistress, this homely girl suddenly became a great beauty. But after a while, people became indifferent and no one gave her a second look."

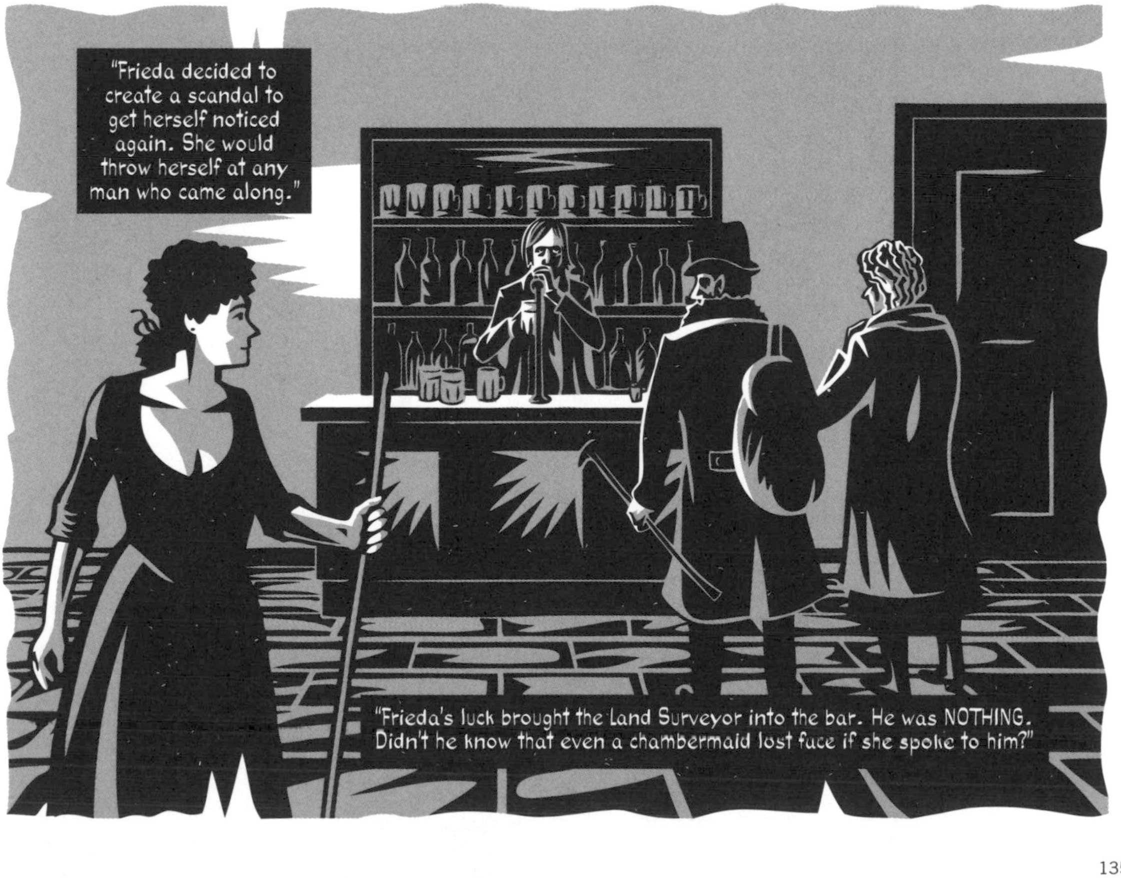
"Frieda decided to create a scandal to get herself noticed again. She would throw herself at any man who came along."
"Frieda's luck brought the Land Surveyor into the bar. He was NOTHING. Didn't he know that even a chambermaid lost face if she spoke to him?"

So you fell into her trap and took that skinny, ugly girl away from KLAMM. And then I could serve behind the bar...

"KLAMM was in the inn, but it was my misfortune that he didn't come down to the lounge."
"If only I could carry KLAMM down to the lounge in my arms. That's one burden I wouldn't collapse under."

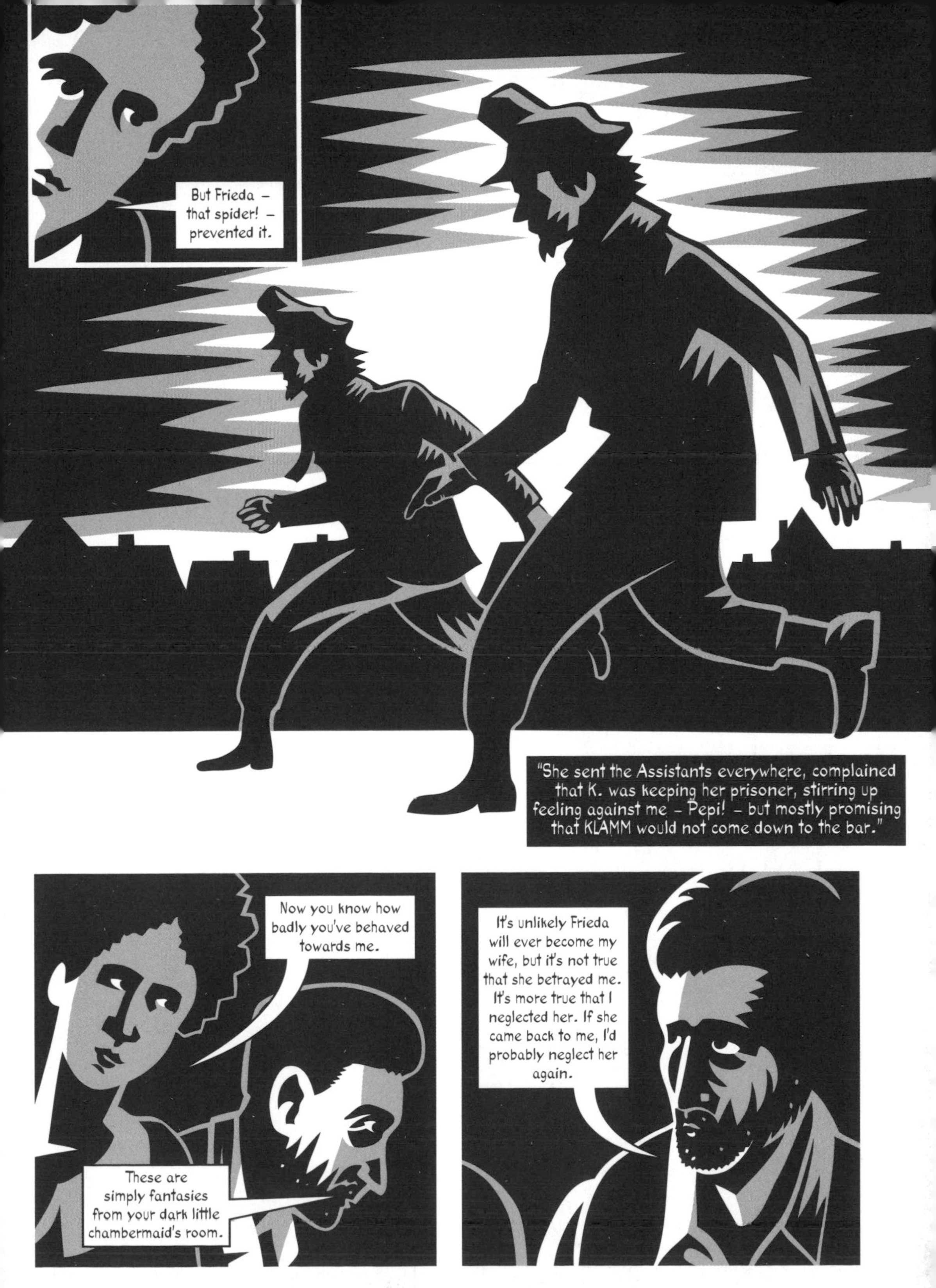
But Frieda – that spider! – prevented it.
"She sent the Assistants everywhere, complained that K. was keeping her prisoner, stirring up feeling against me – Pepi! – but mostly promising that KLAMM would not come down to the bar."
Now you know how badly you've behaved towards me.
These are simply fantasies from your dark little chambermaid's room.
It's unlikely Frieda will ever become my wife, but it's not true that she betrayed me. It's more true that I neglected her. If she came back to me, I'd probably neglect her again.

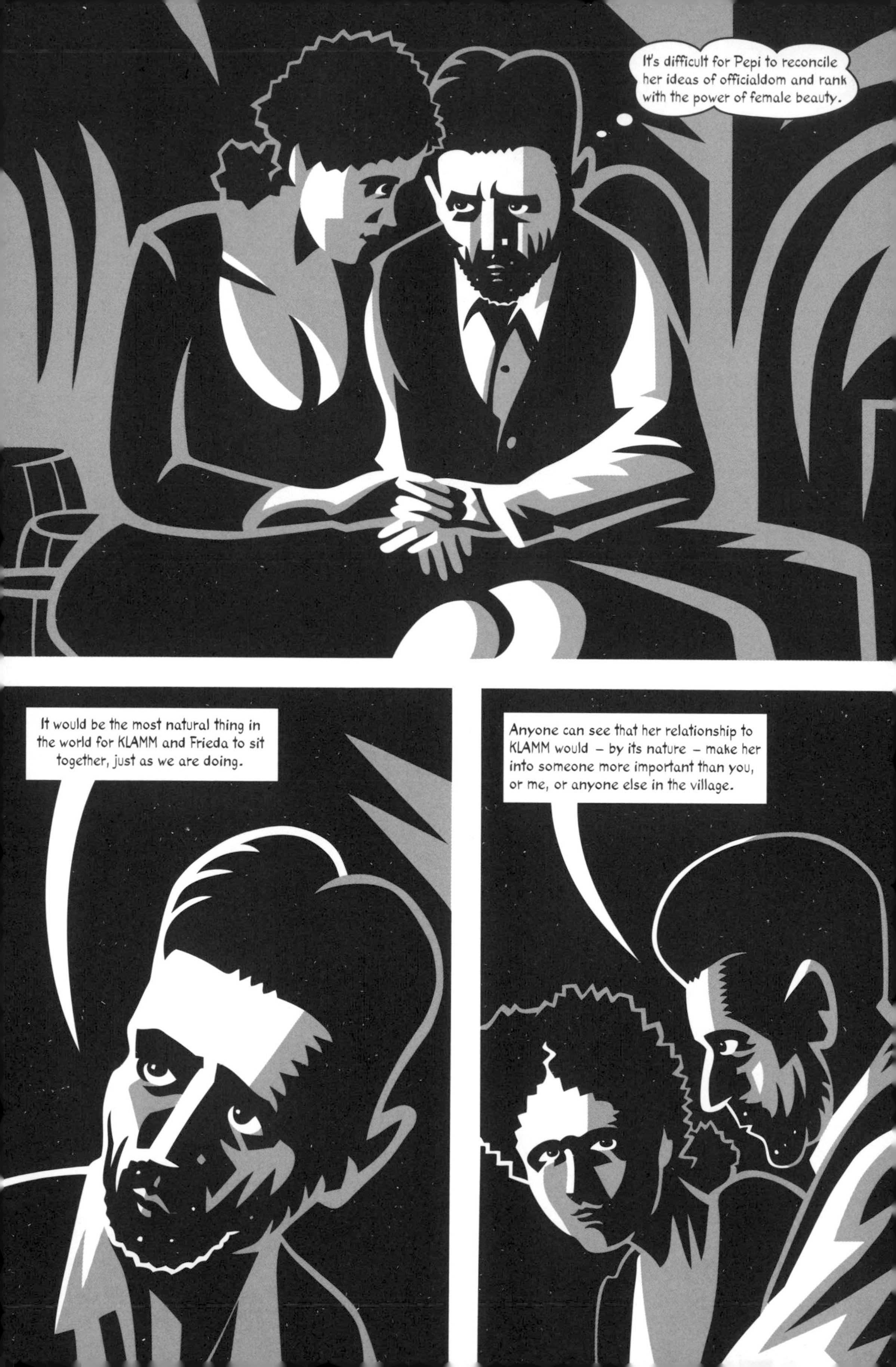
It's difficult for Pepi to reconcile her ideas of officialdom and rank with the power of female beauty.
It would be the most natural thing in the world for KLAMM and Frieda to sit together, just as we are doing.
Anyone can see that her relationship to KLAMM would – by its nature – make her into someone more important than you, or me, or anyone else in the village.

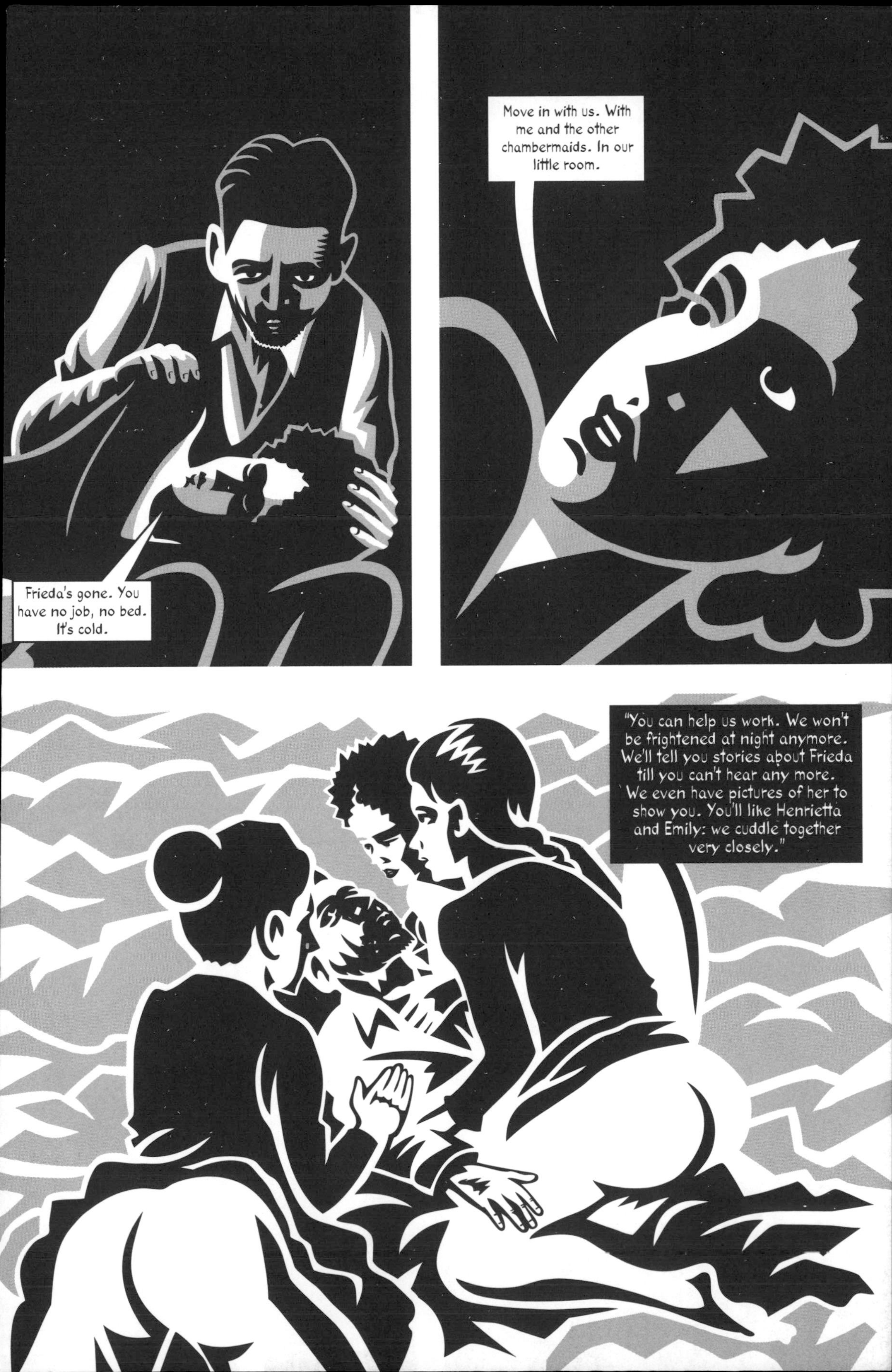
Frieda's gone. You have no job, no bed. It's cold.
Move in with us. With me and the other chambermaids. In our little room.
"You can help us work. We won't be frightened at night anymore. We'll tell you stories about Frieda till you can't hear any more. We even have pictures of her to show you. You'll like Henrietta and Emily: we cuddle together very closely."

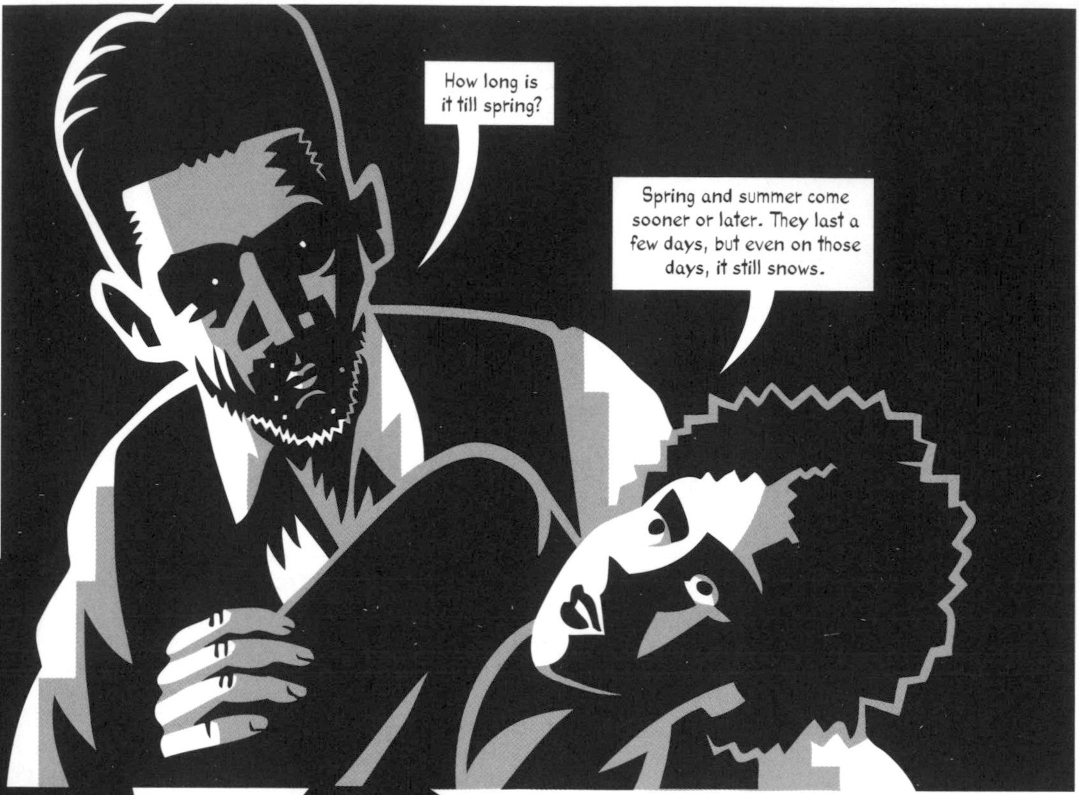
How long is it till spring?
Spring and summer come sooner or later. They last a few days, but even on those days, it still snows.
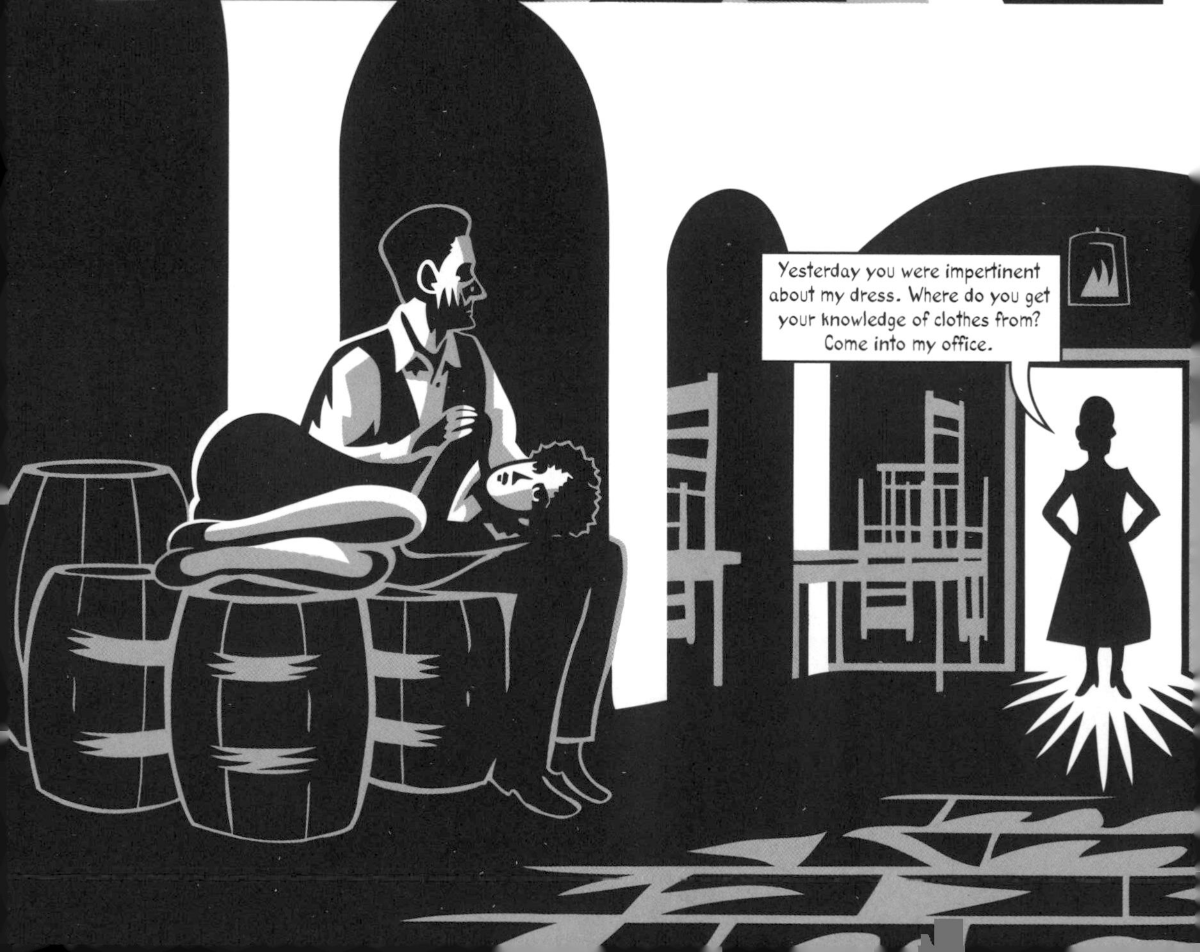
Yesterday you were impertinent about my dress. Where do you get your knowledge of clothes from? Come into my office.

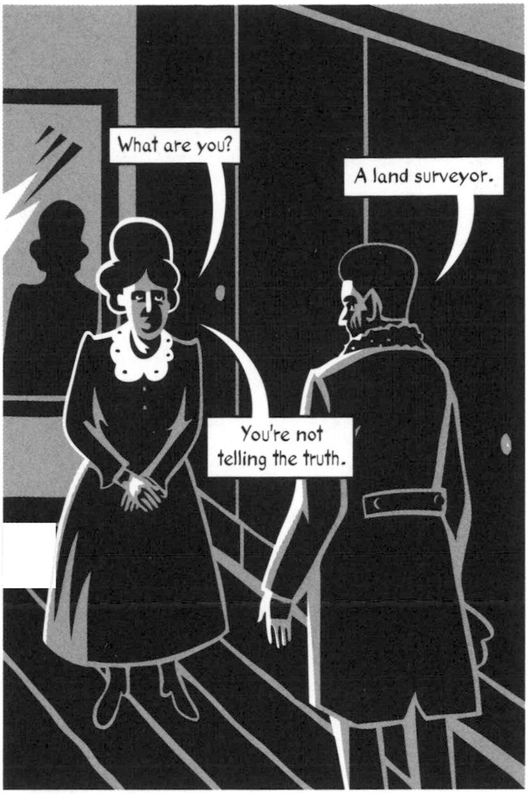
What are you?
A land surveyor.
You're not telling the truth.

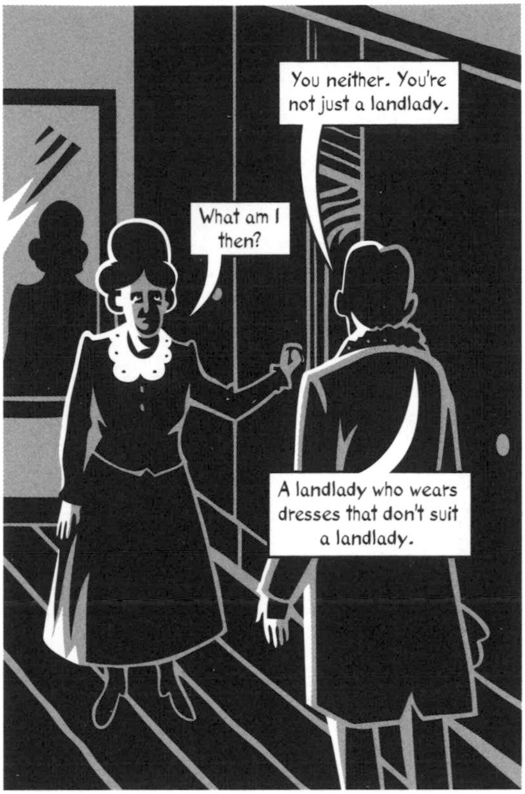
What am I then?
You neither. You're not just a landlady.
A landlady who wears dresses that don't suit a landlady.

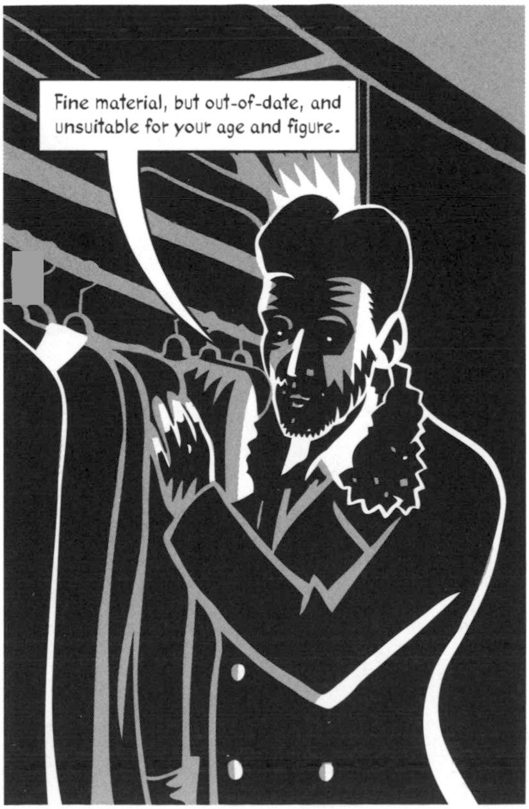
Fine material, but out-of-date, and unsuitable for your age and figure.

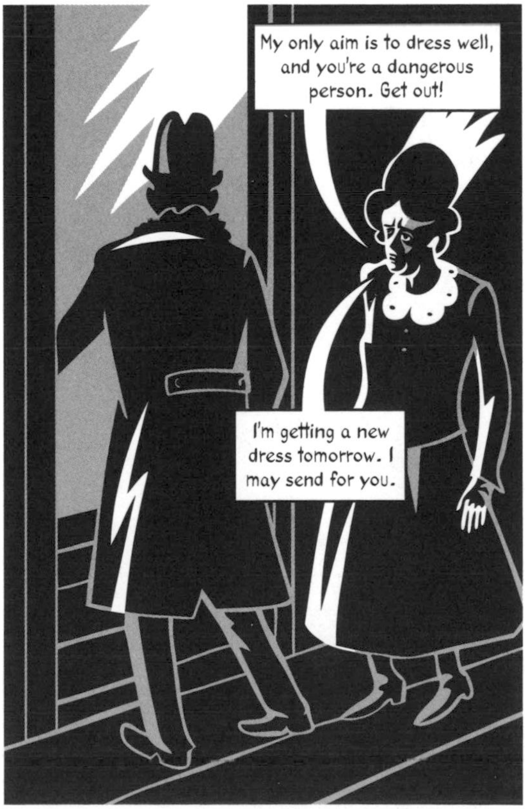
My only aim is to dress well, and you're a dangerous person. Get out!
I'm getting a new dress tomorrow. I may send for you.

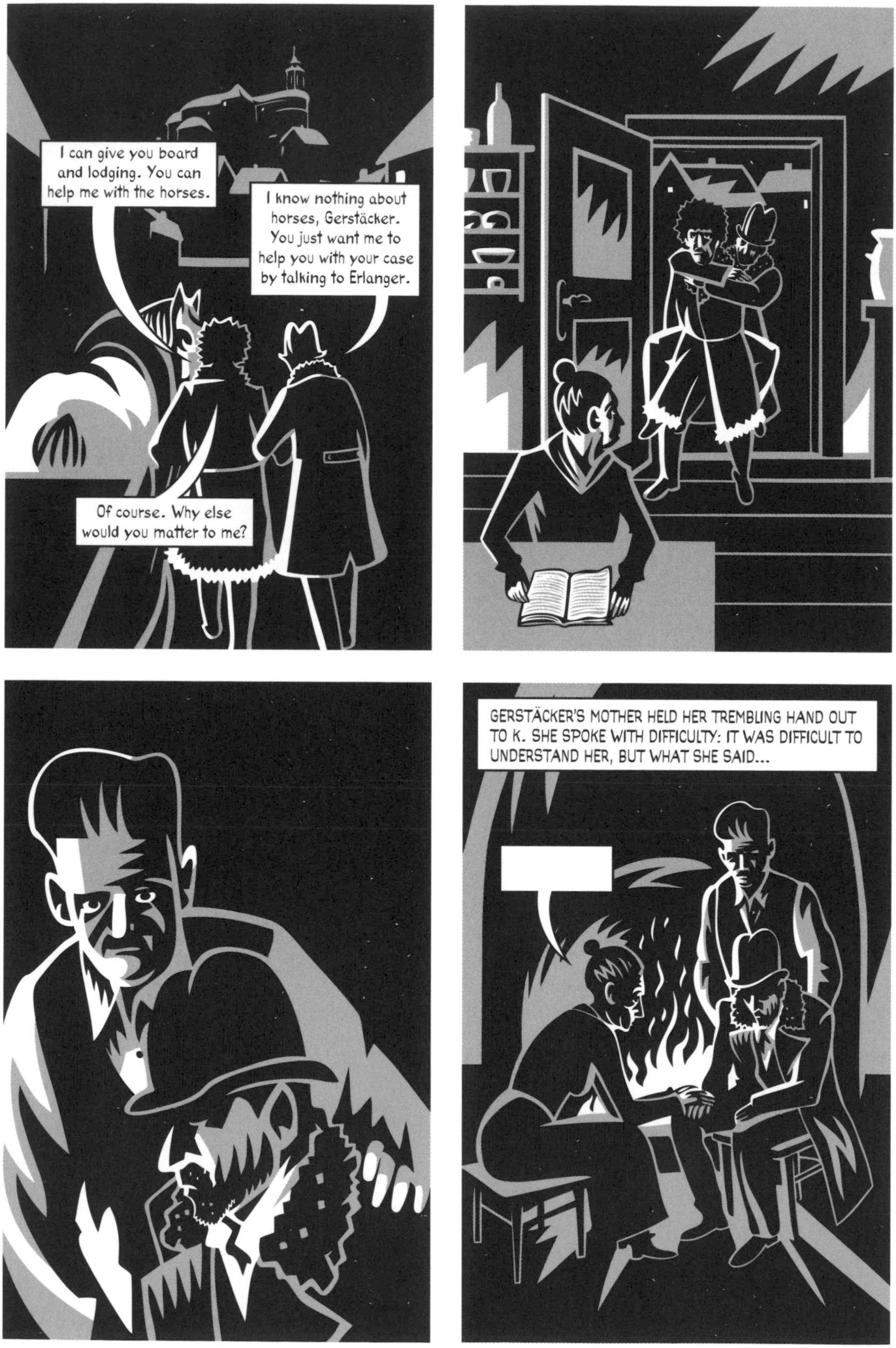
I can give you board and lodging. You can help me with the horses.
I know nothing about horses, Gerstäcker. You just want me to help you with your case by talking to Erlanger.
Of course. Why else would you matter to me?
GERSTÄCKER'S MOTHER HELD HER TREMBLING HAND OUT TO K. SHE SPOKE WITH DIFFICULTY: IT WAS DIFFICULT TO UNDERSTAND HER, BUT WHAT SHE SAID...

Sie reichte K die zitternde Hand und ließ ihn neben sich niedersetzen, mühselig sprach sie, man hatte Mühe, sie zu verstehen, aber was sie sagte

Kafka's text stops here.